From childhood services to adult provision the needs of an individual with autism develop and change yet the literature addressing specific adult requirements is scarce. This volume sets out to fill this gap and provides practical help and guidance specifically for those caring for the growing recognised population of adults with autism.

Issues of theory and practice from both local and international perspectives are included. Subsequent chapters analyse the implications arising from inflexible thinking and behaviour with emphasis on the management of transition and bereavement. Models for practice in employment and further education and also pharmacological and educational approaches to mental health problems, epilepsy and challenging behaviour are concluded by a practitioner training programme in residential settings.

This book is an essential guide for all those concerned with the care and well-being of adults with autism including parents, researchers, practitioner and community care workers.

Adults with autism

a guide to theory and practice

Adults with autism
a guide to theory and practice

Hugh Morgan
West Midlands Autistic Society

with invited contributors

Foreword by Geraldine Peacock
Chief Executive to the National Autistic Society,
United Kingdom

CAMBRIDGE
UNIVERSITY PRESS

Published by the Syndicate of the University of Cambridge
The Pitt Building, Trumpington Street, Cambridge CB2 1RP
40 West 20th Street, New York, NY 10011-4211, USA
10 Stamford Road, Oakleigh, Melbourne 3166, Australia

First Published 1996

Printed in Great Britain at the University Press, Cambridge

A catalogue record for this book is available from the British Library

Library of Congress cataloguing in publication data

Morgan, Hugh.
Adults with autism: a guide to theory and practice / Hugh Morgan,
with invited contributors; foreword by Geraldine Peacock.
p. cm.
Includes index.
ISBN 0 521 45070 5 (hardback). – ISBN 0 521 45683 5 (pbk)
1. Autism. 2. Autism – Patients – Services for. I. Title.
[DNLM: 1. Austism. 2. Social Support.   WM 203.5 M848a 1996]
RC553.A88M67 1996
616.89′82–dc20
DNLM/DLC
for Library of Congress   96–13982 CIP

ISBN 0 521 45070 5 hardback
ISBN 0 521 45683 5 paperback

TAG

Contents

Contents

Contributors

David Clarke, *Dept of Psychiatry, University of Birmingham and Queen Elizabeth Psychiatric Hospital, Birmingham*
John Corbett, *Dept of Psychiatry, University of Birmingham and Queen Elizabeth Psychiatric Hospital, Birmingham*
Gwenn Edwards, *City of Birmingham Education Department*
Rita Jordan, *School of Education, University of Birmingham*
Lynn Mason, *Matthew Boulton College, Birmingham*
Alison Matthews, *Employment Training Unit, Nailsworth, Gloucestershire*
Eve Matthews, *West Midlands Autistic Society*
Stuart Powell, *University of Hertfordshire*
Bob Reynolds, *National Autistic Society*
Gill Wainscott, *Queen Elizabeth Psychiatric Hospital, Birmingham*

Foreword

Geraldine Peacock,
Chief Executive,
The National Autistic Society

T HE FIRST generation of adults with autism, who were being diagnosed as children, are now in their mid-forties. It took a long time for autism to be recognised as a condition and there is still an enormous amount to learn about ways to work with, and empower, adults with autism.

Hugh Morgan's book is particularly timely in providing a comprehensive introduction to the needs, philosophies and research that exist currently in this field.

Whilst adults with autism have many needs in common with other people with disabilities, the complexity of the condition also dictates that specific needs must be recognised and worked with if real progress is to be made. Adults with autism do not fit neatly into existing systems. This book helps to identify specific special needs, why those needs exist and ways forward to help people understand and work effectively with this client group.

Not only because autism is a complex condition, but also because it is a spectrum condition, understanding and the development of relevant approaches are made even more crucial. For the first time, Hugh Morgan and his contributing authors try to identify knowledge and good practice on a national and international level. They pull together the thinking that guides our understanding of adults with autism and provide fascinating examples of innovative practice from all over the world.

Recognition of autism and Asperger syndrome is growing all the time, but very little has been written about work in this field. This useful book summarises the rapid development and progress in recent years.

There are potentially 300 000 people with autistic spectrum disorders in the UK. As there is, at present, no cure for autism, children with autism become adults with autism. Thus it is vital that the advances that have been made in diagnostic and educational services, which provide early recognition and positive intervention, are followed through with appropriate services for adult life.

The principles of care in the community can only truly work if the complex needs of adults with autism are understood and acknowledged. Whilst the opportunities for innovative practice development are greater than ever before, these opportunities will not be grasped without a greater awareness of autism on the part of the public, politicians and professionals. This book will make a significant contribution towards addressing this and in providing a real reference point for those working in the field, examining as it does the key areas of research, therapeutic interventions, models of practice and highlighting a huge range of issues that need to be explored. I welcome the publication of this book, which I am sure will be of enormous value in ensuring we work more effectively to enable adults with autism to fulfil their potential.

Preface

Professor John Corbett and Hugh Morgan

O VER THE past three decades, major advances have been made in the recognition of, and responses to, autism. Within the United Kingdom, the first generations of children who have been diagnosed in early childhood have been moving through from specialist schooling into adult provision. There is also an increasing recognition of the needs of more disabled young people with autistic impairments in communication, social interaction and repetitive stereotyped activities who, in the past, would not have received specialised care or been institutionalised and are now moving into the community.

Although, by definition, autistic problems date back to early childhood and much has been written about the needs of children, knowledge of the needs of adults and the best ways to help them are poorly documented. This book sets out to provide practical help and guidance specifically for adults and those caring for them.

One measure of the efficacy of specialised services will be in their capacity to demonstrate that the child with autism, who has great difficulties in communicating with and responding socially to others, is able to learn some of the ground rules by which they can make sense of their world as they mature into young adults and subsequently pass into middle and old age.

Currently, the biggest gap in service provision concerns the paucity of community-based services and it is clear that an increasing number of adults with autism will come to the attention of generic services, e.g. further and higher education, employment and Social and Health Services. It is also apparent that such services are likely to have very little knowledge of the continuum of autism disorders and of the types of support systems that will need to be developed if adults with autism are not to be failed. It is essential that bridges be built between childhood and adult services so that young people with autism can safely negotiate the developmental hurdles into adult life.

The essence of this book is its exploration of many of the key issues in service provision for adults with autism, both in residential and in community-based settings, providing examples of good practice from the mainstream of autism.

It does not target on one particular subgroup but rather, by its emphasis on the middle-ground, suggests that insight may be gained which will be helpful when working with high-functioning adults with autism or those with more severe and profound learning disabilities and autism. It is, therefore, a book which emphasises theoretical considerations and the practical lessons to be learnt from work with adults with autism, and also takes account of the underlying structural issues in terms of the dynamics of residential work, and the need for underpinning guidance for practitioners.

'Adults with Autism' draws upon a breadth of material from psychology, education, psychiatry and social work, and it is hoped that the practitioner, parent and researcher will find something to interest them within its covers.

Introduction

Hugh Morgan

PEOPLE WITH autism have severe deficits in social communication and imaginative skills (Wing and Gould 1979). The majority of people with autism also suffer from brain damage and, as a result, have additional learning disabilities. Le Couteur (1990) considers autism to be an organic neuro-developmental disorder involving fundamental cognitive and social deficits that are more common in males than females.

People with autism spend most of their lives as adults yet, by far, most of the literature relating to autism has reported on research and practice with children. This publication seeks to contribute to the evolving dialogue specifically relating to theory and practice with adults with autism. There is, I believe, a need to move beyond the increasingly tired rhetoric of generic ideology and practice and, for those who plan and deliver services, to demonstrate understanding of the unconventional pattern of learning of people with autism. By doing so, services and intervention strategies may be established which reflect and respond to the needs of individuals with autism rather than simply apply the social values of wider society.

This book seeks to describe and evaluate what is currently happening in services for adults with autism and to propose models of practice. Vignettes illustrate practice throughout the text although pseudonyms are used to retain the anonymity of the individual. The reader may wish to know that the content of the book is divided into five distinct sections; the first three chapters investigate, describe and evaluate the provision and philosophies of service design from both international and national perspectives. Much research and practice in the field of autism has concentrated upon difficulties in communication and socialisation, but the common thread running through Chapters Four to Six is the sometimes neglected third attribute of Wing and Gould's (1979) Triad of Impairments, an inflexibility in thinking and behaviour. It is suggested that this may be of critical and underpinning significance in the way in which daily living programmes are designed and support systems are developed to meet the needs of people with autism. Two significant areas of increasing opportunities for adults

1

with autism in the UK are in employment and further education, and models of innovative practice are reported in Chapters Seven and Eight. The three subsequent chapters contain intervention strategies from both medical and educational perspectives of autism. The final chapter presents a model for practitioner training, which not only draws upon many of the conclusions of the earlier chapters, but which is representative of wider issues and practice. Throughout, the book is written from the perspective of the practitioner employed in work with people within the autistic spectrum. The term practitioner is used in preference to other designations to describe those people working with adults with autism, be they care staff, managers, teachers, psychologists, and so on. It is believed that this book will hold something of relevance for practitioners, researchers and parents. A guide to each chapter is as follows:

Internationally, there is a distinct pattern to the development of services for adults with autism and, in *Chapter One*, the key features in this pattern of service delivery are outlined. The work of several organisations is described, illustrating the world-wide movement in the field of autism. Examples of innovative practice are presented from Europe, South America, Australasia, Southern and Eastern Asia. Particular attention is ascribed to the evolving situation in Greece, which is proposed as a paradigm for action, echoing the circumstances in the UK 25 years ago.

The underpinning philosophy behind the design of services for adults with autism is critically evaluated in *Chapter Two*. The ideology of normalisation is placed into historical and political context, and some specific difficulties in application to people with autism are outlined. It is clear that current ideology has failed to bring parents alongside in the move towards greater self-determination for people with learning disabilities, and this is especially striking in the field of autism, where the international development of services has been largely pioneered by parents. By reference to the autobiographical contributions by people with autism, it is proposed that 'normal' practice is simply not good enough.

How can the quality of services for people with autism be evaluated and how can parents and purchasers know that organisations actually deliver a service which is sensitive and attuned to the specific needs of adults with autism ? Quality audit and accreditation schemes have been in existence for many years, particularly in North America and Australia, and in the UK such schemes are becoming increasingly common. Accreditation should not be confused with local authority or State inspection procedures, which seek to apply minimum standards. Until recently there has been no objective measure, in any country, of the performance of a service in meeting the specific needs of people with autism, as distinct from generic care practice. *Chapter Three* describes the background and the process of the Autism

Quality Audit and Accreditation Programme in the UK before presenting and evaluating the findings following the first two years of operation. Recommendations are made for the future development of this continuously evolving programme.

The third aspect of the Triad of Impairments (Wing and Gould 1979), i.e. the lack of flexibility of thought and behaviour, has been afforded relatively little attention in relation to practice with adults with autism. In *Chapter Four*, Rita Jordan and Stewart Powell argue that this lack of flexibility should be recognised as a major factor in the lives of adults with autism as it underlies many of the features of thinking and subsequent behaviour. There are clear implications for the way in which practitioners recognise and respond to this lack of flexibility and this can be seen in the planning of suitable environments and appropriate daily programmes for individuals with autism. Jordan and Powell then propose that practitioners also have a significant role in developing the flexibility in their clients and suggest a model for helping to overcome this fundamental difficulty.

Chapter Five further develops the theme arising from the impact of lack of flexibility of thinking and behaviour, and explores the significance of attachment and loss for adults with autism. It is clear that lack of flexibility may directly and adversely influence any process of change for people with autism. Using research into bereavement and psychosocial transitions as reference points, a psychological model of attachment and loss for adults with autism is presented, with particular reference to the transition from child to adulthood and from one home to another. The practical implications for both transition and bereavement are discussed and it is stressed that practitioners need to understand how and why attachments are formed, plan the timing, sequencing, synchronisation of transitions based upon this understanding, and of the individual circumstances. Practitioners can then anticipate the problems that may occur founded upon this underlying knowledge.

Action research can be a valuable tool for informing about practice with adults with autism. Eve Matthews presents one example of how this may be achieved, in which she tests the hypothesis that, due to perceptual and processing difficulties, adults with autism may have a specific inflexibility in perceiving visual clues in the same way as others. In *Chapter Six*, she describes an experimental methodology employed to explore whether there is a specific difficulty in recognising symbols of age, status and gender purely on the basis of visual clues. The implication of this research leads Eve Matthews to suggest that the absence of an intuitive grasp of the age, gender and status of another person would be likely to impact upon consequential communication and social interaction. Eve Matthews also considers some of the recent psychological debates in the field of autism which have proposed that the features of autism occur as the result of one underlying deficit, since the results of her Visual Clues experiment will inevitably have implications for these theories.

In *Chapter Seven* the first of two models illustrating methods by which adults with autism may be supported in ordinary settings is presented. The findings from the development of a support system, which has enabled two adults with autism with associated moderate learning disabilities to extract a valuable service from a large college of further education located in a densely populated inner city area, are described. Since 1989, many individuals with autism have attended further education colleges within the city of Birmingham, not always successfully, and this project was specifically set up, with the support of public funding, to identify and evaluate the difficulties, strategies, process and benefits to individuals with autism of access to colleges of further education. Recommendations are made for future work. The collaborative model that is presented has, as its core, the development of support systems, which include a staff development programme and the close link between the college and home of the two adults with autism. The project also led to college staff achieving a greater awareness of the specific difficulties of autism, thus demonstrating the importance of collaborative links enabling the sharing of information to take place on a regular and consistent basis.

Supported employment schemes designed specifically for people with autism in the UK are few and far between, yet it is likely that, as in the case of access to colleges of further education, such schemes will increase in significance in years to come. In *Chapter Eight*, Alison Matthews reports the findings from the first three years of one innovative employment scheme, operating in the heart of rural Gloucestershire. She draws clear comparisons with the vocational options programme operating in North Carolina but also, interestingly, identifies weaknesses in the current assessment process used by Placing Assessment and Counselling Teams (PACT) which may have led to some people with autism being placed in employment settings in which they are ill-equipped to cope. Such findings are likely to have significant implications for the raising of awareness of autism of PACT officers and serves to emphasise the importance of networks of practitioners as a means of obtaining specialist advice for people with autism.

In *Chapter Nine*, Professor John Corbett and Dr Gill Wainscott investigate the often neglected issue of physical health in relation to adolescents and adults with autism. They consider the nature of the medical assessment, focus on preventative medical and dental care, pay special attention to the association between epilepsy and autism, and look at the effect of maturation upon physical health in autism.

Dr David Clarke explores the usage and efficacy of pharmacological approaches to the treatment of autism in adulthood in *Chapter Ten*. He begins by identifying the factors which predispose and maintain seriously self-injurious behaviour and other behavioural disorders found in autism. In particular, David Clarke describes the features of psychiatric disturbances which can occur in adulthood for some individuals with autism. He emphasises that pharmacological interventions play a significant part in the treatment of psychiatric illness sometimes associated with autism, but may also play a role in the treatment plan for adults with autism experiencing challenging behaviours.

Chapter Eleven begins by briefly appraising some of the difficulties in traditional intervention strategies which have tended to respond to symptomatic behaviour alone, rather than appreciating the style of learning by people with autism as a foundation for intervention. Practitioners can anticipate and avoid much of the symptomatic challenging behaviour displayed by those with autism by creating 'signposts' which respond to the cognition of adults with autism. That is, by providing answers to their questions, 'where should I be ?' 'when will it start and finish?' 'what do I have to do?' etc. in concrete situations and locations. By adopting alternative forms of communication, i.e. visually augmented systems, we may make messages and meanings more understandable. By doing so, we may also, of course, anticipate and prevent many of the displays of behaviour which challenge services. It was, however, recognised and acknowledged that sometimes difficult situations do develop in work with people with autism and that practitioners are under great pressure to find solutions quickly. Practitioner stress is acknowledged and discussed, and practical guidelines presented for responding to the symptomatic and challenging behaviour.

The final chapter of this book investigates the training of residential practitioners working with adults with autism. It is proposed that practitioners require skills in generic care practice, but also, significantly, in autism-specific practice. Essential components and strategies for developing a training programme seeking to imbue such skills are presented. Several themes from the earlier chapters of this book are used as the basis of training topics, as are those derived from wider practice. Also identified and explored is the development of professionally qualifying courses providing autism-specific training for practitioners and a profile of one such course operated by the University of Birmingham is delineated.

The epilogue seeks to identify a few future trends in practice with adults with autism within the UK alone, but is by no means a definitive list. Within a political and economic context, support to families and to high-functioning adults with autism, influencing the public sector, respite services, practitioner training, 'miracle cures' and the utilisation of new technologies are all briefly considered and are deserving of greater detail.

So, this book explores some, but admittedly not all, of the key issues involved in therapeutic work with adults with autism. What are likely to be the burning issues for the next decade in this line of work? Future research leading to the development of models of practice should include comparative evaluations of the differing types of service provision within and between countries, and longitudinal comparisons of autism-specific provision with non-autism-specific services. There will be a need for considerable practical input into the development of informed, enabling strategies for self-determination and also increased understanding of, and responses to, sexuality. The development of innovative outreach schemes focused on the primary rather than the secondary care level, which will aim to provide support for adults with autism in their own homes, will, in market-led economies, be far more cost efficient than residential care. Inevitably though, residential services will continue to play a significant role in supporting a minority of adults with autism, therefore the training of practitioners involved in supporting adults with autism in the wider community and also those within specialist residential and day settings should be placed at the very top of management agendas. Training and practice should be consistently developed and delivered from an ever increasing understanding of the distinct style of thinking and learning of people with autism.

BIBLIOGRAPHY

Le Couteur, A. (1990). Autism: current understanding and management. *British Journal of Hospital Medicine*, **43**, 448–452.
Wing, L. and Gould, J. (1979). Severe impairments of social interaction and associated abnormalities in children: epidemiology and classification. *Journal of Autism and Developmental Disorders*, **9**, 11–29.

1

Services for adults with autism: an international perspective

Hugh Morgan

T HIS CHAPTER sketches the international pattern of services delivered to adults with autism and is divided into three related sections. It will identify recurring themes, before then presenting snapshots of the developmental progress of services in countries including Chile, India, Japan, Australia, Iceland, Luxembourg, Spain and Portugal. The final part of Chapter One, 'Profile: the Greek experience', will profile the early formative stages of service development in Greece. Developments in Greece may be viewed as a paradigm for action and may, in years to come, serve as a model for the simultaneous development of provision for both children and adults with autism and their families. For the Greek nation it will mean condensing the developments which have taken place in the UK over the past 25 years, into five years.

RECURRING THEMES

In many, if not all countries influencing the provision of services for people with autism, the following factors seem to apply consistently:

1 The experiences of the adult with autism and of his/her family tends to be much the same.
2 Where service developments for adults have taken place, these have largely resulted from the efforts of interested professionals and especially from the innovative hard work of parents.
3 Progress has often been very slow and it would appear that services for adults have usually developed many years after services for children have originated.
4 In only very few countries can examples be found where attempts are being made to consistently apply specific methods of teaching to both children's and adult's settings.
5 No country provides a full range of services sufficient to meet the individual needs of all adults with autism living within that country.

7

Before presenting snapshots of service development within various countries it is important to look at the differences in recognition and classification of autism.

International recognition of and responses to autism have developed from the efforts of two distinct groups, namely parents with autistic children and professionals with a special interest in autism. In some cases these same practitioners are also parents and thus have a dual interest in the condition. Psychologists and psychiatrists were the first professional groups to be interested in autism, interpreting and explaining the condition in terms which they understood and which reflected attitudes current at the time (Shattock 1993) and a good example of this can be found in the development of services for people with autism in the UK.

Over the last 50 years or so, two divergent views of the aetiology of autism have evolved and particularly in the early post-war years, the focus of the professional perspective in many countries was to view autism as a psychogenetic illness, resulting from 'refrigerator' parenting. This perspective lays blame – not that there should be blame apportioned – firmly on parents and mothers in particular. Parents became demoralised and the psychoanalytical techniques employed were no panacea for the child with autism (Schopler and Hennike 1990). Whilst countries in Central and Northern Europe, North and South America and Australasia have tended to move away from this theoretical perspective, the psychoanalytical approach still pervades and influences services in several countries in Western and Southern Europe, including parts of France, Germany, Spain, Italy and Greece. This theoretical stance is an anathema and illogically flies in the face of the significant body of evidence from the majority of 'autism-friendly' countries indicating that autism is likely to derive from an organic neurodevelopmental disorder involving fundamental cognitive and social deficits that are more common in males than females (Le Couteur 1990), and can be defined on the basis of seemingly stringent diagnostic criteria (Gillberg 1990). Shattock (1993) suggests that the reasons for the adherence by Southern European countries to psychoanalytical explanations and treatments may have more to do with political and professional expediency than from any deep seated theoretical perspective. Evidence from Eastern European countries is beginning to emerge. For example, professionals at the Institute of Correctional Pedagogics, the Russian Academy of Education in Moscow, have studied autism since 1978, with a view to influencing the delivery of treatment (Lebedinskaya and Nikolsaya 1994). Prior to 1978 in Russia, autism was recognised, but treatment was largely by the administration of drug therapy.

Despite differences in the recognition, classification, and consequential provision of services for people with autism (Everard 1987), people with autism exhibit almost exactly the same patterns of behaviours wherever they live. The problems of the individuals and their families are virtually the same, and the required responses are quite similar (Shattock 1993). Take the following quotations:

Parent of a young man with autism in Greece

'The parents of the autistic adolescent become isolated from friends, they have different interests, different situations and even non-existent free time. At this point, it is possible that the other children in the family may begin to experience problems. In our house, there is a different pace of life compared to the pace of life in our friends' homes; there is a tension and there are problems.'

Parent of a young man with autism living in England

'The problem of late adolescence can strike a family with quite devastating results. Our family experienced a period of comparative calm then, quite (seemingly) suddenly, the situation changed and we were having to cope with a young man exhibiting extremely challenging behaviour. At this point our family circumstances altered, caused by a number of uncontrollable events, and this may have been the trigger for the change in behaviour. The problem for the parents was where to turn to for help and advice. The help that was then given was, at best, unsatisfactory and, at worst, harmful and damaging. For a period of about seven years the family had to cope as best they could. (The happier outcome after this traumatic period was the provision of specialised residential care. As a result, the family have seen a substantial change in both the behaviour and outlook of our autistic son.)'

SNAPSHOTS OF DEVELOPMENTAL PROGRESS AROUND THE WORLD

So it can be seen that there are likely to be similarities in the experience of autism and stresses and strains felt by families. In Central and South America the movement specific to autism has been in the very early stages of development for some time. Everard (1987) reported that associations have evolved, only to disappear. Nevertheless, contact points have emerged in Brazil, amongst others. ABRA, the Brazilian association for people with autism was founded ten years ago with the aim to bring together the parents and friends of people with autism within that country. ABRA plays an important political role in securing the rights of people with autism in Brazil and, reflecting the development of the movement specific to autism in many other countries, have concentrated their initial efforts on lobbying for the provision of services for children with autism. Subsequently, parent/professional groups, frustrated by political indifference, have set up services themselves. Services for adults with autism are planned and it is intended to follow the same general philosophy of care used with children with autism, i.e. to assess and diagnose autism, and to devise intervention plans based on educative processes with the aim to improve quality of life, and social independence.

Chile

In Chile an impressive endeavour aimed at influencing services for children and young adults with autism was formally started in 1981, when the Asociacion Chilena de Padres y Amigos de los Autistas was formed by a small numbers of parents with autistic children. Almost 15 years later an impact is beginning to be made on services for young adults with autism, albeit in a very limited way. In 1987 the first programme for children with autism in the country opened, staffed by volunteer special education teachers and assistants, and by 1991 it had received limited government recognition and support. Currently, the educational and leisure programme is attended by 25 people with autism aged 5-22 years and an outreach service is provided on a monthly basis to a further 17 from neighbouring towns. The programme emphasises affective contact, socialisation, communication and hygiene. Activities include swimming, using public transport, walks to parks, markets, visits to concerts, sailing, etc. At any time in the programme, parents get together to share mutual concerns and to discuss caring strategies.

Asociacion Chilena de Padres y Amigos de los Autistas has recently increased its scope of influence in the development of services for people with autism, organising seminars and workshops and sharing their experiences to encourage other associations to develop their own services. In 1993 the association founded a school for 50 children and adolescents with autism from differing social and financial statuses. Although the association includes young adults in the programmes, there is currently no service specifically designed for adults with autism – the oldest person with a diagnosis of autism in Chile in 1994 was believed to be 26 years old. It is suggested that older people, as yet with no diagnosis of autism, reside at home or in psychiatric hospitals.

In Southern Asia, services to adults with autism are at extremely early stage of development, where awareness of the condition of autism has filtered into only a few sections of society.

India

Knowledge of autism in India is still very limited, and autism is regarded as just another kind of mental retardation. The diagnosis has often been limited to 'non-communicative', 'hyperactive' and 'attention deficit', and clinicians have tended to view autism as a form of mental handicap which has existed only in the Western World (Dewan 1992). What knowledge there is does not keep pace with the evolving and changing understanding of autism and, with limited awareness amongst the medical profession, individuals with autism remain largely undiagnosed. Those few children diagnosed as autistic attend schools for the mentally disabled and, as yet, there are no specific provisions designed to meet the distinctive needs of children with autism. A handful of very high-functioning children with autism (who do not exhibit 'socially unacceptable' behaviour) attend regular school usually in a special section for the more able mentally disabled.

There are no residential institutions; the concept of institutionalisation is not as prevalent in India as in the West and most families would prefer to keep their autistic child at home. With little or no diagnosis there are no residential facilities for the adult with autism and, indeed for the disabled in general, as services provided by the State are limited. These include a few state-run schools and a few concessions to families in the areas of travel, income tax, etc. Non-governmental organisations working in the field of disability can apply for a government grant to fund the services they provide. The last decade or so has seen the formation of a few parents' groups and currently most vocational and rehabilitation centres are run by them. Going by current trends it would appear that eventually most services will be run by parents groups.

'Action for Autism' is one organisation in India attempting to work specifically for people with autism. Operated by parents with a few professionals in New Delhi, it forms networks of families, provides a volunteer parent support/counselling service, seeks to influence the training of practitioners, and in 1994 started a school 'Open Door' for children with autism which has been combined with a training programme for teachers. For adults with autism, consideration is being given to community-based schemes, and the development of vocational training, rather than to residential projects.

One has to turn to Eastern Asia to find a greater, but still far from complete, realisation of service provision to adults with autism.

Japan

In common with many other countries, Japan is beginning to develop community-based facilities for people with learning disabilities, attempting to shift the emphasis away from large, long-stay institutions. Whilst progress has been made over the past ten years, service delivery to people with learning disabilities is still largely centred upon institutionalised care. Currently there is no legal basis for an autism-specific service in Japan. Again, in line with many other countries, social welfare policy is based upon three defined areas: for those with physical disabilities, mental disabilities, and learning disabilities. Despite the lobbying efforts of the autistic society in Japan for a separate law to address the special needs of people with autism, the Ministry of Health and Welfare prefer to address the issue of disability collectively, rather than for each type of disability.

Day programmes for adults with autism in Japan are provided in three main areas: day centres attached to long-stay institutions, in Day Activity Centres, and in small sheltered workshops. Attendance at the Day Activity Centre programmes is free of charge and participants receive a small, nominal payment of about 1500 yen (about £10) per month. Those attending perform simple tasks such as assembling ball-point pens or, in some cases, produce craft work for sale to the local community. Staff ratios must conform to the national regulation of one staff to every 7.5 persons. However, local authorities sometimes provide additional subsidies enabling a ratio of 1:5 to be reached. Information provided by the association of parents of adults with autism living in the Kanagawa Prefecture show that almost 5% of adults with autism are in employment. Kanagawa Prefecture established a job guidance centre five years ago which sought to assist people with disabilities to obtain job placements and for these placements to be sustained. The Japanese Ministry of Labour is currently studying such types of innovative practice.

There is no autism-specific residential provision for adults in Japan. However, group homes for children with autism have been established in recent years through the efforts of parent associations. In 1995 it was believed that there may have been as many as ten group homes for children with autism across the country and it is hoped to open three to four facilities each year. By contrast, many adults with autism live in residential settings, including long-stay hospitals, where their cognitive restrictions and unconventional styles of thinking and learning are therefore not understood, and the required management responses are not appropriate. In Yokohama, which has a population of around 3.5 million, parents are increasingly attempting to keep their children and young adults with autism at home, rather than place them in long-stay institutions. For those families, whose son or daughter with autism is presenting severely challenging behaviour, there are additional problems, as many cities, including Yokohama, do not have the expertise to manage such behaviour, and consequently, individuals are often shunted from one establishment to another. In 1993, the Japanese government decided to respond to this predicament and started a pilot programme known as 'special treatment for those with severe behavioural problems'. By early 1995 the programme catered for 20 people, most with a diagnosis of autism, in five institutions. A further major concern of parent associations is to address the current lack of service provision for people with Asperger syndrome.

Services for adults with autism are also beginning to develop in Australia where six States already provide services for children with autism and their families.

Australia

Each State differs in philosophy and in the practical services that are delivered and the organisational structure of individual States is correspondingly different (Leekam and Richdale 1990). All States within Australia provide some services for people with autism with the exception of Tasmania (Patterson-Coates 1992). One example can be found in Victoria where the State Autistic Association currently supports the work of local associations operating in separate regions of the State. The Victorian Autistic Children's and Adults Association (VACAA) co-ordinates the activities of several local associations and also lobbies and advises government and other 'key' agencies on the needs of locally based services for people with autism. In addition to educational programmes (which mainly focus on early intervention and integration into mainstream schools) and respite care designed for children with autism, a 16+ unit is provided enabling adults and adolescents with autism to undertake pre-vocational and vocational training programmes. Further, an outreach scheme designed to provide consultative support to agencies caring for people with autism has been established.

One of the few examples of services for adults with autism in Australia has been developed by MACCRO (Mansfield Autistic Centre Committee for Residential Options). This association provides accommodation and a day programme for six adults with autism, who were previously students of the Mansfield Autistic Centre (residential) during their school years. Two adults live independently in a small house supported by about 4 hours of staff time per week to supervise their budgeting, shopping and housekeeping. The remaining four live in another house a few streets away with a resident supervisor. Initially, the day part of the flexible programme was funded by MACCRO and a range of activities were provided combining independent living skills and vocational training with community access and recreation. A third house was purchased for use as a workshop, office and showroom and a garden ornament business was started together with external contract work. Eventually, government assistance was obtained and an outreach worker was employed. Currently, MACCRO feel that the balance of the day care programme has become heavily weighted towards paid employment, with a diminished focus on personal development.

In North America, as in the UK, residential services for adults with autism have been described extensively in the literature, for example see the descriptions of the Benhaven programme by Lettick (1983) and by Simonson and Simonson (1987), or of the Jay Nolan Center community-based programme (LaVigna 1983), and for comparisons of services in the USA and UK (Van Bourgonien and Elgar 1990). Descriptions of Group Homes in North Carolina and of farm communities for adults with autism have been presented by Wall (1990) and by Kay (1990), respectively, and reports have been made on the main features of farm-type communities in Europe and the USA (Giddan and Giddan 1991, 1993). This exposition does not seek to echo yet again descriptions of services in the USA and in the UK, but there are at least three common 'key' themes shared between these two geographically distant countries. The role of parents as collaborators with professionals in the development of services for adults with autism; the fact that services for children were developed first; and that 'pockets' of practice provide limited evidence of continuity of teaching methods from children's to adult's services.

The consistency of specialised support and teaching methods from childhood through to adulthood can be found only in a few cases, the most obvious and formalised example being the TEACCH programme (Division for the Treatment and Education of Autistic and related Communication handicapped CHildren) in operation in the North American State of North Carolina and in the increasing use of this model by other countries. In the UK, pupils in schools for children with autism will sometimes be placed in specialist adult establishments – reflecting a degree of consistency in staffing provision but not necessarily in teaching methods.

In Northern Europe and also in Iceland, the main thrust of services for adults with autism has been in residential care and has reflected the shift from large-scale institutionalised care, to small 'ordinary' homes. In Sweden, institutionalisation has been reduced dramatically and a recent attempt to establish a small community for people with autism had to be abandoned because of adverse media exposure which deemed the community an 'institution' (Shattock 1993). Like Sweden, services for adults with autism in Denmark reflect the philosophical shift towards normalisation and the same applies in Iceland.

Iceland

The total population of Iceland is now just over 265 000 and the birth-rate per year is around 4600 (1994, 4623). A survey of children born between 1980 and 1991 showed that there are, on average, three children per year who have received a diagnosis of autism.

Before 1982, there were no services in Iceland designed or provided especially for children or adults with autism. The National Autistic Society was founded in 1977 and it sought to influence the authorities, so that a group home could be established for the children who had been diagnosed and treated at the Child Psychiatric Clinic in Reykjavik. In 1980, a new Act of Law on the affairs of the handicapped was passed opening the possibility of establishing residential accommodation for people with autism.

All people with disabilities in Iceland enjoy the same basic rights as other members of the society. In addition, a special Act of Law (Act on the Affairs of the Handicapped, no. 59, 1992) was implemented to secure special services that are needed. According to Art. no. 1;

The objective of this Act of Law is to ensure to the handicapped equality and living conditions comparable with those of other citizens, and to provide them with conditions that enable them to lead a normal life.

Adults with autism in Iceland make use of the various services for people with disabilities that are specified in the Act, but certain services are specifically designed to meet the needs of a limited number of adults with autism in the Reykjavik area. These services are operated by the State. There is the National Autistic Society of Iceland which, although it does not operate its own services, does indirectly influence the development of services by the State and has approached the Ministry of Social Affairs with its ideas for future services. The Icelandic system is therefore most unusual, but not unique, when compared to that in many other countries, in that the State takes a key role in the development of services for adults with autism. The other striking example of services being provided almost exclusively by public agencies can be found in Norway, where the Landsforeningen for Autister (LFA, i.e. the National Autistic Society, Norway), is described as a 'watch dog and messenger', rather than as a service provider (Anonymous 1995 in *Link*).

The first residential service for people with autism was opened in 1982 and there are now three residential group homes for adults with autism, serving a total of 13 individuals. Their abilities, social competence and patterns of behaviour cover a wide range. Some are able to work with limited supervision and have a fair degree of self-care skills and social competence. Others require a great deal of staff support at all times, because of their limited ability, few social skills and, at times, marked behavioural problems. Ten of the adults with autism from the group homes attend a sheltered workshop operated by the same organisation which, by early 1995, had at least 15 places available. Group home residents make use of various educational and leisure opportunities which are usually planned and organised from the group homes. The staff to client ratio in the workshop is 1:2, but ratios tend to vary in the group homes depending upon the needs of the adults with autism cared for. In two of the homes it is usually 1:2, and occasionally 1:1. In the third home, the residents (two men and two women) have gained more independence than those in the other two homes and now require less supervision. Each home has one waking night staff on duty.

The philosophy of care for adults with autism in these settings is in line with the Icelandic goal to provide people with disabilities with, 'living conditions comparable with those of other citizens ...'. Each group home resident has his or her own room and usually shares facilities, such as kitchen, living room and a bathroom, with the others. The aim is to ensure that each resident is provided with the training and the assistance to enable him/her to take part in as wide a range of life experiences as possible. In recent years the TEACCH principles, developed in North Carolina, have increasingly influenced practice in the Heimili og vinnustofa einhverfra (i.e. Group Homes and Workshop for People with Autism) homes. Since 1993 the emphasis has shifted towards living conditions which provide each and every one with the possibilities of having more privacy in his or her own home. It is anticipated that in the near future, the group homes will consist of a cluster of small individual apartments, which also share certain facilities.

In Central Europe, particularly in those countries falling within the European Union (EU), details on services for adults with autism are comparatively easy to find in the literature, largely as the result of the work of an umbrella association, known as 'Autisme-Europe'. If the development of services for adults with autism is to develop within the less prominent EU countries, then parent-founded organisations such as Autisme-Europe will have a major lobbying role to play (an example of which will follow later in this chapter). In addition to playing a link role as a mechanism for communication between several European countries, Autisme-Europe holds a large and impressively organised conference every four years. The 1992 Congress was held in The Netherlands, and attracted over 130 lectures and workshops with over 2000 participants from 40 countries throughout the world. The opportunity to mix and chat with practitioners and parents hailing from many differing countries serves to emphasise the international perspective of autism.

An investigation on behalf of Autisme-Europe of the legal rights of people with learning disabilities living in European countries was undertaken by Vogel (1988) which he then compared with the procedures inherent in the legal system of the USA. Vogel found a dilemma in his extensive study and one for which no country has had sufficient awareness of learning disability to find a satisfactory answer: to legally recognise that a person has a learning disability, to enable her/him to obtain legal amenities and specific services, or to insist upon the legal equality of all persons, regardless of their medical or psychological condition. Shattock (1993) has written that Scandinavian systems are based upon a greater recognition of the needs and wishes of the individual.

Luxembourg

Luxembourg has a population of 375 000 and is a multicultural society. This has many implications for the education and treatment of people with autism, who are continually exposed to two spoken languages – mainly Luxembourgish (a spoken dialect) and French. If they learn to read and write then they would be expected to do this in French but also in a third language, German.

The Society to help people with autism (known as APA) was created in 1981 and has since been active in developing and establishing structures for children and adults with autism. Official recognition of autism came after a government decree in 1988 which set up The Institute for Autistic and Psychotic Children in Luxembourg (The Institute). The decree stated that the specialised education given to children, adolescents and adults with autism must aim at maximum educational, social and professional integration (Memorial Journal Officiel du Grand-Duche de Luxembourg 1988). By 1995, The Institute had responsibility for 33 children and adults with autism, the majority of whom continued to live at home with their families.

The official school leaving age for children with 'special needs' in Luxembourg is 15. After this age greater emphasis is given to job training than to academic studies and further contact with age peers. The Institute currently has one sheltered workshop where the young people are taught carpentry, weaving, printing and pottery at their own pace by specialised staff.

Co-operative Peter Pan

'Co-operative Peter Pan' was recently established which now runs three shops (a grocery, newsagents and giftware shop) as well as stands at local markets. Young adults are encouraged to engage in tasks that demand a high level of contact with people. Unlike the sheltered workshops, the young people are in an ordinary working environment engaged in skills needed to run small shops. Specialised staff encourage normal working relationships with an emphasis on autonomy, choice and decision making. Scott (1995 in correspondence with the author) reported that these young people are coping remarkably well in situations that previously they would have found intolerable. The deficiency of autism remains but self-esteem is raised when the young adults themselves realise their worth in society.

The 'atelier' which provides a more protected environment than that of the Co-operative Peter Pan has young people and adults who have greater difficulty in social contact. Nevertheless, it is envisaged that they too will not be over-protected and can participate in the running of the Co-operative Peter Pan by seeing their work being sold, for example.

Ordinary employment

At the present time two young men are working in ordinary workplaces. One works as a gardener for the Commune (County Council equivalent) while the other works as a librarian.

Residential

The philosophy upon which present and future residential services are to be based is that residential facilities should be on a small scale, that is, that adults should not be housed in large institutions but in family-sized units. Homes should not be isolated in areas where there is no transport or access to community services and leisure activities. One 'Teaching Home', which was set up in 1989 and has six places, is open throughout the year except weekends. Here the young people are being trained to live as independently as possible. Additionally, two adults are living independently in their own flat with minimum assistance.

Adults not provided for by The Institute

There are many adults with autism who are not provided for by The Institute. Usually children educated before the creation of The Institute were provided for in non-specialist settings or simply lived at home with their families. Indeed most of these children were not even recognised as having autism. No one knows the true number of adults with autism or where they all live. Many are probably still at home or in psychiatric establishments. Given the growing awareness of people with disabilities and their rights to be integrated into society the Luxembourgian government is aware that many people with handicaps are not catered for appropriately. Associations dealing with disabilities have been asked to help adults move from psychiatric hospitals to more appropriate placements. Consequently, The Institute has already been approached and asked to help in the mammoth task of reintegrating adults with autism into the community. In spite of Luxembourg being a rich country, there are still many shortcomings in the provision of education, work and accommodation for individuals with autism, in that only a small fraction of people with autism are being catered for adequately. This is probably due to the lack of awareness of autism at all levels of society. However, those being provided for are receiving a first-class service. Work being done with the young adults is especially impressive.

Without unequivocal recognition of autism as a specific disability requiring specific responses, then attempts to provide a service tailored to the individual needs of people with autism will be, at best, piecemeal. In France, where the psychoanalytical model of autism prevails, most adults with autism requiring residential care are placed in psychiatric hospitals or in non-specialist forms of residential and day care facilities. Sheltered employment opportunities are very limited, as are placements in work aid centres (i.e. Centre d'aide par le travail). However, innovative projects such as, 'L'Hermitage' (Le Relais 1996) will do much to redress the balance.

One of the founder members of Autisme-Europe, the Irish Society for Autistic Children, had been formed in 1963, and in 1982, following a national public appeal, raised sufficient funds to purchase a farm which quickly developed to provide a rural community for adults with autism as described in Giddan and Giddan (1993). The Irish example appears unusual compared to the development of services in other countries in that adults' as opposed to childrens' services were the first to be developed. This project – the Dunfirth Community – provides both residential and day programmes for up to 27 adults, 18 of whom take part in vocational training programmes including horticulture, farming, joinery, etc. It is anticipated that several adults with autism can be encouraged to take part in employment away from Dunfirth, and in co-operative or other supported work-based situations (Matthews 1994).

In Germany, the Autism Institute in Hamburg provides out-patient facilities for around 100 children and adults with autism, with the emphasis on diagnosis and communication development. In what was formerly West Germany, a total of five residential homes and three small residential and day centre communities provide specialist facilities to a small number of adults with autism, although solely autism-specific day units do not exist in this country. The former East Germany appears to have had no specialised facilities for people with autism (Spivack 1992). In Hamburg there are three workshops financially supported by the German government, providing sheltered employment to 138 people, with learning disabilities, including 13 with autism. At the Winterhuder Werkstatten workshop, employment opportunities include metalwork, printing and pottery, the products then being sold from a shop directly to the public. No specialised programmes for the employees with autism are provided. The residential communities of Weidenhof-Seerau and Hof Meyerweide provide full-time support for a total of 24 adults with autism, consisting of 15 males and nine females. These communities are typical of the rural-type communities often found in the UK and USA, providing supportive residential and day care programmes including traditional craft work such as weaving, carpentry, land work, etc. Unlike Hof Meyerweide, which is located in Etelaen near Bremen and which is open all year, Weidenhof-Seerau is closed for holiday periods. The Association 'Hilfe für das autistische Kind' (Help for the child with autism), which is the national society in Germany, assists in co-ordinating the work of 28 regional organisations, consisting of over 2500 members (Pohl 1993). A farm community for adults with autism was recently established as a pilot scheme in Bremen (Frank 1995). There are plans to develop two more homes for adults with autism, although developments in the areas of education and employment are unlikely to occur in the near future due to additional economic pressures following the unification of the former East and West Germanies.

Spain

In Spain there are 18 regional societies, six of which are affiliated to an umbrella organisation, the Asociacion de Padres de Ninos Autistas (APNA). Two other associations, GAUTENA – the Spanish Basque association and APAFACC – based in Catalonia are, like APNA, member associations of Autisme-Europe. APNA, based in Madrid, estimates that approximately 7400 people with autism are living in Spain. In addition to diagnostic and educational facilities, APNA provide one adult residence (numbers unknown), with gardening, workshop and farm facilities, and also training courses and conferences for professional staff and parents. APAFACC manages a subsidiary foundation, CONGOST, which provides a range of diagnostic, educational, respite and residential facilities in La Garringa in Catalonia.

Set in the Basque country in Northern Spain, GAUTENA was founded in 1978 at the time of an international meeting about autism held in Madrid, which led to the development of similar societies in other parts of Spain. GAUTENA (the Guipuzcoa Society of Parents of Children with Autism and other Pervasive Developmental Disorders) is based in Guipuzcoa, a small province of 700 000 inhabitants, which is located on the border with France and is one of the regions of the Spanish Basque country. The late 1970s were pioneering days in the post-Franco era in Spain and changes in administrative and legislative structures led to a decentralisation of services; the Basque country having greater control over the direction and provision of services. Like many other societies, GAUTENA was founded by a small group of parents together with well-motivated professionals.

Sixteen years after inception, GAUTENA has established a range of services. Psychiatric clinics, providing assessments which lead to the development of community based treatment programmes, are located in three towns in the province, with parents needing to travel no further than 20 km to their nearest clinic. The special educational needs of children with autism are met by GAUTENA who provide autism-specific classes both with their own school and in mainstream schools. GAUTENA also offers both specialist day and residential facilities to adults with autism. Following a visit to GAUTENA in early 1994, it was reported that a total of 189 families were being provided with support (Scott 1995).

Funded largely by the Governmental council of Guipuzcoa and also by contributions from clients, the DAC (Day Activity Centre) provides a service for adults with severe learning disabilities and autism, often with associated medical, psychiatric or behavioural problems. Following initial assessment, an individualised programme of activities is constructed drawing upon a range of activities, some of which are offered in the DAC itself and others in associated agencies. The activities include further education, communication skills, music and dance, workshops, carpentry, occupational skills, handicraft activities, sports and other recreational activities, gardening, socialisation and life skills. Regular reviews involve parents and carers. The DAC is managed by an occupational therapist supported by other practitioners on a 1:6 staff to student ratio. Aspirations for the future include the construction of more DACs and the further development of a recently established supported employment scheme. Mirroring the trend within Social Education Centres in England and Wales, the DACs believe that increasing numbers of adults with autism with severe behavioural problems will be provided with a service in the centre.

Like the DAC, the community living programme is financed mainly from local government and client fees. Designed to provide sheltered and small group living accommodation for adults with autism, GAUTENA seeks to provide a family-style home life. In the sheltered apartment, which is located alongside other apartments in an ordinary living area, three members of staff work a 24-hour rota system achieving 1:6 staff to client ratio. In the more intensely staffed group homes the professional staff are supported by volunteer staff to provide a service for 12 adults with autism, ten men and two women, aged 17–30, who live in two semi-detached houses in the village of Urnieta. Scott (1995) reported that the daily programme is structured with use made of visual augmented communication systems for all daily living skills. Weekend activities were more relaxed and the home was well accepted by the local community.

Portugal

The Asociacao Portuguesa Para Proteccao Aos Deficientes Autistas (APPDA) was created in 1971 by a group of parents and friends of autistic children. Regional branches of APPDA are located in Lisbon, Porto and in Coimbra, and the association has played the leading role in the development and management of services for children and adults with autism. Since 1976, 300 people have received a diagnosis from the medical services of APPDA and most people with autism live at home with their families or in residential provision, including those services provided by APPDA. A report presented in Lisbon by Cottinelli Telmo (1995), illustrated that the association provided residential homes for both children and adults with autism in Zambujal, and in Alto da Ajuda. As an illustration, the project in Zambujal is home to three children and two adults and is situated in Carcavelos, which is only five minutes by car from the beach, and 20 kilometres from the APPDA centres in Lisbon. The accommodation is located on four floors and there is a staffing ratio of one member of staff to every three persons with autism. For five days of the week, a bus collects the five at 07.30 a.m. and transports them to the two APPDA day centres in Lisbon. They return them home for 18.00p.m. The five usually spend their weekends away with their families.

As in virtually every other country, there is no specialist qualification for practitioners working with children or adults with autism in Portugal. On-the-job training has been the main training route for most residential practitioners, whereas several of their colleagues in the day centres had a teaching diploma. Input from psychologists has helped with training and there has been a particular emphasis on behavioural methods. For the future, APPDA plan to develop further resources for adults with autism, and are hoping to locate day provision next to residential homes.

In Eastern European countries the development of services for adults with autism is at an early stage although, by late 1994, a small group home for adolescents with autism had opened in Budapest, Hungary. In Russia, there are no services specific to adults with autism, many people with autism still live in large, long-stay institutions, together with people with other types of disabilities. Determined attempts involving parental and professional collaboration to establish services are being made in many Eastern

European Countries – Ukraine, Poland, the Czech Republic and Estonia, but are being hampered by the lack of any modern information on autism. Already it is apparent that these countries will need to rely on advice, support and finance from the West. Exchange, training and financial initiatives via the Erasmus, Tacis, Phare, Horizon and Helios programmes are leading to co-operation between countries.

So far in this chapter, themes have been identified and snapshots presented of the current state of service development for adults with autism in several countries and across several continents. But, what pressures do families with autism face, what barriers are placed in their way and what are the thoughts and aspirations of parents seeking to develop services?

PROFILE: THE GREEK EXPERIENCE

Living with an autistic child in Greece can, in the best circumstances, be described as only 'a problem' and in the worst as a 'disaster.' However, living with an *autistic adolescent* in Greece and especially in the provinces, can be described, putting it mildly, as living in despair.

Written in 1993 by the mother, of a young man with autism from Larisa, a city situated in Thessaly, central Greece.

This profile investigates the past and present experience of autism in Greece and identifies the aspirations of the recently formed Greek Society for the Protection of Autistic People (the *Greek Society*). Responses were collated and edited from contributions made by parents and, especially, from Professor Christos Alexiou, President of the Greek Society. It will be seen that, for the Greek Society, there are major obstacles which hinder the development of services for both children and adults with autism, not least of which are the philosophical differences in the recognition and classification of autism.

Incidence of autism in Greece

It is not known how many people with autism there are in Greece and estimates can only be based on information obtained from epidemiological studies undertaken in other countries. In Britain (1993), for example, the National Autistic Society estimates up to 115 000 people with autism from a gross population of 60 million. Application of such estimates can lead to the extrapolation that there may be around 12 000 people with autistic-spectrum disorders living, today, in Greece.

Awareness of autism in Greece

Until recently, there has been little publicity about autism in Greece, reflecting a lack of awareness of the condition amongst professionals and politicians. The result is that parents in Greece receive no information about autism and thus receive little help to develop coping strategies, especially from adolescence onwards. There is no normal, prepared transition from school to an adult environment, or from a permanent residence (the family home) to another permanent residence (a sheltered autistic community) because there are no adult communities specifically for autistic people.

Provision for adults with autism in Greece

Where are these people? Writing for this chapter in 1993, Professor Alexiou stated,

Most children, adolescents and young adults up to the ages of 30 and 40 years, stay with their families. People over this age may be found in asylums such as on the island of Leros, or in psychiatric hospitals like Daphni. Some others have to survive through the charity of their local community, through which they wander, stigmatised by the label 'the mad person'. One parent talks about the problems faced by their family with an adolescent son with autism.
'An autistic child in the provinces is condemned to not having an education. The child simply exists and hangs about all day in the house without being specifically occupied. The conscientious efforts of the family start to diminish and despite all goodwill, the child becomes an unbearable burden.'
Especially when both parents work, they cannot cope with even simple practical problems. As the child grows up and he/she stops being 'the little autistic', the problem becomes more intense. Who will be willing to look after an autistic adolescent? Even if a person is found for the morning hours, the rest of the day is tension-filled in the family because there is no relief; the tiredness becomes agony, becomes despair. There is no care and no support from the state. A lot of couples usually separate when the children enter adolescence or during pre-adolescence. This is the time they finally realise what it means to live with an autistic child and they see no way out anywhere. Some parents say that it takes a lot of courage to stay if you know what you have to cope with. Things are even worse when parents have not adopted the idea that their autistic child is not a second-class citizen but one who has rights in this world as do all citizens... In this way they lose the opportunity to fight, to struggle, to impose on their fellow-men the existence of their child ... to demand help for the founding of schools and for the right places of residence.

Another parent commented

Parents of autistic children in Greece cannot afford the luxury of being ill themselves.

Therefore it can be observed that there are little or no support services in Greece. Some small private centres have been established in Athens and Thessaloniki and, if parents can afford them, then they can leave their young offspring for a few hours every day. This offers no solution for the vast majority of parents and it is the family who continually care for the person with autism.

Within the cities in Greece, the problem of taking around children without any kind of disability, never mind children or adults with a learning or physical disability, can be an absolute nightmare. Urban society in Greece is simply not planned with any attention paid to the needs of people with disabilities and their carers. Cars park on the pavements, forcing pedestrians to walk along the sides of heavily congested roads and public buses on popular routes are often packed to overflowing.

For some families, it is preferable to live in rural settings where the adolescent or adult with autism has the opportunity to become known and accepted by the local community. From Crete, one parent explains that, despite there being little or no educational opportunities,

Living in the provinces has helped our son, especially at becoming a little more independent. He can walk around alone in Heracleum, certainly not without any danger but he can manage. There are also our acquaintances who accept him and will even help him with his education, for example the clerks at the local supermarket and also the people who give us a rest by staying with him for a few hours.

Nevertheless, problems grow as he grows older. Now we see that our son has learned some things but the lack of systematic special education is obvious in his behaviour which has become problematic, and in the development of his abilities and knowledge ... he will work only when he wants to, due to the lack of a strict programme in his life. Such a programme would help a lot in his case but it would have to be implemented in a school and not at home.

Another problem we face as he grows up is that it becomes much more difficult to leave him somewhere and go away for a few days. And of course the common anxiety we all suffer from 'What is going to happen to him when we cease to exist?

Political backcloth

The Greek Constitution of 1975 explicitly acknowledged the social rights of people with special needs and the legislature is obliged to provide care for all disabled people – whether they are war- or peace-time disabled and those who suffer from an incurable mental or physical disease. Yet the Ministry of Health and Social Affairs in Greece is currently unclear as to which section of the ministry people with autism should be classified. They have two choices: either the section of welfare designed for people with special needs, or in the section of health and specifically in the section of mental health. In practice, however, this is not a dilemma peculiar to Greece, for in the UK, whilst services for people with autism tend to fall under the umbrella of services for people with learning disabilities, many people with autism are provided (often inappropriately) with services for people with mental health problems.

Professional support is lacking and psychiatrists who are experienced in dealing with autism in Greece are few, as are the psychologists, social workers, nurses, teachers and special therapists who have had no training for or experience in work with people with autism and their families. Many practitioners who do work with people with autism have received a training heavily biased in psychodynamic approaches and thus take a vastly different practical approach to therapeutic approaches to autism to those of their colleagues working in the majority of other, 'autism-friendly' countries (for example, compare the approach of Athanassios and Panopoulou-Maratou 1995, in Greece with that of Peeters in Belgium 1995).

Financially, there is very little support for families from the Greek government's welfare policy. As there are no clear authorised provisions in the law, the allocating of allowances and specific amounts is left to the Ministries of Finance and of Health and Social Affairs. This then falls subject to party or other expediencies which determine the priorities of the economic policy of each government. There is a monthly allowance given to people with autism whose degree of disability is assessed at being more than 67%. This works out as about 20 000 drachmas, the equivalent of £50 a month. It is obvious that this allowance does not cover any of the major expenses that a person with autism and his or her family will incur. The State claims it has a social welfare policy, but in reality, the costs are met by the family.

In very recent years diagnostic centres have been set up in the major cities of Athens and Thessaloniki. Between the mid 1970s and the academic year 1991–2, 186 special schools were established in Greece – a figure which also includes four vocational training centres. Despite the Ministry of Health and Social Affair's indifference to the condition of autism, the establishment of all these schools is a development which shows an impressive change in the policy of the Ministry of Education towards children with special needs. This is important because until 1975 there was no such policy. However, by taking into account the Ministry's assessment (based on international statistics) of at least 10% of the student population (i.e. between 180 000 and 200 000) needing special education, then the policy is relatively impotent. By 1992, 12 383 children with special needs attended non-specialist services. No school or vocational training centre provides a service specifically designed for children or adults with autism. In Greece people with autism are not even mentioned as being people with special needs.

1992 – The Greek Society for the Protection of Autistic People receives legal approval

To work for the rights in life of autistic people, these being people who present the syndrome of autism and other similar conditions in which autistic elements are the most important, and to determine the needs of their everyday life, education, therapy and their life-long protection.

The stated goal of the Greek Society for the Protection of Autistic People.

Building on the experiences of parents of autistic children the Greek Society for the Protection of Autistic People was founded in November 1992. The President of the society, Professor Christos Alexiou, is the father of twin autistic children, one living in England and the other in Greece, and was Secretary of Special Education in the Ministry of Education for more than three years. Membership has come from parents living in cities, towns and villages across Greece and a further membership section, equivalent to a 'Friends of' category, enlists the support of those other than parents who wish to contribute in any scientific, economic or moral way.

The Greek Society sets out to realise their goal by any legal means and specifically by the dissemination of information to members of the Greek Society, to appropriate governmental authorities, to local authorities and to the EEC in all matters that concern autistic people and their families. They also vow to bring to their government's attention the rights of people with autism as laid down by declarations of international organisations which the State has signed and thereby made law.

As with associations in several other countries, the Greek Society intends to play an active role in the organisation of lectures, discussions, educational meetings and conferences and will publish leaflets so as to inform parents, teachers, and specialists of the problems which people with autism face and the coping strategies that may be employed. The Greek Society also plans to be in a position to morally and financially support innovative programmes of applied research in matters of diagnosis, education, care and rehabilitation of people with autism.

It is quite clear that in their struggle to develop services, the Greek Society will require the active support of the European and International movements already working with people with autism and, in 1993, the Greeks commenced their journey along this path when they were elected as members of Autisme-Europe.

The future

It can be seen that development of services for people with autism in Greece is currently at an extremely early stage. Following the well-worn path laid in other countries it is the formation by parents of an association which is likely to lead to pressure being brought to bear upon government and other sources for services to be developed for children and adults with autism. Not content to undertake the lengthy process of evolution displayed by many other countries where services for children are the first to be established, the Greek Society intends to simultaneously develop residential services for adults with autism, many of whom currently live at home with parents. An urgent task will be to identify and train 'key' practitioners to lead the way in the development of services, but maybe this cannot be fully realised until a consistent and agreed approach is made to the aetiology and treatment of people with autism.

The task ahead in Greece is a unique undertaking but one which may be hampered by its uncertain political climate. However, by the autumn of 1994, the process had commenced when funding from the EEC 'Horizon' programme enabled a series of visiting professionals to undertake training sessions with volunteer professionals and parents in Athens, covering many of the aspects inherent in the provision of services for children and adults with autism. The first international conference on autism was held at the University of Athens in January 1995, and plans are being laid to develop up to five centres of excellence. Mirroring the innovative practice shown in places such as Chile, the Greek Society hope to establish a community support network for families – an outreach scheme – particularly to those living in rural settings.

It is clear that the Greek Society will continue to need the active co-operation – both financially and morally, of its European partners. As a member of the EEC, Greece not only signed the European Community Charter of Recognition of the Fundamental Social Rights of the Disabled and all the related legislation of the EEC for people with special needs, but also fought for the enactment of European Community Help Programmes. These programmes aim to aid countries under development, such as Greece, to achieve the appropriate education, vocational rehabilitation, social integration and life-long protection of people with special needs.

CHAPTER SUMMARY

Despite differences in the recognition and classification of autism, the experience of autism for the person him/herself, for the families and others who care for the individual, is the same. The influence of parents within the development of service provision as providers themselves, or as a vociferous and determined lobbier of public authorities, has been impressive, but even so, there is no country that can claim that it provides a truly individual service to all its children and adults with autism. Services for adults with autism are consistently the last to be developed and in many countries have yet even to be planned. What is the way forward? Bryson (1994) stresses that strong and determined lobbying for services should be directed at a local level, but that this lobbying by both parents and practitioners using one voice must dovetail with government policy for new service development. Such policy is likely to require innovative and cost-effective alternatives to what already exists and against increasingly stiff competition. Indeed, several of the examples described in this chapter illustrate that innovative practice can occur in countries with little tradition of service providers for adults with autism.

ACKNOWLEDGEMENTS

Professor Christos Alexiou, University of Thessali, Greece. Eulalia Monge de Barros, Asociacion Chilena de Padres y Amigos de los Autistas, V Region, Chile. Dr Anna Balazs, Autism Research Group, Budapest, Hungary. Merry Barua, Action for Autism, New Delhi, India. Helen Blohm, Help for Children with Autism, Germany. Deusina Lopes Da Cruz, Presidente Associacao Brasilia De Autismo (ABRA). Joan M. Curtis, MACCRO Victoria, Australia. Dr Joaquin Fuentes, GAUTENA, San Sebastian, Spain. Tessa Hall and Geraldine Peacock of the National Autistic Society, London, UK. Sigriour Lao Jonsdottir, Group homes and workshop for people with autism, Iceland. Andrea McCleod, West Midlands Autistic Society, Birmingham, UK. Elizabeth Scott, The Institute, Luxembourg. Minoru Sekimizu, Director, Higashi Yamata Kobo, Yokohama, Japan. Masako Suzuki, Tokyo, Japan. Reena Sen, Spastics Society of East India, Calcutta, India. Paul Shattock, Autism Research Unit, University of Sunderland, UK. Muriel Woodhouse, West Midlands Autistic Society, Birmingham, UK.

BIBLIOGRAPHY

Anonymous. (1995). Portrait: Landsforeningen For Autister (LFA). *Link*, **16**, 4–8.
Association Le Relais (1996). Presentation of the Community Home L'Hermitage. *Link*, **18**, 4–7.
Athanassios, A. and Panopoulou-Maratou, O. (1995). The operation of the thera-peutic community 'Little Garden' for psychotic and autistic children. Paper presented at The First European Conference for Autism, University of Athens, 13–15 January 1995.
Bryson, S. (1994). *Serving Adults with Autism: Identifying*. Ontatio, Audio Archives of Canada.
Cottinelli Telmo, I. (1995). APPDA Residences – May 1995. Paper presented to delegates on Helios Exchange Programme, Lisbon 12 May 1995. Lisbon, APPDA.
Dewan, S.K. (1992). The family with autism and community care in India. In *Living with Autism: a Collection of Papers*. Durham, National Autistic Society and Autism Research Unit.
Everard, P. (1987). An international perspective. In D.J. Cohen, A.M. Donnellan and P. Rhea (eds.) *Handbook of Autism and Pervasive Developmental Disorders*. New York, Wiley and Sons Inc.
Frank, K. (1995). Therapy between stable and bed. *Deutschland*, March, 50–52.
Giddan, J.J. and Giddan, N.S. (1991). *Autistic Adults at Bittersweet Farms*. New York, Howorth Press.

Giddan, J.J. and Giddan, N.S.(1993). *European Farm Communities.* Toledo, Ohio, Medical College of Ohio Press.

Gillberg, C. (1990). Autism and pervasive developmental disorders. *Journal of Child Psychology and Psychiatry,* 31, 99–119.

Kay, B.-R. (1990). Bittersweet farms. *Journal of Autism and Developmental Disorders,* 20, 309–338.

LaVigna, G.W. (1983). The Jay Nolan Center. A community-based programme. In E. Schopler and G.B. Mesibov (eds.) *Autism in Adolescents and Adults.* New York, Plenum.

Lebedinskaya, K.S. and Nikolsaya, O.S. (1994). Brief report: analysis of autism and its treatment in modern Russian defectology. *Journal of Autism and Developmental Disorders,* 23, 675–679.

Le Couteur, A. (1990). Autism: current understanding and management. *British Journal of Hospital Medicine,* 43, 448–452.

Leekam, S. and Richdale, A. (1990). Autism down under: research and services in Australia. *Communication,* 24(2), 53–55.

Lettick, A. (1983). Benhaven. In E. Schopler and G.B. Mesibov (eds.) *Autism in Adolescents and Adults.* New York. Plenum.

Matthews, P. (1994). Profile of the Irish Society for Autism. *Link,* 12, 4–7.

Memorial Journal Officiel du Grand-Duche de Luxembourg (1988) Arrete grandducal du 4 mars 1988 portant creation d'un institut pour enfants autistiques et psychotiques. Reglement grand-ducal du 4 mars 1988 portant organisation de l'institut pour enfants autistiques et psychotiques, pp. 125–126.

Patterson-Coates, D. (1992). Services to people with autism in Australia. Paper presented at the fourth Congress Autisme-Europe, The Hague, the Netherlands, May 1992.

Peeters, T. (1995). The best treatment of behaviour problems in autism is prevention. Paper presented at The First European Conference for Autism , University of Athens, 13–15 January 1995.

Pohl, E. (1993). Help for the Child with Autism. *Link,* 12, 4–7.

Schopler, E. and Hennike, J.M. (1990). Past and present trends in residential treatment. *Journal of Autism and Developmental Disorders,* 20, 291–298.

Scott, E. (1995). GAUTENA: an exemplary system of services. *Link,* 16, 9–12.

Shattock, P. (1993). Epilogue. In J.J. Giddan and N.S. Giddan. *European Farm Communities.* Toledo, Ohio, Medical College of Ohio Press.

Simonson, L.R. and Simonson, S.M. (1987). Residential programming at Benhaven. In D.J. Cohen, A.M. Donnellan and P. Rhea (eds.) *Handbook of Autism and Pervasive Developmental Disorders.* New York, Wiley and Sons Inc.

Spivack, R. (1992). A visit to Germany. *Communication,* 26 (1), 7–8.

Van Bourgonien, M.E. and Elgar, S. (1990). The relationship between existing residential services and the needs of autistic adults. *Journal of Autism and Developmental Disorders,* 20, 299–308.

Vogel, L. (1988). *Systems of Representation and the Legal Protection of the Mentally Handicapped.* Technical Report. Brussels, Autisme-Europe.

Wall, A.J. (1990). Group Homes in North Carolina for children and adults with autism. *Journal of Autism and Developmental Disorders,* 20, 353–367.

2

Underpinning philosophy in the provision of services for adults with autism: a critique of global values related to specific practice

Hugh Morgan

IN CHAPTER one, several common themes behind the development of services for adults with autism throughout the world were identified. The aim of this chapter is to evaluate critically the underpinning philosophy behind service design and to identify certain difficulties in application for people with autism.

Chapter Two will begin by taking a historical look at educational approaches to people with learning disabilities and then describe the comparatively recent development of the ideology of normalisation. It will be suggested that proponents of normalisation have failed to bring parents/carers alongside them in the move towards the greater perceived autonomy for people with disabilities, and that this is of particular significance in the field of autism, where, as was described in Chapter One, so many services have arisen largely through the efforts of parents. It will be seen that practitioner training has concentrated too heavily on ideology and far too little upon developing the skills which are relevant to people with autism. Whilst normalisation enjoys general acceptance amongst practitioners, and especially in the training of social workers, nurses and psychologists, there has been a lack of consistency in the development of philosophies and standards of services within and between countries. It may be better for practitioners to recognise and understand the specific restrictions that people with autism have in making sense of their world, to discover what type of services people with autism would find meaningful to them, and then to design services accordingly. This chapter considers some of the difficulties in the application of recent approaches to the design of services for people with autism, and describes the findings of a small survey which asked people with autism, already living in specialist residential accommodation, to identify characteristics of their environment which were important to them. Finally, the issue of independence is briefly explored by looking at employment from the perspective of the person with autism, as a means of illustrating that even for high-functioning people with autism, there is likely to be the need for empathetic and specialised support systems.

UNDERPINNING PHILOSOPHY

There has been a tendency over the past quarter of a century to view the increased trend in the transfer of people with learning disabilities from large, long-stay institutions to smaller, more individually responsive group-living homes as the direct result of the influence of a philosophical set of values, widely referred to as normalisation. Just how fair is this assumption and how applicable can normalisation theory be to the needs of adults with autism, a client group who tend to have a very different perception of their world from that of others? It may be helpful to explore the roots of humanistic and educational models of service design and then to look at how normalisation theory has developed.

THE ROOTS OF HUMANISTIC THEORY: A HISTORICAL PERSPECTIVE

There was sense of trying to break with a dark past at the turn of the nineteenth century and medical opinion on the treatment of 'idiots' began to sway towards the theories of Pinel, Esquirol, Sequin and, of course, Jean-Marc Itard. It was the latter's educational and somewhat behavioural programme for Victor, the so-called 'Wild Boy of Aveyron' (who had been captured in the forests of Aveyron in 1800, aged 13 years), and thought now by some to be autistic (Bettleheim 1967; Corbett 1990; Frith 1989),[1] that inspired Sequin in 1846 to say

whilst waiting for medicine to cure idiots, I have undertaken to see that they participate in the benefit of education.

(Reynolds 1981)

In the UK the energies of those who set up the first asylums and schools for 'idiots' were directed more to towards finding successful methods of education, and the claims for their humanity were part of the reforming initiative of the mid-nineteenth century. 'Moral Management', as it was known attempted to replace the traditional reliance on mechanical restraints for controlling patients with non-physical methods (Nolan 1993). But the abolition of physical restraint was not uniformly accepted by all, and proponents, including William Cullen, saw that restraint was necessary as a method of both control and remedy. However, justification for reform in the treatment of 'idiots', in terms of their possible transformation into individuals able to find greater acceptance from others, has been one of the main

---

[1] However, Lane (1976) maintains that the retrospective diagnosis of autism relies on selective use of the available evidence. Even so, Itard's programme for Victor was not wholly successful, an indication that perhaps strengthens the case that Victor was autistic and therefore was not able to respond appropriately to Itard's programme.

arguments of reformers ever since. The enthusiasm and fine intentions surrounding the establishment of the early asylums and schools, which, at the time, were seen as model environments, were characterised by standards of care in which any kind of force was considered repugnant. Teachers and attendants were required to have patience, their task was to concentrate upon sensory and muscular development, nutrition and exercise, and to provide those in their care with the opportunities to take part in leisure activities. In the UK, the first report of the 1842 Lunacy Act recommended that every county was to build asylums for those for whom other means of subsistence were not available - the so-called 'pauper lunatics'. These asylums were to undergo regular inspections, individual case notes were to be maintained and there was to be the removal of all forms of mechanical restraint. The writings of the first half of the 19th century are full of rich case histories and individual success stories (Phillips 1980).

After this early promising period, practices in the following century were characterised by language which included widespread use of the terms 'lunacy', 'asylums', 'workhouses', 'attendants' and 'moral defection'. As hysteria was whipped up by the influential and eugenically motivated 'Lunatics Friends Society' (a name which now seems in appallingly bad taste), public opinion and attitudes turned against 'Moral Management', as evidenced by the service provision between 1850 and 1913. Public perception of people with disabilities was further influenced by the negative and terrible portrayals in classic English Literature including Charlotte Bronte's '*Jane Eyre*'.

Major acts of legislation from the late nineteenth century through to the Second World War, especially the 1913 Mental Deficiency Act, served to emphasise the segregation of people with learning disabilities from the wider populace. But there was a reaction against this in the years immediately after the second world war, which was buoyed by the pioneering spirit of change of the returning veterans, who had themselves witnessed dreadful suffering. This, together with Scandinavian influences, led quickly to the development of a humanitarian theory, which later developed into normalisation. In the USA, returning Vietnam war veterans, disabled by the war, led persuasive civil rights campaigns in the fight to obtain equal opportunities for people with disabilities in employment, transport, education and so on. In the pioneering era of de-institutionalisation, the ideology of normalisation has contributed significantly to the move away from large-scale institutionalised care practices. For example, in the UK, the 1950s saw the introduction of the 1959 Mental Health Act, perhaps the most significant legislative change of UK social policy in the twentieth century directly affecting the lives of people with psychiatric and learning disabilities.

APPRAISING NORMALISATION

Based upon the work of Bank-Mikkelsen (1969), Director of the Danish Mental Retardation Service, Nirje (1969) emphasised that people with disabilities should be enabled to experience a 'normal lifestyle'. This implied that the individuals with disabilities need a normal pattern of daily life. Taking holidays each year, having the opportunities to engage in the open employment and educational markets and to pursue an appropriate daily pattern of life were important. Nirje saw that the application of the principle of normalisation was not to make people with learning disabilities 'normal', but that life conditions should be made as normal as possible taking into account the degree of disability, competence and maturity, as well as the need for the provision of appropriate services. Nirje stressed that it was likely that only relative independence and integration were likely to be attained, enabling an existence which would be as near to normal as possible. Wolfensberger's (1972) subsequent and more involved interpretation of normalisation moved some way away from the original concept proposed by Bank-Mikkelsen, which, by this time, had itself quickly become part of a legislative decree for services for people with disabilities in Denmark. Wolfensberger saw that there was a need to translate a broad philosophy into action and that the key to this was through influencing the administrative and organisational structures providing services for people with disabilities, thus creating the conditions to enable people with disabilities to take part in 'normal' life situations. In a sense, Wolfensberger appeared to be saying that should a society organise itself in terms of its social values, then the platform would be created for people with disabilities to take advantage of new opportunities. Wolfensberger (1980) proposed that culturally normative methods should be used to establish, enable and support behaviours, appearances, experiences and expectations. The thrust of emphasis, therefore was shared by the self-determination of the individual, normative organisational structures within society, and normative methods of assisting individuals to achieve culturally normal lives. In terms of service design, Wolfensberger highlighted at least three key issues which needed to be considered in service design, namely isolation versus integration; dehumanisation versus personal dignity; and age-inappropriateness versus age-appropriateness. It seemed a logical step forward and is often credited for the heightening of public and professional awareness, which has led to the transfer of people with disabilities from large-scale institutions into smaller, more individually sensitive, community-based living situations over the past 20 years or so.

Today, the ideology of normalisation and its extension, social role valorisation, creates many differing emotional responses, depending upon the viewpoint of the individual. For practitioners, particularly those in field work posts, it has become the focal point for a moral stance – the rights of the individual with disabilities to make his or her choices which may include where and with whom to live and the opportunity to engage in personally meaningful employment and leisure activities. The normalisation movement has placed before us an agenda for certain ways of communicating and behaving towards people with learning disabilities.

Normalisation, though, has been essentially a global framework of values awaiting clearly defined translation into practice. One influential set of values was presented by O'Brien (1987), who, using normalisation as a basis, has developed principles on lifestyle planning, focusing on social interaction and networks. He initially identified five accomplishments (which have recently been extended by two more). The original five accomplishments can be summarised as: Community Presence, Choice, Competence, Respect and Community Participation. But, Shattock and Burrows (1995) caution that O'Brien's focus on service-users' rights, dignity, employment prospects, and social and sexual relationships may deflect attention away from more fundamental issues which predispose, and will ultimately determine, the quality of a person's life, that is people's most immediate physical and material needs. Mesibov (1990) argues that the theory of normalisation is perceived as *the* goal rather than as one of a number of possible intervention strategies. Indeed, he argues that the goal of normalisation is vague and unattainable, serving only to discourage a wide range of service responses to the individual needs of people with learning difficulties. Indeed, this then is beginning to 'get at' the nucleus of the problem, for the global values embodied by normalisation may serve to deflect attention away from the very areas in which people with disabilities need most support. This can be seen most damagingly in areas of practitioner training and in relationships between practitioners and parents.

Normalisation and parents

For many parents, normalisation has been perceived as a nightmare, creating scenarios in which parents feel that their adult offspring, already vulnerable because of disability, are being moved in situations which concentrate more on individual rights than on the practical issues of support. The language of normalisation – the jargon of social work 'speak' – has helped to create a division between practitioners and parents, for although normalisation has functioned as a desirable ideology for many practitioners, it does not appear to have brought parents alongside. Indeed it appears to have been divisive, serving to highlight divisions between parents and practitioners. As an exercise in public relations it has failed miserably. This is of particular importance in the field of autism, in which so many parents have been instrumental in leading the development and on-going management of services. Rimland, an academic and also a parent of an autistic son, provides an illustration of this divide

..here in the U.S., and I imagine it is also true to some extent in Europe as well, there has arisen a dangerous, militant movement of ideologically-motivated, self-appointed 'advocates', who are convinced that they, and only they, know what is right for handicapped people, and who believe that their views must prevail for all of the handicapped.....They are very much like other political extremists, not only in their single-minded dedication to promoting their ideology, but because they attempt to control other people's thinking by insisting that everyone use 'politically correct' language. I refer to these people as 'advozealots' – zealots who pose as advocates.

(Rimland 1993, p. 1)

The delicate balance between protection and risk-taking may have been perceived by some parents as tipping too far in the direction of risk-taking.

Normalisation and practitioner training

Practitioner training has become 'awash with social values' (Doherty 1995) and the focus on 'ordinary living' has sometimes been used as a justification for a lack of specialist training. It is the chasm between the value system and its translation into practices reflecting the very particular needs of individuals with disabilities which has been worryingly characteristic in the training of practitioners working, in residential and day settings with people with autism over recent years. A predominantly value-based, even ideological training, rather than the provision of training curricula founded upon the skills that the client will need to improve their quality of life, may have the effect of eroding the skills of professional staff, who will not have the levels of understanding and the knowledge base to respond to specific situations. In such situations we are left to rely upon practitioners who gain knowledge solely by their practical experiences at work, not through any underpinning wisdom. The conclusion to be reached is that we are no better at training our practitioners than we were 30 years ago.

Celebration of differences

It is the failure of 'normal' people to take account of the differences (rather than deficits) of people with disabilities which may be at the core of the current debate on normalisation. Following many years of almost blind acceptance, lack of rational appraisal, and almost evangelical zeal in seeking to implement normalisation, the debate is beginning to open up. Corbett and Barton (1992) make the point well when they say that the normal model negates the celebration of differences. Duffy (1990) describes her experience of living with a disability

I have learned slowly that how I feel about my body, my life, is not really very different from how non-disabled people feel about themselves. It's simply that they wear the cloak of normality, a concept which renders me naked.

(Duffy 1990, p.75)

There is, therefore, a need to become more receptive to the perspective of people with disabilities who now reject a concept of normalisation defined solely by 'normal' people. A disabled academic (Oliver 1992) questions the abilities of the non-disabled to discuss disability when they lack direct experience

As a disabled person and academic, I am in favour of academic debates about the nature of disability, what concerns me about this one is that it is yet one more example of people with abilities attempting to speak authoritatively about us.

(Oliver 1992, p. 20)

Those within the deaf community are now rejecting 'normality' as a concept that can be determined only by non-disabled people, preferring to think that the only difference between non-disabled and disabled people is the physical one. But, for people with learning difficulties, there is not always a visible difference, and they are often not the most articulate at demonstrating their viewpoint. Despite this, in 1972, the first of the 'People First' self-advocacy groups was formed, which have since made headway in the UK, making their views, wishes and needs known to local authority planners and others (Van der Gaag and Dormandy 1993). Whilst there has been much research extolling the virtues and successes of these groups, as yet, there appears to have been a lack of specific research evaluating the role and influence of the practitioner as a 'facilitator' in 'Peoples First' groups.

Normalisation, the concept of 'self' and autism

Normalisation is reliant upon changes in political and economic structures taking place which are far beyond the control of the individual. Even so, in many aspects of everyday life, for example, in further education and in employment, adults with learning difficulties are expected to develop self-reliance, self-control and self-advocacy. In these situations the concept of what is 'normal' is intrinsically linked with the concept of 'self'. The emphasis of success or failure is far removed from wider political and economic forces and determined by the individual's capacity to cope with their situation. Yet the individual perspective gives rise to an individualisation of the problem and does not give grounds for the provision of research tools in order to change the economic, social and physical structures in society (Reindal 1995). Unfortunately, normalisation now conveniently nestles in

right-wing political philosophy, although this was never the intention !
Wolfensberger (1994) attacks 'modernists' who, he writes, acclaim 'the self'
which is embodied by characteristics including selfishness, and which is
inextricably linked to how productive people are and the economic benefits
that can be gained from their work. Herein seems to lie a dilemma for the
advocacy movement. Whereas advocacy can be seen as the representation of
the interests of an individual or group by another individual or organisation,
self-advocacy may be seen as the individual representing him/herself without the influence of another person or organisation. In self-advocacy, which
is an extension of the process of empowerment, it is therefore the responsibility of the individual to achieve parity in society and is consistent with the
demands of modernism, of which Wolfensberger is so critical. Self-determination is a laudable objective, but the emphasis placed upon 'the self' reeks
of political expediency, taking the pressure away from society to provide services for the disadvantaged minority. Self-advocacy will require greater
rather than fewer resources if people with disabilities are to be given greater
say over their own lives.

The concept of empathy appears to be integral to self-advocacy.
Understanding of 'the self' and of others is essential within the process of
empowerment for, without empathy, autocracy may occur. How do adults
with autism measure up in this respect? There is already strong evidence
that people with autism lack the ability to appreciate the feelings, thoughts,
emotions, motives, intentions, desires and beliefs of others. This poverty of
empathy is often referred to as an inability to develop a theory of mind, a
phrase first used by Premack and Woodruff (1978) in relation to their work
with chimpanzees, and then applied to and developed in research with children with autism (for example, Baron-Cohen 1992; Baron-Cohen *et al.*
1985). Samet (1993) argues that there should be an identification of the
role of 'self' in the development of the theory of mind. He sees understanding of the concept of 'self', as a 'beholder' of beliefs and desires, as an
important, but as yet largely unexplored, component in our appreciation of
the building of reciprocal relationships with others.

For the adult with autism, there is a need to impose regularity on what,
for them, is an especially irregular and unpredictable world (Powell *et al.*
1994). They appear to find it difficult to make links between individual
items of experience and thus find great difficulty in predicting their world
(Wing 1994). This may largely arise from a failure to 'experience to self'
(Powell and Jordan 1993) or from an inability to perceive the emotions and
attitudes of others and thus of themselves (Hobson 1993). Accounts
recorded by adults with autism provide graphic descriptions of the difficulty
that people with autism have in making sense of their world (e.g. Sinclair
1992, Donna Williams, interviewed on Australian television by Eric Walters,

1992). But the implication is clear, for without the opportunity to gain some control and therefore to elicit predictability within their living environment, life for the person with autism may become confusing and ultimately terrifying. In an unfamiliar and unpredictable environment, particularly where a loss of familiarity has occurred, the adult with autism may often withdraw into themselves and engage in internalised routines, which although providing them with some limited degree of security, may severely challenge service provision.

It is therefore clear that the foundation for self-advocacy (as defined and determined by normal people) is impeded by cognitive restriction and by the individual's unconventional expectation of the world around them. This can be observed practically when the adults with autism make choices for themselves. Choice-making is at the heart of normalisation ideology. To be in a position to make a choice, one must know what choices are available and the means by which these can be enacted. The capacity to think abstractly, to weigh up the options that are available, and to make a judgment based upon the advantages or disadvantages of a particular recourse are essential if genuine choices are to be made. Many people with, and even without, learning difficulties find this process difficult, but given sufficient time, and perhaps also guidance, they are able to think abstractly and make their choices accordingly. One can only respect an individual's free choice if that individual is capable of making a meaningful choice. The person with autism is likely to have difficulty in thinking in anything other than concrete terms and the presentation of abstract choices can send them spiralling into anxiety. This, of course, does not mean that adults with autism cannot make choices, but that the options, about which a judgment can be made, must have already been experienced and are therefore concrete rather than abstract. It may be more respectful of the dignity of adults with autism if we recognise their extreme difficulties in social learning and set out to give them greater access to meaningful choice through direct and positive teaching approaches (Jordan and Powell 1994). Take two examples of the implications for the design of services:

VIGNETTE 2.1

Current social work practice in the UK dictates that 'clients' with learning difficulties attend and contribute to any review about themselves. For the individual with autism this process presupposes the capacity to reflect upon past progress and to make choices about future aspirations – to listen to people talking about oneself and to contribute to the meeting both verbally and perhaps in writing, and to respond spontaneously to questions, often from people who will not be familiar to the person with autism. These tasks will be daunting for many adults with autism whose irregular or poorly developed sense of 'self' will inhibit their capacity for self-reflection. Furthermore, Sinclair (1994) graphically illustrates the need to establish clearly defined ground rules prior to new meetings taking place. There needs to be a lot of pre-planning, explanation and negotiation. He says, 'We don't just walk into a meeting and have things click'. The individual with autism may need to know whether it is required to shake hands, to talk, where to sit, whether to look at other people, what will happen if self-stimulatory or self-injurious behaviours occur? etc.

So, for many people with autism the Individual Programme Planning review meeting is a somewhat artificial format for obtaining their views and choices, though, with considerable preparation and skilled support, the more able person may be able to take part in meetings in which they are at ease with the other participants. However, for many people with autism, there will be better ways of obtaining their views and choices in situations in which they are confident, secure and relaxed, on a daily basis, but this requires a high degree of autism-specific knowledge and well-developed observational skills of the practitioners who work with the individual.

VIGNETTE 2.2

The integration edict of normalisation dictates that people with learning difficulties should live in 'ordinary houses' in 'ordinary communities' with easy access to all the amenities including shops, leisure outlets and health care facilities. Indeed those living in such environments find such amenities important. But again, the spectre of the difficulty in understanding their 'self' impacts upon service delivery for adults with autism. It has been recorded that adults with autism are very poor at recognising when they are ill[1] so how relevant is it for the 'ordinary' home to be close to the General Practitioner? Certainly, should illness occur, it is obviously important for a doctor to be contacted quickly and close proximity to a health surgery may help, but before this can happen the symptoms of illness must be recognised. This information is unlikely to be volunteered by the person with autism, and again recognition of the illness will be dependent on the quality of relationships that the person with autism has with others, and particularly on the observational skills of a person knowledgeable about autism. This is particularly relevant for those more able adults with autism living in independent or semi-independent situations, who have relied upon their parents dropping in on a regular basis, but who, when their parents have died, will have no one to perform this monitoring role.

Interpreting normalisation: issues of service design

In Chapter One it was seen that services for adults with autism were being developed in the State of Victoria, Australia, by MACCRO. Curtis:

There have been great changes in the philosophy of care for the intellectually handicapped in Australia, with rather mixed results. It is policy to avoid all forms of 'congregate care' for intellectually handicapped people. They should live in normal houses, among normal people if possible. If you do set up a house specifically for

---

[1] Morgan, S. H. and Beddow, M. (1992). Unpublished survey of adolescents and adults living in semi-independent or independent living situations. Birmingham, West Midlands Autistic Society.

them it should not house more than four, it should be in a socially 'valued' neighbourhood and it must not, on any account, be adjacent to any other service for the handicapped such as a special school, activity centre or workshop – or even a hostel or elderly citizens hostel. As you can imagine this prevents any economies of scale, and also disadvantages organisations such as ours who purchased several acres of rural land to build a school and hopefully have space for several cottages for residents with a landscaped campus.

Current philosophy also dictates that everyone should work -not vocational training, not domestic duties around their own home, not voluntary work, not part-time work, but full-time work for independent employers who award wages, or a percentage thereof, based on productivity. This places service providers under great pressure to come up with programmes that meet these criteria and I think even the government is beginning to wonder if these policies may be a little unrealistic.

(J. Curtis 1994, personal communication)

Whilst it was seen in Chapter One that there are common and recurring themes in the development of services for adults with autism, there are likely to be differences in the design of services and these will be dependent upon political, economic and philosophical considerations. In Europe, for example, a comparative survey by Demeestere and Van Buggenhout (1992) found that the design of specialist services which took account of the autism-specific needs of individuals was dependent upon the political system, the financial possibilities and the legal framework within a country. Demeestere and Van Buggenhout say that it is the better resourced countries which appear to pay greatest attention to normalisation. Even so, attempts to normalise environments can be vulnerable to bureaucratic interference. Shattock (1993) points out that there are differences between the way in which each country interprets and imposes health and safety regulations in establishments providing services for people with learning difficulties. In some situations he feels that the over-zealous application of rules and regulations can inhibit the ability to establish home-like environments. Shattock calls for the, 'standardisation of acceptability', that is the formulation of rules which are comprehensible and acceptable to all, as a priority. He hopes that as standards of acceptability are developed, the criteria will relate to the quality of the service provided and not merely to the administrative details of the accommodation or the qualifications of the staff. For a starting point in the design of services for people with autism, Bryson (1994) says that we should begin to develop services by seeking to discover, from people with autism and their families, what types of services they would like to receive. So let us make a start:

What do adults with autism themselves seek in service design?

Whatever the political standpoint of practitioners and the perspective of parents, there surely must be a general agreement that we should all aim to be sensitive to the needs and views of adults with autism and to respond appropriately. With this in mind, a small, informal study was undertaken[1] to identify some of the views of 'service-users' in relation to what they considered to be important issues in the establishments in which they lived. A total of 31 service-users living in three establishments in the Midlands, the South and the North of the UK were asked to give their views. The methodology employed was not controlled. However, in each case, the questions were posed in settings in which the individuals with autism were familiar and relaxed and the questions were set by people whom they had known on a daily basis for several years. Those living in the three units were asked questions either on a group basis as part of the usual 'people's meetings' or, on an individual basis, for which attendance at a meeting did not take place. It was acknowledged that opinions were not obtained from those who were unable to verbally articulate their opinions. It was also recognised that other service-users may have been unwilling to contribute to the survey. In one establishment, those who contributed to the survey were also asked to give their opinions as to the views that they believed other service users would find important.

Summary of findings

The findings of the informal survey (detailed in Appendix 2.1) strongly indicated that the views of service-users were extremely pertinent and should be taken into account when the design of the location and the daily regime takes place. Key areas included views given on:

1 Access to amenities within the locality, e.g. being near to a post box, shops, etc.
2 Staff, e.g. more choice in new staff.
3 Compatibility and involvement with peers, e.g. choosing who to go on holiday with.
4 Environmental factors within the home, e.g. to be able to go to one's own room and not be disturbed.
5 Food, e.g. choosing food and drinks.
6 Social life, e.g. being able to go out, to stay in.
7 Leisure activities, e.g. having the opportunity to develop new interests.
8 Communication factors, e.g. needing help to communicate better.
9 Views expressed on behalf of non-verbal peers who did not convey their views included the perspective that there should be a lack of surprises.

[1] Lorimer, C., McCormick, J. and Morgan, S.H. (1995). Unpublished survey of service-user views on quality of life issues. Leeds, Nailsworth and Birmingham, National Autistic Society.

The data obtained helped also to remind us that practitioners should always remember that establishments are first and foremost the homes of the service-user and secondly a place of employment for staff. However, we do adults with autism a disservice if we accept such findings at face value and believe that all we need to do is to alter the system around them to reflect their views. One must move beyond simply creating the conditions of opportunity and remember that, for people with autism, being able to take advantage of opportunities and to interact in 'normal' ways with others is likely to depend on the calibre of support and teaching that is provided. It is clear that the quality of the physical environment will be matched by the substance of the relationship that each person experiences.

THE QUALITY OF THE RELATIONSHIP BETWEEN CARE-GIVER AND THE PERSON WITH AUTISM

The most important influences on the day-to-day lives of people with autism will be those who spend most time with them, i.e residential practitioners, or family, and this has been demonstrated on many occasions by researchers looking at the quality of staff training for those working with people with learning disabilities (e.g. Mittler 1984). It is especially important within these relationships that the understanding of autism will contribute significantly to the quality of teaching. Attwood (1986) suggests that people with autism have unique learning problems and find it particularly difficult to make sense of incoming perceptual information. Jim Sinclair, a man with autism, tells us that indeed the process of learning for people with autism is significantly different than that for others. He wrote

Being autistic does not mean being unable to learn. But it does mean there are differences in *how* learning happens.....autism involves differences in what is known as *without* learning.

(Sinclair 1992, p. 295)

Sinclair failed to understand what others took for granted,

I understand a lot about not understanding. I usually understand when I don't understand something, and I'm beginning to recognise gaps between what I actually understand and what other people assume I understand.

(Sinclair 1992, p. 295)

So the quality of support, the relationships that are formed and the teaching strategies that are employed will be of critical importance in helping adults with autism to experience everyday life. The way in which teaching strategies are applied to, for example, social skills training in autism is a good illustration of where 'normal' practice is not enough. Baron-Cohen and Bolton (1993) identify that teaching an adolescent with autism how to make a telephone call should not purely focus on the physical aspects of the task, i.e. how to dial a number, but should impart the social conventions involved, such as how to start, maintain and finish the telephone call. The capacity to engage in reciprocal communication on the telephone must be a tremendously difficult concept to grasp for individuals whose disability renders them unable to perceive the feelings and emotions of others. It is clear therefore that 'normal' teaching practice, as applied to people with learning difficulties, is not the best way to teach new skills to people with autism. The process of teaching is significantly different and it is not enough to respond at the level of behaviour alone.

INDEPENDENCE AND AUTISM

The notion of independence for people with autism is complex and complicated by the apparent absence of a theory of mind. The implication is that people with autism have great difficulty in identifying the expectations that others have about the way they should be behave. To achieve independence, one must be able to think and act without reference to other people, to accept a level of measured risk and a good level of competence will need to be gained across a range of levels of skill. The achievement of a balance of skill levels is likely to be uneven for the adult with autism, strong in some areas like verbal skills, particularly those skills learned by rote, but weak in others such as social interaction and being able to work empathetically with others. One activity considered important, if one is to achieve independence, is employment. The person with autism may well have specific difficulties which will affect their ability to successfully undertake employment in the open market. Howlin *et al.*(1995) highlight the problems in the workplace arising from communication difficulties, failure to appreciate social rules, failure to work independently and to spontaneously develop new work practices, the development of inappropriate work patterns, obsessional behaviours and resistance to change in routine, coping with promotion and mistreatment by others. Howlin *et al.* (1995) report that such difficulties can be balanced by evidence, from the TEACCH organisation in North Carolina that large companies value the low absenteeism, reliability and trustworthiness of employees with a diagnosis of autism.

The writings of adults with autism in employment provide us with an unusually frank insight into specific problems that adults with autism have in attempting to achieve independent living. Anne Carpenter, a woman with autism and a graduate librarian, wrote of her difficulty in employment, within a library, which was arranged by the local vocational rehabilitation services

..In early June of 1982, I was asked to leave because of my inappropriate behaviour. In a conference with my counsellor, it was revealed that I had interrupted the supervisor several times because I did not know what to do next, conversed with other staff members at the wrong times, and needed constant help with the IBM Selectric typewriter. I became upset very easily and was never quite sure how to handle certain situations. It is very difficult for even a high-functioning autistic adult to know exactly when to say something, when to ask for help, or when to remain quiet. To such a person, life is a reason.

(Carpenter 1992, p. 291)

Matthew Griffin, a man with autism, attempted to try to explain his specific difficulties of autism to his non-disabled colleagues at work. Up to this point he had found that his colleagues 'normal' approach to him had led to considerable conflict:

It's not nice having a label but it's even worse when other people just think you're stupid, lazy or deliberately rude when you behave in unexpected or inappropriate ways. So what distinguishes the more able autistic individuals? There are four key areas and the most important concerns communication and understanding social situations. Those of you who have worked with an autistic person perhaps think that they talk too much at times – so where is the communication problem? It concerns the non-verbal part of communication. You were born with the capacity to rapidly read other people's moods and reactions. You probably don't even realise it but you are constantly and automatically adjusting your behaviour and responses – depending on the people you are with and the situation you are in. For people with autism that's a great problem, we have great difficulty recognising and reacting to these subtle and constantly changing signals. With help and hard work it is possible to improve our understanding of this complicated process but mistakes will unfortunately continue to be made. When they do, patience and a few words of explanation from you could make all the difference.
Routines and order are very important. It takes an autistic person longer than most to learn a job but we have a good memory for detail. The trouble comes when a routine is changed or one is expected to make a common sense adjustment for an unforeseen circumstance. It may be common sense to you but it is not obvious to us. A clear routine is safe and it builds confidence. Change unsettles and leads to anxiety. Anxiety is the third key area. Events which seem trivial to you can trigger disproportionate concern for an autistic person. And this is particularly true in the work situation where skills of communication and common sense (difficult areas for us) are constantly put to the test. Fear of making mistakes is an ever-present source of anxiety. It saps confidence and reduces our effectiveness.
Odd behaviour. Autistic people seem sometimes to retreat into their own world where they re-enact events, talking and giggling to themselves. This is odd and perhaps a little frightening to a bystander but it is not intended to be threatening.
Well, I hope this short article has given you some idea of what it is like being an autistic person, in the world of work.

(M. Griffin 1994, personal communication)

From these two autobiographical writings, it may seem that even for adults with autism who have achieved high skill levels within a clearly defined area of work, there is likely to be a need for on-going, but not intrusive, systems of support to ensure that there is consistency of expectations from both the person with autism and his or her work colleagues and employers. The development of networking between employers and external organisations knowledgeable in autism is one way of approaching the many issues involved in the clarification of expectations and the prevention of misunderstandings.

CHAPTER SUMMARY

The ideology of normalisation has proven to be an influential framework of social values, helping to shape the global design and delivery of services for people with learning disabilities in many countries. The roots of normalisation can be traced back to educational models of care in operation at least 200 years ago. Because normalisation is an ideology, having an easily recognisable name and a few 'key' messages, it has been employed as a rallying banner under which humanitarian issues of the design of services are placed on the public agenda. Because it is a populist theory, however, the opinions of the minority, who are critical of some components of the theory, tend to be attacked and marginalised.

It is frequently stated that normalisation is not about making people 'normal' but the fact remains that it is an ideology that has been defined in 'normal' terms by non-disabled people. In the world of autism, normalisation has become something of a 'red-herring', deflecting attention away from the areas of support that people with autism require as a result of their specific cognitive and perceptual differences, and onto to broader areas of general philosophy. Parents, who have been the prime movers in the development of services for people with autism in many countries across the world, have been distanced by normalisation.

This chapter has looked at the development of normalisation theory and identified some areas of concern where the theory does not sit easily with the characteristics of autism. It was seen that normalisation is inextricably linked with the concept of 'self' but that for people with autism, whose sense of 'self' may be at least unconventionally experienced, the focus of attention should be on the support systems that enable them to take part in society. Even so, their experience of society may be qualitatively different to our own, due to their difficulty in appreciating and understanding the basic conventions of communication and sociability. Quality of life should therefore be judged by what is meaningful to the individual with autism and not necessarily to ourselves. Practitioners should focus upon the actual delivery of services and on the quality of the relationship between themselves and the person with autism. The critical issue will become the quality of training that is available to practitioners who work with people with autism, which should be based upon analyses of the skills that people with autism require to make their lives more meaningful to them, and not be determined by a set of global values devised by others. Whilst there are important humanitarian messages in normalisation theory, which will need to be passed on in practitioner training, the success or failure of individual adults with autism in society will depend more upon the skilled networks of support that can be put in place which accept and understand the specific perceptual difficulties of people with autism. Based upon this underlying knowledge, systems of support can be developed to enable adults with autism, not as Nirje (1969) says, 'to achieve an existence as close to *the normal* as possible', but to achieve an existence which acknowledges their specific difficulties and creates the environments in which they can learn and experience everyday activities, in line with their very individual wishes and skills. Clearly, normal practice by itself is not good enough for people with autism.

ACKNOWLEDGEMENTS

Matthew Griffin, West Midlands Autistic Society.

APPENDIX 2.1

Survey of service-user views on quality of life issues

C. Lorimer, J. McCormick and S.H. Morgan

Summary of the findings from an informal survey of the views of service-users living in three establishments for adults with autism in England, $n=31$

1 Access to amenities within the locality
Being close to:

A post-box
Bus stop
Video shop
Hairdressers
Newsagent
Pubs
Shops
Parks

Being able to:

Mix with people outside the home
Go out
Go to college

2 Views on staff

Dislike staff turning the TV off
More choice in new staff
Having experienced and qualified staff
Having the right level of support
Don't like being told what to do
Being able to trust staff to look after one's affairs when away, i.e. staff to look after room and possessions, mail, etc.
Staff who have left should keep in contact
Dislike being stopped from habits (twiddling pieces of string – why is this different from the behaviours of other residents?)
Staff should make family and friends welcome when they visit

3 Compatibility and involvement with peers

Having a choice about who you live with
Living with others one could 'get on with'

People shouldn't put buttery knives into the marmalade
Choosing who to go on holiday with
Dislike being interrupted by others when the TV is on

4 Environmental factors within the home

Right to privacy
To be able to go to one's room and not to be disturbed
Right to relax and not to be told what to do
Own space
Sleep
To live in a calm and secure home
Peace and quiet
Concern that clothes were sometimes damaged in the laundry
Dislike piles of ironing always in the sitting room
Washing/ironing own clothes
Decent central heating
Rules on smoking
Being able to wash-up by hand and not by dishwasher
Having a push, rather than mechanical, lawn mower.
Not having to miss TV programmes
Ornaments are special
Everything should be nice
Easy to use jug kettle is better than old water geyser
Should have small nail scissors instead of using toe nail clippers for
cutting finger nails
Photos of family

5 Food

Dad being invited to lunch
Good food
Cooking our own food
Being able to make snacks
Choosing food and drinks
Being able to eat on my own

6 Social life

Being able to go out
To stay in
Seeing family
Going to pubs

Day trips
Meals out (especially for birthdays)
Shopping trips
Holidays
Going to other people's homes
Important to visit family and friends

7 Leisure activities

Having the opportunity to develop new interests
Learning German
Video games, e.g. Sega megadrive
Going to the races (horse racing)
Relaxing
Music

8 Communication factors

Need help to communicate better
Writing letters home

9 Views expressed on behalf of non-verbal peers, who did not convey
their views

Privacy
Access to water and tactile activities
Music
Peace
Lack of surprises
Visit to pubs
Computers
Radio One
Attention
Affection
Help to communicate
To go out or to stay in
To visit people at weekends
To trust staff

BIBLIOGRAPHY

Attwood T. (1986). 'Do autistic children have unique learning problems?'. *Communication*, 20, 9–11.

Bank-Mikkelson, N.E. (1969). In R. Kugel and W. Wolfensberger (eds.) *Changing Patterns in Residential Services for the Mentally Retarded.* Washington DC, Presidents Committee on Mental Retardation, Government Printing Office.

Baron-Cohen, S. (1992). The theory of mind hypothesis of autism: history and prospects of the idea. *Psychologist*, 5 (1), 9–12.

Baron-Cohen, S. and Bolton, P. (1993). *Autism: the Facts.* Oxford, Oxford University Press.

Baron-Cohen, S., Leslie, A. and Frith, U. (1985). 'Does the autistic child have a theory of mind?' *Cognition*, 21, 37–46.

Bettleheim, B. (1967). *The Empty Fortress: Infantile Autism and the Birth of Self.* New York, Free Press.

Blunden, R. (1988). Quality of life in persons with disabilities: issues in the development of services. In R.I. Brown (ed.). *Quality of Life for Handicapped People.* New York, Croom Helm.

Bryson, S. (1994). *Serving Adults with Autism: Identifying.* Ontario, Audio Archives of Canada.

Carpenter, A. (1992). In E. Schopler and G.B. Mesibov (eds.) *High-Functioning Individuals with Autism.* New York, Plenum Press.

Corbett, J. (1990). The aetiology of autism. Paper presented at a conference organised by the West Midlands Autistic Society, May 1990. University of Keele.

Corbett, J. and Barton, L. (1992). *A Struggle for Choice – Students with Special Needs in Transition to Adulthood.* London, Routledge.

Demeestere, G. and Van Buggenhout, B. (1992). *Comparative Evaluation Survey of Structures and Services in the E.C. For People with Autism.* Belgium, Autisme-Europe.

Doherty, H. (1995). Paper presented at the Workshop on Training for Staff Working with People with Disabilities, 29 June 1995. University of Keele.

Duffy, M. (1990). In J. Corbett and L. Barton. (1992). *A Struggle for Choice – Students with Special Needs in Transition to Adulthood.* London, Routledge.

Frith, V. (1989). *Autism: Explaining the Enigma.* Oxford, Blackwell.

Hobson, R.P. (1993). *Autism and the Development of Mind.* Hove, Lawrence Erlbaum Associates.

Howlin, P., Jordan, R.R. and Evans, G.(1995). Module 3. Unit 3, Distance Education Course in Autism (Adults). Birmingham, University of Birmingham, School of Education.

Jordan, R.R., and Powell, S.D. (1994) Module 1. Unit 3, Distance Education Course in Autism (Adults). Birmingham, University of Birmingham, School of Education.

Landesman, R., Dwyer, S. and Knowles, M. (1987). Ecological analysis of staff training in residential settings. In P. Mittler and J. Hogg (eds.) *Staff Training in Mental Handicap.* London, Croom Helm.

Lane, H. (1976). *The Wild Boy of Aveyron.* London, George Allen and Unwin.

Mesibov, G.B. (1990). Normalisation and its relevance today. *Journal of Autism and Developmental Disorders*, 20 (3), 379–390.

Mittler, P. (1984). Evaluation of services and staff training. In J. Dobbing (ed.) *Scientific Studies in Mental Retardation.* London, Macmillan.

Nirje, B. (1969). The normalisation principle and its human management implications. In R. Kugel and W. Wolfensberger (eds.) *Changing Patterns in Residential Services for the Mentally Retarded*. Washington DC, Presidents Committee on Mental Retardation, Government Printing Office.

Nolan, P. (1993). *A History of Mental Health Nursing*. London, Chapman and Hall.

O'Brien, J. (1987). A guide to life-style planning: using the activities catalog to integrate services and natural support systems. In B. Wilcox and G. Thomas Bellamy (eds.) *A Comprehensive Guide to the Activities Catalog: an Alternative Curriculum for Youth and Adults with Severe Disabilities*. Baltimore, Paul H. Brookes.

Oliver, M. (1992). Intellectual masturbation: a rejoinder to Soeder and Booth. *European Journal of Special Needs Education*, 4 (1), 20–27.

Phillips, J. (1980). Kaspar Hauser. The Times, Saturday 16 August 1980, p. 7.

Premack, D. and Woodruff, G. (1978). Does the chimpanzee have a theory of mind ? *Behavioural and Brain Sciences*, 1, 515–526.

Powell, S.D. and Jordan, R.R. (1993). Being subjective about autistic thinking and learning to learn. *Educational Psychology*, 13, 359–369.

Powell, S.D., Matthews, E. and Morgan S.H. (1994). Flexibility in Thinking and Behaviour. Module 1. Unit 4, Distance Education Course in Autism (Adults). Birmingham, University of Birmingham, School of Education.

Reindal, S.M. (1995). Discussing disability – and investigation into theories of disability. *European Journal of Special Needs Education*, 10 (1), 58–69.

Reynolds, D. (1981). The development of the British Welfare State. Course Paper. Cardiff, University College.

Rimland, B. (1993). Prologue. In J.J. Giddan and N.S. Giddan. *European Farm Communities for Autism*. Toledo, Ohio, Medical College of Ohio Press.

Samet, J. (1993). Autism and theory of mind: some philosophical perspectives. In S. Baron-Cohen, H. Tager-Flusberg and D.J. Cohen (eds.) *Understanding Other Minds: Perspectives from Autism*. Oxford, Oxford University Press.

Schopler, E. and Mesibov, G.B.(eds.) (1992). *High-Functioning Individuals with Autism*. New York, Plenum Press.

Shattock, P. (1993). In J.J. Giddan and N.S. Giddan. *European Farm Communities for Autism*. Toledo Ohio, Medical College of Ohio Press.

Shattock, P. and Burrows, T. (1995). Promoting Physical and Material Well-Being. Module 2. Unit 3, Distance Education Course in Autism (Adults). Birmingham, University of Birmingham, School of Education.

Sinclair, J. (1992). In E. Schopler and G.B. Mesibov (eds.) *High-Functioning Individuals with Autism*. New York, Plenum Press.

Sinclair, J. (1994). *Keynote Address: Autism First Hand*. Ontario, Audio Archives of Canada.

Van der Gaag, A., and Dormandy, K. (1993). *Communication and Adults with Learning Disabilities*. London, Whurr Publishers Ltd.

Wing, L. (1994). The Autistic Spectrum. Module 1. Unit 1, Distance Education Course in Autism (Adults). Birmingham, University of Birmingham, School of Education.

Wolfensberger, W. (1972). *The Principle of Normalisation in Human Services*. Toronto, National Institute on Mental Retardation.

Wolfensberger, W. (1980). Overview of normalisation. In J. Flynn and K. Nitsch (eds.) *Normalisation, Social Integration and Community Services*. Baltimore, University Park Press.

Wolfensberger, W. (1994). The growing threat to the lives of handicapped people in the context of modernistic values. *Disability and Society*, 9 (3), 395–413.

3

Evaluating services for adults with autism: the Autism Quality Audit and Accreditation Programme

Hugh Morgan and Bob Reynolds

IN MANY countries, services for adults with autism are subject to statutory regulations imposed by local authority or State registration departments (e.g. Kelly and Warr 1992; Wall 1990). Guidelines for inspection have been largely formulated upon minimum requirements for practice within services for people who are elderly, mentally ill, or with learning difficulties. Usually, these formal assessment processes take little account of the nature and manifestation of autism and the consequential implication for the design and delivery of support services.

This chapter begins by considering the development of quality assurance systems in social care and seeks to identify those characteristics which determine the quality of a service. It reviews the general factors which need to be included in a quality audit programme evaluating social care provision; acknowledges the specific benefits of quality audit to service-users and to employees, before introducing one model of quality audit, known as accreditation. The major part of this chapter then describes and evaluates a Quality Audit and Accreditation Programme for services for people with autism which has attempted to move far beyond the minimum standards of practice required by the statutory bodies. Particular emphasis is given to the composition and task of the accreditation team, the process of accreditation and of the gathering of evidence. The experiences of individuals involved are described and the findings of the first two years of operation are presented and evaluated. Suggestions are made for the further development of this model of accreditation.

SETTING THE SCENE

The current trend towards quality assurance must not hide nor dismiss the fact that the concept of quality existed in social care provision well before systems of measuring quality became prominent. In recent years, the achievement of quality through the process of quality assurance has become increasingly significant in the design, organisation and delivery of social care provision. Quality assurance is essentially an evolving process, but an enduring characteristic in a time of great change in the provision of services for people with learning difficulties and other vulnerable groups. The process of quality assurance now offers an opportunity to formally evaluate and measure the design and delivery of services, and, by so doing, to provide the means by which action and change can take place within organisations.

Historically, the concept and process of quality assurance applied to the provision of health and social care is not new (Tresnowski 1988) and has been around since the first years of the twentieth century. Internationally, the language and delivery of quality has taken place within a context that includes national legislation, in which personal litigation and the rights of clients have become key issues. In a climate of fiscal regulation, contract specification and competition, professional regulation, accreditation and the setting of standards, consumer advocacy and service design are all of increasing concern and significance (Richards 1992). Experience in the USA has influenced the development of quality assurance systems in several countries, including the UK, Australia and Canada, with heightened awareness and, in some cases, programmes in many other countries including Japan, China, Italy, Spain and The Netherlands (Scrivens 1995).

It may be observed that in market-led economies, two polarised perspectives have developed over the past 20 years, embodied by those who are concerned to ensure the quality of health and social care in the face of cost-containment, and those who see cost-containment itself as the definition of quality. The debate is not assisted by the language increasingly used and references to the 'customer' or 'consumer' rather than to 'patient' or 'resident' seem to represent a move away from the medical model to a commercial definition of health. The rhetoric does nothing to assuage the impression that, without a qualitative social definition of health and social care, the individuals themselves lose out, and that market forces, with their inherent competitive drive, determine the ultimate goal of health care.

SHARPENING THE CONCEPT OF QUALITY

Which characteristics determine the quality of a service?

Dunnachie (1992) draws on literature from commercial enterprises which he then applies to social care settings, to conclude that a quality service should be led by customers and that there should be a commitment to, and ownership of, the idea of quality throughout the agency. People, rather than statistics, should be valued and there should be higher rather than lower spending on staff supervision, development and training. Dunnachie goes on to say that the agency should be explicit and disciplined about goals, roles and standards at all levels.

What general factors need to be included in a quality audit programme evaluating social care provision?

Richards and Heginbotham (1992) have developed a checklist of questions which seek to elicit the value of a quality assurance programme. These questions are as follows:

1 Does it have a repetitive cyclical path and focus on enhancement in preference to maintenance?
2 Is it highly participative, including users and professional staff to contribute to quality management by increasing communication, shared values and objectives?
3 Does it take account of user/consumer statements?
4 Does it involve 'peer review' by staff?
5 Is it linked to standard setting exercises?
6 Does it involve observation of services in operation?
7 Is it outcome-orientated and does it explore causal links with service structures and processes?
8 Can it compliment but stand independent of cost data, and other quantitative data?
9 Is it action-orientated in applying its findings?
10 Does it embody its values, principles and make them explicit to participants?
11 Does it have a transparent and learnable methodology?

Richards and Heginbotham believe that a quality assurance programme should be a highly participative, cyclical review (cited in Donabedian 1988) which enhances the responsiveness of the service to the individuals for whom it cares for. Its methodology should include the direct observation of services, and should pay particular attention to statements made by clients. Dunnachie (1992) says that a quality assurance programme should play a key role in preventing rather than detecting problems, within an organisation.

What are the potential benefits to service-users?

A quality assurance system should seek to measure whether a service is organised in such a way that it can appropriately and effectively meet the individual needs of each person using the service. This process will help to focus practitioners' attention upon the specific needs of their clients. It seems also that a further benefit would be its use as a helpful tool to reassure parents/carers/advocates that the services provided for their sons/daughters/friends are responsive to individual needs, and will be supported and encouraged to respond more appropriately.

What are the potential benefits to employees?

The benefits to employees working in those services evaluated by quality assurance systems have been identified (Clough 1992). He believes that it will lead to an evolving framework for staff development, training and supervision, and an improved clarity of purpose for work brought about by appropriate leadership and management. Clough writes about the benefit for employees working within services which undergo quality audit, but if we refer again to the characteristics of an effective design for quality assurance systems (listed on p. 55) then it can be seen that one of the distinctive features is the process of peer evaluation. This, by itself, has great potential for use in the process of staff development, and it will be seen in the example which follows that the methodology of peer evaluation does, in fact, play an extremely important role in this process. Even so, current evidence from the USA, Australia and, recently, the UK indicates that, increasingly, peer review of professional education will be favoured less than a model of external, policing review, which will focus more on surveillance and on guarantees of public protection (Scrivens *et al.* 1995).

THE ACCREDITATION MODEL

The accreditation model is a leading example of a quality audit system which uses peer review as a tool for collecting evidence about the quality of a service. Accreditation has been described as a process of self-regulation in which an independent body defines and monitors the standards of those organisations who voluntarily elect to participate in the scheme (Scrivens *et al.* 1995). The process of accreditation – of self-regulation – is distinct from the alternative model of imposed regulation, by which inspection of a service is necessary for the service to continue to receive funding.

The introduction of accreditation systems to hospitals has been the precursor of the accreditation programmes employed in other health and social care systems and it would be helpful to spend a little time exploring these before looking at a similar programme used specifically in services for people with autism.

In 1905, Ernest Codman, a surgeon at the Massachusetts General Hospital in Boston, USA, sought to measure the outcomes of health care in the hospital in which he worked. Codman christened this process the 'End

Result Idea' which, by 1917, had influenced the development of the Hospital Standardisation Programme. By the early post-World War two years, over half of the hospitals in the USA had enlisted in the scheme, known as the 'Joint Commission on Accreditation of Hospitals'. The process was controlled essentially by the medical profession as a means to usurp the previously dominant role of hospital administrators and trustees. Whilst State legislation in, for example, Pennsylvania and Colorado has mandatorily required hospitals to release to the public their performance indicators on medical outcomes and severity of illness, the medical control of the process of accreditation continues today with the re-named 'Joint Commission on Accreditation of Health Care Organisations'. The application of accreditation systems to health and social care is prominent in Australia, Canada, the UK as well as the USA, which Scrivens (1995) describes as a pioneer of accreditation.

Why have an accreditation system?

Any service in the health and social care sector should to be accountable to the individuals who use the service and also to the purchaser of those services. The accreditation process can be used to acknowledge and validate the knowledge and practice of staff via the implementation of appropriate and agreed standards. The process can promote continuity and consistency in service delivery and can be particularly helpful when service development plans are drawn up and reviewed.

Application of an accreditation system to services for adults with autism

A recurring theme in this book is the reference to the perception of the world, and its constituent parts, held by the person with autism. The implication is that the designers of services must first understand and empathise with the autistic perspective in order to begin to address the issues of service design. Whatever service is provided for people with autism, there must be some capacity to measure objectively the quality of the service. Furthermore, this measurement must be one which gauges the quality of life for the person with autism by taking into account his/her perception of the environment in which she/he lives. It will need to be demonstrated that a service must be responsive to current and changing needs of service-users, consistently fit for its stated purpose, and operating to agreed standards. It has been shown that quality audits are increasingly being used in the caring field, but, without autism-specific measures, the sensitivity of such methods when applied to people with autism may lead to false conclusions being reached.

ONE EXAMPLE OF SERVICE EVALUATION: THE AUTISM QUALITY AUDIT AND ACCREDITATION PROGRAMME

Background

In 1991, the National Autistic Society (NAS) began a process to identify the characteristics of local autistic societies (LAS) which were already, or wished to become, affiliated to the NAS. For example, in 1992 there were, in addition to the NAS, no less than 72 local regional autistic societies, some with small but others with a large membership (Peacock 1992). One area quickly pinpointed was the need to ensure that societies providing practical services were responding to the needs of people with autism in an empathetic and meaningful way. It was agreed that an evaluatory process would be looked at which measured the autism-specific quality of a service. Meetings were convened for both LAS and NAS representatives and were co-ordinated by a skilled independent chairperson, who himself led a national agency working on behalf of people with learning disabilities. The initial meeting led to the formation of a steering group, whose task was to specify measures and standards of quality which could be used to assess services provided for people with autism. Before the process of measurement, that is the production of a standardised format, could be identified and agreed, the committee had to answer key questions including:

What is quality?
How would it be recognised?
How should it be measured?
How could it be independently verified?
How could quality be established and developed?

Inherent in the process of answering these and other questions, was the necessity to clarify what the accreditation process would seek to achieve:

It would not be:

An inspection (to minimum standards)
A pass or fail process
A way of comparing one service with another
A requirement to work to specific styles of practice
An alternative management system
An alternative grievance/complaints system.

Following a pilot study, the accreditation programme was ready for implementation, and national and most local societies agreed to the review of their specialist services. The accreditation process was tailored to meet the differing needs of children's and adult's services. The overall goal of The

Autism Quality Audit and Accreditation Programme has been to assist, encourage and support all education, all care and all support services for people with autism to attain and retain accreditation. Achievement of this goal should mean that every person with autism could be assured that he/she will receive appropriate support from an organised service that meets standards including a capability for provision of services which understand and respond to the specific needs of people with autism.

Services wishing to achieve accreditation would become registered in the programme indicating their commitment to working towards and achieving the standards required for accreditation. The service would receive support in planning and implementing its development from the Accreditation Programme Manager and from networking with other services in the programme. Arrangements would subsequently be made for each service to receive an in-depth visit from an accreditation team during the first year, then shortened follow-up visits during years two and three and, in the fourth year, a second in-depth review of their services. The scheme was to be funded by contributions from NAS and LAS and was initially kick-started by a grant from the National Department of Health. What follows is an account of the review process for adult services only.

The accreditation team

The quality audit teams were selected from an established pool of team members by the Accreditation and Support Services Manager. Pool members included experienced practitioners from participating services and other relevant professionals who, on occasions, have been local authority registration officers. Professionals were usually seconded by their employers. A team leader was appointed, who was always a highly experienced practitioner in the field of autism, and the other members of the team were selected to ensure a spread of expertise and interests relevant to the establishment under review. The quality audit team of, say, four people (the size of the team was dependent upon the size of the establishment) spent up to one week within an establishment.

The objectives of the accreditation team

The main aim of the quality audit team was to look at the organisational framework in which the service is provided and to identify how the service understands and responds to autism. The review process attempted to elicit data from the perspective of the service-user by looking at how the individual service addressed the social, physical and emotional well-being of the user. Finally, the review team looked at how the service accounted for its practice through the records it maintained – both general records of the whole service and of records relating to the individual. The broad areas are summarised in Figure 3.1.

How evidence was gathered

The evidence gathered related to the criteria outlined above, all of which were specific to the understanding of autism and to the underlying knowledge base of the responses required.

Evidence was acquired by several methods. Written material, describing the project, giving financial details, staffing, admission criteria, etc., was provided by the service managers in advance of the visit. During the visit itself, the members of the review team focused on their own specific areas of expertise, and observed, discussed and interviewed members of staff, parents, users, and others who were relevant to the evidence-gathering process. Team members were provided with a checklist of questions against each standard, which, when asked, were designed to elicit responses which helped to build up sufficient evidence to determine whether a standard had been reached.

The evidence

To achieve accreditation, the service must provide evidence that they meet the following criteria:

1 An autism-specific body of knowledge
2 Evidence that the body of knowledge is consistently applied to the way the service is organised and delivered
3 Evidence that the body of knowledge is consistently applied to the work of individuals
4 Evidence that its specialised services are related to the individual needs of each person.

The evidence of criteria for achievement was gathered against 38 standards applied to the following areas:

The owner or provider of the service
The organisation of the service
The understanding of autism
The specific organisational responses to autism
Individual service plans for service-users
The physical well-being of the service-users
The social well-being of the service-users
The emotional well-being of the service-users
Record keeping and monitoring of the service.

THE PROCESS

Service registers in the programme

⋆

Accreditation Manager visits service

Plans to prepare for, or to start, review

⋆

Service to prepare pre-review information

for review team – 5 copies

Team leader and team selected and advance

service information circulated

⋆

Programme for visit arranged by

Team leader and service manager

⋆

Team training and review visit

⋆

Team leader compiles report

Feedback from team, feedback from manager

Report with recommendations goes to Committee

⋆

Accreditation committee decision

⋆   ⋆

Committee accredits service   Committee does not accredit

and issues certificate   service – action detailed

⋆   ⋆

Follow-up

Team leader visits annually x2

⋆

Full service review again after three years

Figure 3.1 *The audit process*

So, the format of the audit process had four clear phases: the circulation of written material to the team in advance of the audit team visits, the initial opening interview with the senior practitioner, leading to three days or so of data collection, followed by the concluding interview. At the concluding meeting, which has evolved into a general de-briefing session, limited feedback was given to the same practitioners who had attended the initial meeting on the very first day. Details of the complete process is outlined in Figure 3.1.

Who makes the decision whether to accredit or defer an establishment?

Following the review, the team leader presented a report – completed in the standardised format, and with the full agreement of all team members – to an arms-length committee which was appointed to oversee the operation and delivery of the quality audit review programme. The arms-length committee then made decisions about the report so that it would be seen as an objective and independent response. The managers of establishments would then have been informed of the decision reached, and provided with an opportunity to respond to any suggestions made.

Many services reached the standards set, but, inevitably, some services failed to achieve the required level of quality, and the issue of deferment has been an extremely sensitive one. In such cases, by the end of the final day's de-briefing session, it should be clear to the establishment that deferment is a strong possibility, and confirmation will usually follow from the arms-length committee. Services in this position have, to date, been deferred rather than failed. It would not serve the interests of those adults with autism living and/or working within a 'suspect' service, to be left unsupported in the hands of an organisation which has been shown to be failing them. The remedial approach to this problem has been firstly to provide the organisation with a statement of those areas where their service has required improvement and, secondly, the facilitation of structured support organised by the Accreditation and Support Services Manager, enabling them to subsequently achieve accreditation status. Should the establishment – and – by implication – their Society, fail to respond appropriately to the suggestions made, then the service will not be able to obtain affiliation status to the NAS. To date this has not occurred.

EXPERIENCING ACCREDITATION

A parent's perspective

The first parent to become a member of an accreditation team, Ann Lovell, described her experiences (Lovell 1994). The following extracts illustrate her apprehension for the task ahead, and the process in which she was engaged. Names are changed to preserve anonymity.

When the Accreditation Programme Manager telephoned me to ask if I would join the accreditation team due to visit the White House, my reaction was one of extreme caution. I could not think why he was approaching me. What on earth can I possibly contribute? I asked him. My only real qualification for becoming a team member was that I have been a mother of a man – who has autism – for some 31 years, written a book about him and had been involved in his life at school and then, once it was founded, in his adult residence. This, it seemed, was precisely the experience that the Accreditation and Support Services Manager wanted. Parents have a different perspective from professionals – however deeply the latter may care – and it is necessary to include that perspective in order to obtain a complete picture of the workings of a centre, be it the White House or the school up the road. Thus reassured, though still very apprehensive, I agreed to go.....

Ann Lovell describes the preparation of the team for the process, and then the initial meetings. She later continued:

The Centre had also taken great care to prepare their residents for our visit so that the advent of our strangers might not prove too worrying. We, for our part, did our best to take ourselves off quietly if it seemed that someone was beginning to be disturbed by our presence. We met just about everyone – even the cook and the cleaning ladies. I, for one, was particularly pleased to meet a whole group of parents and to listen to their views.

Altogether we spent just under three days on the visit. All of us felt that we had come through an extraordinarily interesting experience and agreed that, once we had recovered, we would be more than willing to do it again – with less nervous 'wear and tear' next time.

For me it was particularly marvellous to be given a chance to look into the workings of a centre totally different from, yet in many ways like the centre in which my son lived; to consider its philosophy and practice; and to store away at the back of my mind several of its many excellent ideas.

As for her role, Ann Lovell says:

I was, after all, of use – not perhaps so much at taking the lead in interviews but at bringing forward ideas for discussion and voicing my reactions to replies we had been given, as well as at supporting the others when delicacy of approach was needed. It had not seemed to matter in the least that I was the oldest of the four of us, or the least able-bodied. Somehow, we all very quickly became a team and what mattered most was that we, as well as the staff of the White House, were all working on the same side for the same end.

A team member's perspective

Initially, I was extremely excited to be selected as a member of an accreditation team. However, as the week approached I became slightly apprehensive, what if everyone knew more than me? I need not have worried. The accreditation team met in relaxed surroundings, a beautiful hotel in a village. The 'getting to know you' exercise was extremely valuable – each person sharing information about themselves with the group. The team was made up of people from very different backgrounds, for example, social work and nursing, but all had experience of working with people with autism.

I found the accreditation process to be stimulating, tiring and at times worrying/concerning. The service being audited appeared to believe that their service was being inspected rather than accredited, this was one of my reasons for concern. Clearly, the management team were not enjoying the process nearly as much as my own management team had, some months earlier. Nevertheless, throughout the four days of the audit, many 'positives' came to the fore, i.e. good practice, attitudes and philosophies. I would heartily recommend that people providing a service to people with autism participate in the accreditation process. The experiences certainly broadened my knowledge base and should be regarded as essential staff training for those working with adults with autism.

A Service Manager's perspective

My management committee had always fully supported the idea of accreditation and quality audit. Most of the members of my management committee were professionals – a director of nursing, a team leader from social services, a solicitor, an accountant, the chairman was a former deputy director of social services, a housing association development officer, and two parents of adults with autism. I had little doubt that any opposition to the process of accreditation would fall on stony ground, and as I was more concerned about appearing abnormally defensive to others I resigned myself to the thought that my own establishment would be open to minute inspection – warts and all. A little reluctantly, I recognised that an in-depth review of our establishment's capacity to meet the autism-specific needs of the adults living in it would demonstrate and reassure parents and local authorities that we, as practitioners, were performing our jobs properly.

Preparation for the visit seemed to be the key to me and there were four areas which required work: preparation of all the staff so that they knew what to expect from the accreditation team, preparation of the adults with autism living in our establishment, preparation of the parents and, finally, as the date of the visit drew nearer, so we also became aware of the need to brief the accreditation team of what we expected of them, in terms of their sensitivity to our situation. The aims and methods of accreditation were discussed with all 45 staff members, both individually and on a group basis. It was a lengthy process but it helped to reassure staff who learned that nothing out of the ordinary was being expected from them – they were to carry out their own duties in their own styles as usual, but when asked questions by individuals of the team were free to respond as they believed appropriate. We did a bit of refresher training on the 'Triad of Impairments' and on our approaches to those adults with autism whose behaviours challenged our service, but we were due to do this anyway as part of our own in-house rolling training programme. We introduced the forthcoming visit to those living in the unit again both on an individual and on a group basis – we gave them the names of the members of the team and referred to them as visitors and guests who wished to see their home and what they did in the day centre and out in the city. The forthcoming visit was discussed with parents at the bi-monthly parents meeting and I did say that whilst we would not seek to influence the process, it was important that all the parents/carers took the opportunity to convey their feelings about the place as a home and workplace for their sons or daughters. The first evening of the accreditation process was seen as a chance to make it clear to the team that, whilst we understood that they had a job to do, we expected them to be sensitive to the needs of our 'people'. Anxieties were anticipated from both those living and working in our establishment but the depth of our preparation seemed to work well, and the accreditation team were never intrusive and sensitively moved away from situations where our clients were showing signs of undue anxiety.

After three days the process had finished and we awaited the initial feedback meeting prior to the departure of the audit. The visit went as smoothly as we could have hoped and the team appeared to have collected information from a wide number of staff, parents, outside professionals including our General Practitioner and, of course, from their own observations of our work with the adults with autism living in the establishment. The feedback session was useful and served to allay some of our own anxieties, providing some positive comments about our overall work practices, but questionably, in my view, tried to be too prescriptive about one or two areas – our work is not an exact science and individual, even innovative solutions to specific problems are not necessarily wrong – just because the very limited literature on autism tells us something different. But overall, we, that is the parents, those working and living in the establishment, and the many contacts that we have outside the establishment, including our local authority registration department (whose registration officer was a member of the team), found the accreditation visit to be a very worthwhile process. It concentrated our minds wonderfully on our task of caring for adults with autism and it was reassuring that a totally independent team who were themselves knowledgeable about autism should feel that we, as practitioners, were providing a genuinely therapeutic service and together we were also able to set achievable targets for further progress in agreed areas.

FINDINGS FROM THE FIRST TWO YEARS OF THE PROGRAMME

The findings from the Quality Audit and Accreditation Programme were initially presented at a conference held at the University of Aston in October 1994. In what had clearly been an evolving process, it appeared that there were great similarities in looking at any service – the distinction came when looking at the way in which each service interpreted their task and responded to the individual needs of service-users. This could be seen in the way in which they put into practice educational and social programmes, and responded to difficult behaviour, etc. By the end of the first 24 months, 25 adult establishments in the UK had been reviewed, four of which had been deferred, but which were receiving support to bring them up to the standard of quality expected by the Quality Audit and Accreditation Programme. The number of services in the Programme has steadily increased since April 1993 when the Programme was first started (Table 3.1). It is anticipated that the number of services in the Programme will continue to increase as expertise and credibility is demonstrated. The number of services in the Programme (including schools) is shown in Table 3.1, the owners of those services in Table 3.2, and the outcome of the first two years of accreditation audits of adult care establishments in Table 3.3.

Identified advantages

It appeared that the accreditation process was producing some clear advantages over and above the rather arbitrary distinction of affiliation to the NAS:

1. The findings have demonstrated that the measures used were autism-sensitive measures. This means that the structured and consistently applied approach achieves the aim of evaluating the means by which a service understands and responds to the people with autism for whom it cares.

2. The responses from parents/carers from societies whose establishments have been reviewed have been generally positive. Parents appeared reassured to learn that the services provided for their sons/daughters were responsive to their needs, or will be supported and encouraged to respond more appropriately.

3. For practitioners who become team members, the opportunity to look closely at the workings of another establishment presented an invaluable opportunity for staff training. Innovative practice, even differing approaches to similar problems, were able to be analysed and evaluated by team members. Team members took a global approach to the survey of the workings of the organisation under review, an opportunity which they will not have had previously in their own establishments, where the specifics of their usual role will have precluded close investigation of areas outside their immediate tasks.

4. Too often, establishments work very much in isolation from each other. The method of accreditation by peers and parents serves as one approach of bringing together establishments and their personnel, parents and service-users. The development of a publication of innovative practice, which would then be shared amongst the network, may be one method of confirming and reinforcing the new contacts and methods of working enabled by the accreditation programme.

5. It is likely, although not certain, that accreditation of a service, via the quality audit process, may well help to increase the lobbying power that a service has to influence the funding authorities with which it negotiates. This official seal of approval is especially important when negotiating annual fee levels. Collectively, the measures used in the accreditation programme have led to an explicit clarification of what is special about autism and of the responses that are required. This enhanced definition should enable other organisations and even local and national government to understand the condition better.

Table 3.1 *Number of services in the Quality Audit and Accreditation Programme (including schools)*

Three-year rolling audit programme	Schools	Adult care	Total
Year one 1993/4	14	32	46
Year two 1994/5	13	36	49
Year three 1995/6	14	40	54

Table 3.2 *Owners/providers of services in the Quality Audit and Accreditation Programme at the end of year two, April 1995*

Owner/provider	Service	
	Schools	Adult care services
National autistic society	5	8
Local autistic societies	8	26
Other charities	1	–
Privately owned	–	5
Health trusts	–	1
Total	14	40

6. Early findings from the Quality Audit and Accreditation Programme seem to be showing that there is a close link between the capacity to develop good practice and organisational issues. Where, for example, a service is controlled by a management or executive body who are either too subjective, controlling or who are too laissez faire in their managerial approach, then the wrong messages are passed down to the staffing group. Equally, an inexperienced or purely business-orientated manager is unlikely to be able to gain the respect of his/her staff. As will be seen in Chapter Four, which looks at the training of practitioners, it is important that all staff have a grounding in good care practice and also autism-specific practice – for managers this is essential.

Table 3.3 *Number and outcome of the first two years of Accreditation audits – adult care establishments*

Year	Number of		
	Services audited	Services accredited	Services deferred
Year one	13	12	1
Year two	12	9	3
Total	25	21	4

Accreditation % was 84%.
Deferred % was 16%.

Concerns

1. Ownership of the programme and the perceived independence of the accreditation panel are critical issues. It should be remembered that the initial impetus for the development of the Quality Audit and Accreditation programme arose from the desire of NAS to be assured not only of the quality of its own services, but also of the quality of those societies wishing to affiliate to the NAS. The Quality Audit and Accreditation Programme has evolved so significantly during the first two years of operation, that the process of accreditation has moved far beyond the issues of affiliation to become a key determinant of quality for service delivery to people with autism, wherever these services are located and who ever their owners are. There is a clear need for the independence of the accreditation process to be established, in line with many other successful accreditation programmes in Canada, Australia and the USA.

2. The process of accreditation, of setting standards, could become too prescriptive and innovation may be stifled, for there is sometimes a tendency for practitioners and indeed parents/carers to think one-dimensionally rather than laterally for solutions to problems. The capacity of the planners of services to provide individually sensitive approaches in a highly consistent way will be determined by their ability to think flexibly and with a full understanding of the characteristics of autism.

3. A frequently expressed concern has been the lack of service-user participation in the quality audit teams themselves, and, whilst there are plans to improve this, there is need for clarification of how this may be achieved. Again, analysis of this problem needs to take into account the apparent difficulty that the person with autism is likely to have in appreciating the

emotions and beliefs of others. This is very likely to impact upon the capacity to measure objectively the effect of service design upon another individual. There is a danger of 'tokenism' and one may be placing adults with autism in situations in which they are cognitively ill-equipped to manage. However, it should be remembered that only a small proportion of practitioners employed in the field of autism become accreditation team members. Those who are selected are often the most senior practitioners. Likewise, it may be practical to expect only a small proportion of people with autism to become team members. It is also known from research and practice that individuals with autism may have difficulty in experiencing new situations and in empathising with the feelings, beliefs and needs of others. The aim, therefore, should be to recruit a small proportion of people with autism who will be able to make a meaningful contribution to the accreditation process. Lorimer, McCormick and Morgan (1995) investigated the potential for service-user involvement in the accreditation programme and recommended:

i   Only those adults with autism who volunteer should be recruited to the accreditation process.

ii Individuals with autism should be recruited to become supplementary members of accreditation teams.

iii As supplementary members, these individuals will be asked to examine a specific aspect of the establishment visited, e.g. to observe and provide views on one of the activities in a day care programme.

iv It is anticipated that some individuals will require additional support in order to contribute to this process. It is suggested that the support of 'mentors' familiar to the individual may be of help in enabling individuals to make a meaningful contribution to the process.

(Lorimer, C., McCormick, J. and Morgan, S.H. (1995) Unpublished survey of service-user views on quality of life issues. Leeds, Nailsworth and Birmingham, NAS.)

4. The credibility of all team members and especially team leaders is crucial to establishing the status of the Quality Audit and Accreditation Programme and underwriting its acceptance as an objective professional activity able to meet its established aims. Staff seconded from services registered in the Quality Audit and Accreditation Programme to the audit teams are selected on the grounds of qualification and/or extensive experience in a senior or specialist role. Role descriptions and role specifications are being developed for team leaders and for team members and focused training is being provided for larger groups of potential team members, as well as for each team when they come together prior to the audit of a service. The possibility of secondment to the Quality Audit and Accreditation Programme for longer periods of six months or a year is being considered, a practice followed elsewhere, notably, in Australia, where there are more stringent selection procedures.

HOW DOES THE AUTISM QUALITY AUDIT AND ACCREDITATION PROGRAMME MEASURE UP TO CRITICAL DESIGN FEATURES OUTLINED BY RICHARDS AND HEGINBOTHAM (1992)?

1. DOES IT HAVE A REPETITIVE CYCLICAL PATH AND FOCUS ON ENHANCEMENT IN PREFERENCE TO MAINTENANCE?

Yes, the NAS scheme is a rolling three year programme with a built in annual review. The issue of enhancement of quality is closely linked to continuously monitored change (Donabedian 1988), and is referred back to the main objective of the service, that is to provide a service that is informed about, and sensitive to, the needs of individuals with autism.

2. IS IT HIGHLY PARTICIPATIVE, INCLUDING USERS AND PROFESSIONAL STAFF TO CONTRIBUTE TO QUALITY MANAGEMENT BY INCREASING COMMUNICATION, SHARED VALUES AND OBJECTIVES?

The process of the scheme is designed to be participative. Views are sought from the employees at all levels, parents/carers, and the adults with autism themselves. Key recommendations arise from these views, usually indicating the development of strategies to improve communication and heightening the awareness of shared values and objectives.

3. DOES IT TAKE ACCOUNT OF USER/CONSUMER STATEMENTS?

The process, however, is subject to annual review and amendments by participants, and great efforts are made to include parent advocate and service-user views in the planning and continuous development of the process. As an evolving process it will need to become more receptive to the views of service-users.

4. DOES IT INVOLVE 'PEER REVIEW' BY STAFF?

Yes. Accreditation teams consist of professionals who themselves work in services for people with autism or in closely related areas of work. Also, parents/carers can be involved.

5. IS IT LINKED TO STANDARD-SETTING EXERCISES?

Yes. Standards are clearly laid out in the revised format and the accompanying handbook lists questions which the accreditation team member should seek to address in order to ascertain whether the standard has been acquired in a specific area. For example:

The standard

A clearly written statement of the philosophy, aims and objectives confirming its commitment to understanding and responding to the needs of people with autism. This statement must be made available to all service-users, parents, advocates and staff.

The requirement

Does the evidence confirm that the above standard has been met? YES/NO
The evidence

Summary of evidence including sources and ending with any requirements and/or recommendations:

REVIEW NOTES

i   Is there a statement of service aims and objectives?

ii Does the statement of aims and objectives specifically include and address the needs of people with autism?

iii Is there evidence of shared aims and values based on an understanding of autism that informs decisions on resources, policies, practice, internal and external relations?

iv Is the management/operational style effective and appropriate in supporting the above values, aims and objectives?

v   Does staff deployment/ recruitment/structure support the aims?

vi Do staff training programmes and opportunities support the values/aims?

6. DOES IT INVOLVE OBSERVATION OF SERVICES IN OPERATION?

Yes. Evidence must be collected from direct observation of practice and by listening to, and conversing with, practitioners and service users.

7. IS IT OUTCOME-ORIENTATED AND DOES IT EXPLORE CAUSAL LINKS WITH SERVICE STRUCTURES AND PROCESSES?

Yes. By measuring the quality of a service against set standards, the process determines whether service delivery is autism-sensitive or not. It seeks to explore the effect of management and organisational structures upon service delivery and thus identifies the relationship between organisational issues and what can be considered to be good autism-specific practice.

8. CAN IT COMPLIMENT BUT STAND INDEPENDENT OF COST DATA AND OTHER QUANTITATIVE DATA?

Yes. The Quality Audit and Accreditation Programme is not a cost-containment exercise. Nonetheless should a service fail to meet the agreed standards set in the relevant questions on finance, then the emphasis will be upon suggesting ways in which more resources should be acquired and delivered in specific areas.

9. IS IT ACTION-ORIENTATED IN APPLYING ITS FINDINGS?

Yes. At the end of the audit, recommendations are made to the service and plans of action agreed. As the Quality Audit and Accreditation

Programme is a rolling programme, action plans will be annually assessed and reviewed as necessary.

10. DOES IT EMBODY ITS VALUES AND PRINCIPLES AND MAKE THEM EXPLICIT TO PARTICIPANTS?

Yes. The system evolved because of the involvement and contributions of many of those parents and practitioners who wished to see an improvement in the quality of services for people with autism. This was then translated and made explicit to participants in the programme through a process of lead-in discussions with the service managers, through advance-written material.

11. DOES IT HAVE A TRANSPARENT AND LEARNABLE METHODOLOGY?

Yes. The accreditation programme and the audit process are described in great detail in the accreditation programme manual and each team member receives a detailed audit handbook. Each audit therefore sets out to follow the same process, i.e. gathering evidence in the same way and collating the evidence within the framework of four criteria and 38 standards. The documented framework, the detailed process and the team training all provide for a clearly understandable and learnable methodology. It has to be acknowledged, however, that as all services have their own unique experiences and identity, then so do each member of the audit team. This, however, can be regarded as an asset in as much as each audit has the opportunity to make its own contribution to the continuous development of the Autism Quality Audit and Accreditation Programme.

CHAPTER SUMMARY

This chapter has focused upon the relevance and application of quality audit as a means of evaluating services for adults with autism. A quality audit should be seen as complementary to the usual statutory registration inspection procedures. A description of an autism-specific quality audit was provided and evaluation of this programme found it to be a highly participative peer evaluation of a service, which was largely sensitive to the needs of adults with autism. Suggestions were made that the accreditation process should become independent of ownership by any organisation also providing services for people with autism, that it should seek to become more sensitive to the views of service-users, that the identification, selection, training and evaluation of team members should be tightened – perhaps by looking at models elsewhere, and that a publication of working practices and especially innovative procedures should be compiled and circulated.

ACKNOWLEDGEMENTS

Professor Ellie Scrivens, Centre for Health Planning and Management, University of Keele. Ann Lovell, National Autistic Society. Paul Sullivan, West Midlands Autistic Society. The Library of the Kings Fund.

BIBLIOGRAPHY

Clough, R. (1992). Training for quality. In D. Kelly and B. Warr (eds.) *Quality Counts*. London, Whiting and Birch Ltd.

Donabedian, A. (1988). Quality assessment and assurance: unity of purpose, diversity of means. Inquiry. *Journal of Health Care, Organisation, Provision and Financing*, 25 (1), 3–5.

Dunnachie, H. (1992). Approaches to quality systems. In D. Kelly and B. Warr (eds.) *Quality Counts*. London, Whiting and Birch Ltd.

Lovell, A. (1994). Accreditation: how parents can help. *Communication*, 28 (1), 4–5.

Kelly, D. and Warr, B. (1992). *Quality Counts*. London, Whiting and Birch Ltd.

Peacock, G. (1992). Paper presented at the fourth Congress Autisme-Europe, The Hague, The Netherlands, May 1992.

Richards, H. (1992). International perspectives on quality assurance. In D. Kelly and B. Warr (eds.) *Quality Counts*. London, Whiting and Birch Ltd.

Richards, H. and Heginbotham, C. (1992). *Quality through Observation of Service Delivery: a Workbook*. 2nd edition. London, Kings Fund.

Scrivens, E. (1995). *Accreditation – The Way Forward for the NHS?* Keele, University of Keele.

Scrivens, E., Klein, R. and Steiner, A. (1995). What can we learn from the anglophone model? Working paper 1. In E. Scrivens (ed.) *Issues in Accreditation*, Working papers 1–6. Keele, University of Keele.

Tresnowski, B.R. (1988). The current interest in quality is nothing new. Inquiry. *Journal of Health Care, Organisation, Provision and Financing*, 25 (1), 66–67.

Wall, A.J. (1990). Group Homes in North Carolina for children and adults with autism. *Journal of Autism and Developmental Disorders*, 20 (3), 353–367.

4

Encouraging flexibility in adults with autism

Rita Jordan and Stuart Powell

INTRODUCTION

THE EDUCATION and care of adults with autism often focuses on social and communicative behaviours. The difficulties that fall within these aspects of the Triad of Impairments (Wing 1988) persist from childhood to adulthood and are significant in terms of the possibilities of social integration and of learning within various domains. Yet it is also the case that the third aspect of that triad, lack of flexibility of thought and behaviour, persists into adulthood and underlies many of the features of the thinking and the subsequent behaviour of individuals with autism. This lack of flexibility is clearly a major factor in the lives of the adults concerned and the results need to be addressed by those who care for, and work with, them. We recognise the need to take account of this lack of flexibility in planning suitable environments and appropriate daily programmes for individuals with autism, but what we suggest in this chapter is that staff working with individuals with autism can also have a role in developing that flexibility in their clients, and that this will have a major impact on their quality of life and prospects for independence. This chapter then deals with the impact of the lack of flexibility on the lives of adults with autism, ways of ameliorating these effects and finally a programme for helping to overcome this fundamental difficulty.

THE PROBLEMS

Difficulties with change

Typically, adults with autism experience difficulties in coping with changes within their environment. These difficulties are not merely a matter of social preference, but rather reflect a pattern of cognition which depends on the regular. This preference for 'sameness' was noted as a defining feature of autism (Kanner 1943) but it is often misunderstood. In the young child with autism it may well be reflected in a very narrow range of activities and extreme resistance to change, but, with appropriate education, most adults

74

with autism will have come to accept a reasonably wide range of activities and environments with which they are now familiar and so staff may not be aware that the fundamental problem remains. It only becomes a problem (frequently displayed as 'challenging behaviour') when, for example, routines are disrupted for some unexpected reason, or a room needs to be redecorated.

The problem is not just one of 'resistance to change', as if this were an immutable characteristic of autism. As an able young man with autism, Jim Sinclair has written:

Being autistic does not mean being unable to learn. But it does mean there are differences in how learning happens.

(Sinclair 1992, p. 295)

If we are to be effective in helping adults with autism come to accept changes in their environment, we have to reach some understanding of what those changes mean to them and why there is a dependency on routines and familiarity. As Sinclair also notes, it is not just the problems of adults with autism in understanding that leads to difficulties; it is also (and perhaps primarily) our lack of understanding of them.

In autism there is a central deficit in the social cognitive process that leads to shared understanding of the world (Frith 1989; Hobson 1993). So, where the individual with autism learns things, then that learning remains idiosyncratic. It is not so much that the individual cannot make connections, as that the connections made will depend on the way the individual items are interpreted. The meanings of phenomena are not attached to the phenomena themselves, but come to have meanings through the process of early social learning, through which individuals learn about particular human and cultural meanings. In Halliday's (1975) telling phrase, children 'learn how to mean'.

The difficulties in understanding others and sharing their perspective on the world through a sense of inter-subjectivity is fundamental to autism (Hobson 1993) and leads to meanings (whether attached to physical or social phenomena) that are not 'negotiated' in the normal social interactive way. Where the non-autistic child learns to interpret the world through the eyes of his/her care-giver through, for example, explication, modelling and extrapolation the child with autism does not. Autistic learning then remains at the level of the specific; what is learnt in one context will not necessarily transfer to another related context. Nor will the overall 'purpose' of events or activities be grasped, and teaching approaches that focus on one step at a time will add to this kind of piecemeal learning. The outward manifestation of this style of learning, then, is rigid and stereotypical thought and a sense of panic when the meanings that have been constructed around the particular are arbitrarily (from the point of view of the individual with autism) dis-rupted. Note, that it is not all changes that are resisted and many adults with autism welcome complete changes in their environment that may occur with a holiday, for example; it is only changes in routines and environ-ments that have a particular meaning for them where disruption leads to such anxiety and distress.

Of course, as earlier chapters have shown, there are great individual varia-tions in adults with autism, both in their degree of autism and in the nature and severity of any accompanying difficulties in learning and in language development. Those with additional severe learning difficulties will have their problems in adaptability increased simply because each situation has to be learnt afresh, and all learning is hard. Those with additional language problems (which may be specific, or which may accompany the additional general learning difficulties) will have the additional problems that arise from the lack of an effective medium for thought. It is possible, of course, to think visually and many able people with autism achieve remarkable intel-lectual feats through their facility with the visual mode of thought (for example, Grandin 1992). Yet such modes of thinking encourage a style that focuses on particular patterns rather than an analysis of overall meaning and make it more difficult to transfer learning from one context to another. Language not only gives us a way of abstracting principles (which can then be applied in different contexts) from what we have learnt, but it enables us to learn from, and about, other people's interpretations of the situation. The lack of language is even more debilitating in autism, where there is no intu-itive understanding of others and where it may be necessary to explain explicitly about our understandings and interpretations of the world to make them accessible.

Lack of spontaneity and initiative

An apparent feature of the behaviour of many adults with autism is a lack of spontaneity within the social environment. They may follow directions from others well enough and they may follow their own patterns of behaviour, however intricate those may be, without needing to be directed. Yet, they are often unable to choose activities to engage in outside of their own particular interests or habitual learned patterns. Even when put in familiar situations to perform a familiar task, they may behave in an apparently unmotivated way, or as if they have 'forgotten' what to do until they are prompted or cued to start the task. Once the task or activity is underway, there appears to be no problem in carrying it out, but they find it difficult to get started without that initial support, either from a member of staff or from the particular structure provided in the environment.

There may be similar problems in planning their activities or switching from one activity to another. If they do turn spontaneously from one activity to another, then the reason often seems to be at the level of the immediate rather than the considered. Thus, it is as if their actions are prompted by external stimulation or events, rather than from an internal source of motivation and intent. Some have suggested, in fact, that the problem is a motivational one (Boucher and Lewis 1989), but it is our contention that the difficulty is one of establishing a sense of themselves as actors in the world and consequently a difficulty in intending and planning actions, in monitoring their own performance and in consciously switching attentions (Powell and Jordan 1993a). Nor will they have access to other people's intentions (Powell and Jordan 1993b), so it is not surprising that actions and 'chosen' activities are those that are, in effect, not chosen at all but are programmed and set off by some aspect of the environment or by an initial encouraging prompt (or nag!)

Difficulties with creativity and imagination

The lack of spontaneity described above underpins the lack of creativity that pervades the behaviour and the work of individuals with autism. Where, for example, a non-autistic adult with learning difficulties may be able to create 'new' patterns within an overall design, or make up new events within the framework of a story, the individual with autism will typically find these kinds of activities difficult. Such individuals may reach high levels of skill in terms of, for example, reproducing with paint and paper what they can see in the world. But even here the progression in 'skill' is likely to be defined in terms of exactness of copy, rather than kind of interpretation. Park (1922) describes how her daughter's paintings, which are good enough to gain artistic acclaim and earn the painter money, are exact replicas of what has been seen and how even apparent particular talents (such as the ability to draw in perspective from a young age) are in fact a reflection of her daughter's inability to draw what she 'knows' (which is what normally developing young children do) rather than what she sees, or has seen.

Without getting side-tracked into definitions of 'creativity', it clearly involves extending the known or the seen in such a way as to produce a new interpretation or a new view. It involves bringing together different elements to produce a new understanding. The examples we have given above relate to art, yet creativity is an aspect of thought that pervades intellectual activity in its broadest sense. The difficulties faced by most adults with autism in this connection are not to do with being unable to paint expressively; they are to do with modes of thinking locked into what has been taught and being unable to think up solutions or ideas beyond a set learnt response.

Before leaving art as an example, however, it is worth noting that Park emphasises that her daughter did not acquire the artistic skill she has in a natural 'creative' way. Her way of painting expressed her way of thinking and perceiving, but even this had to be taught in explicit ways over the years. Those concerned with fostering the creative arts in autism are often bothered by this aspect of their role, which they see as a denial of the inherent creativity of the individual concerned. So the adult with autism is left to cover the sheet with black paint time and time again because that is seen as his or her 'creative choice'. But any choice is only a real choice if the individual has the knowledge and skill to effect an alternative. So, the first step, even in encouraging 'creative' activities must be to ensure that the individual has a range of skills and techniques at his or her disposal, knows how to use them in this particular context and, more importantly for our thesis, is aware of his or her own knowledge and ability.

However, even at the level of everyday activities, successfully coping requires creative thought, and creative thinking requires the use of imagination. To successfully create a new meaning out of known elements requires that the thinker can imagine what the new meaning will be like.

To be able to cope when, for example, the bus fails to turn up for the adult to go to college means remembering the skills of telephoning for help (and remembering who to telephone, their telephone number and how to telephone, of course) which almost certainly will not have been taught in this context and may have only been taught in a 'role play' way, since actual circumstances of needing to telephone for help are difficult to contrive. At the time of the initial teaching, therefore, the individual with autism needs to be aware of this activity as a strategy that can be applied in situations he or she has not yet experienced. This awareness must include a knowledge of all the skills involved and the capacity to bring them together in an act of imagination to create a new understanding, of how to behave in an imagined scenario.

The individual with autism might have a series of understandings but again these remain specific and disparate, so making sense of them in a connected, and further an extrapolated, way is problematic or impossible. In the example given, it may be too difficult to rely on this kind of imaginative appraisal of what is being learnt, and instead staff will need to set up engineered situations of buses failing to turn up (perhaps by having advanced warning of cancellations or, for those not able to read the publicly displayed timetable, pretending a bus is due at a certain time and instructing the adult about how long to wait and then who to phone, etc.). In short, in autism the prerequisites for creativity are not present. The adult with autism cannot extend the known, or bring together understandings to create new ones, because the known remains confined to the specific context in which it was learnt and the autistic understandings, by their very nature, are disparate and remain disparate. Autistic thinking is of a non-imaginative kind.

Such statements can sometimes seem confounded by some more able adults with autism who do seem able to 'invent' new scenarios and indeed may seem to prefer these inventions to everyday life. Even then, however, there is usually an underlying problem in the interpretations of these 'inventions'. The adult with autism may have difficulty in distinguishing inventions or thoughts from reality, or in realising that his or her own thoughts are not automatically shared by others. They may invent words (neologisms), but then expect others to understand their idiosyncratic meanings, or they may almost literally 'become' a favourite television character and have difficulty in knowing how or when to switch in and out of role. It is not like normal 'play acting' or the trying out of different roles, but it is as if they are the person whose behaviours and mannerisms they are copying so exactly. The teaching problem in this case is to bring them to a fuller understanding of being creative so that they can be aware of what they are doing (which is necessary for true creativity) and thus monitor and control their 'creative' acts.

Stereotypical thought and behaviour

All of the above results in a particular way of thinking. Those who work with adults with autism will recognise a sense in which the thinking of many of their clients seems to be on a meaningless path. Stereotyped thinking may be characterised as thinking that follows a narrow set route, and stereotypes in behaviour are often taken to be classical descriptors of autism. A kind of thinking that does not readily transfer knowledge from one context to the next and which does not have available a facilitatory social learning environment will necessarily remain in the specific and the (socially) meaningless. This is not to say that stereotypes are purposeless; indeed they may serve a useful function for the individual in reducing the stress of a world that continually threatens with new demands. But their meaning is confined to the individual and to a very specific aspect of his/her current situation. Thought becomes stereotypical because the individual is unable to use current understandings and skills to develop new ways of thinking and behaving. There is a sense in which we may all think in ways which are 'typical' and idiosyncratic. In autism, however, stereotypical thought is the rule rather than the exception and pervasive rather than superficial.

PRACTICAL IMPLICATIONS

Creating anxiety-free situations

It is a feature of all behaviour that anxiety reduces flexibility and, under conditions of high anxiety, many of the characteristics that we have called autistic thinking and learning can be seen in any individual. It is clear then that one way of increasing flexibility is to reduce anxiety levels in adults with autism so that they are free to adopt a less rigid approach. This will not be a sufficient condition to ensure flexibility in individuals with autism, but it is a necessary one. The causes of anxiety in autism will be, to some degree at least, idiosyncratic, and it will require individual knowledge of the adult concerned before all sources of anxiety can be eliminated or at least reduced. However, there are some generalisations that can be made about the kind of events that are likely to lead to anxiety in autism and which, therefore, need to be modified. The difference between adults with autism and those with other non-autistic conditions is that the kind of anxiety-provoking events are not predictable from our own intuitive understandings or our knowledge of that which causes anxiety in non-autistic persons.

High on the list of potential causes of anxiety in adults with autism is the social dimension. Almost all other groups will have their anxiety reduced by the presence of peers or by the supportive help of the 'teacher', but adults with autism may find that the presence of others, no matter how well intentioned, adds to the confusion and the level of anxiety associated with the task. Indeed, it may well be that it is the attempts at the social mediation of a task (the staff member 'helping' the client with the task) that is the main source of anxiety. Staff need to remember, therefore, that new tasks, or tasks where a flexible approach is required, will be best tackled in as asocial a way as possible. This may be done in some cases through the use of computer-assisted learning or the task requirements may be presented in a structured visual way that enables the task to be tackled independently.

At the same time, staff should not accept the anxiety-producing effect of others as an immutable result of autism. It is true that social signals are always likely to be difficult to interpret for those with autism, but staff at least can learn to behave in ways that make their social signals easier to interpret and so make them less a source of anxiety and more a potential help and support. They can do this initially by reducing the number of simultaneous social signals (not gesturing or making overt facial expressions while giving verbal instructions, for example) but then using each of those signals, the words, the facial expressions, the body posture, the gestures, separately and with a clear and explicit meaning. In such ways, the signals (of that individual at least) become familiar and understandable and so cease to cause anxiety. In short, it is important when working with individuals with autism to make oneself more predictable. It is also important to remember to slow down the messages given and to wait for a response; too often, the adult with autism is just marshalling a response when the staff member has given up on getting that response and proceeds to rephrase the command or to use gesture or guidance on the assumption that this will help. In fact, it is likely to add to the confusion and anxiety and may result in the individual 'giving up' altogether. The situation where the adult with autism has learnt to wait for the staff member to supply the 'answer' or has reverted to a habitual stereotyped response is not uncommon.

The inability to read the intentions of others means that the individual with autism is faced with real difficulties whenever social situations are constructed upon what others want or intend. Clearly, these kind of constructions permeate most, if not all, social scenarios. So, whenever the client is in a situation where his/her 'next move' is reliant on a reading of the intentions of another, then that client is likely to experience confusion and subsequently anxiety. There is a need, therefore, for explicitness on the part of those working with such clients and for the extensive use of clear markers which enable the client to interpret the meaning of situations more effectively. These markers may be visual, or may include a combination of the visual and the spoken, but they need to be regular and dependable.

Regular routines, written or pictorial timetables and clear marking of activity areas will help persons with autism understand what they are to do next, where and for how long. Failure to understand this basic structuring of the day, while it might seem obvious to the person without autism, is a common source of anxiety for those to whom intentionality is mysterious. Staff may assume that the person with autism will know that activities come to an end and that no one will expect the person with autism to walk or wash up for ever, but the person with autism may understand the open instruction to 'wash up' or that they are 'going for a walk' as a kind of life sentence. It is only when the behaviour of the individual with autism is contrasted with a situation where the instructions are explicit (e.g. 'we are going to walk to the end of the field and then turn round and come back again' or 'I want you to wash up those dishes and cups and cutlery that are piled on the table here') that the degree of their misunderstanding and subsequent anxiety can be appreciated.

Anxiety and frustration are also associated with inability to see the purpose of certain activities such as going for a walk. In such cases, the staff may need to introduce other more tangible 'goals' to an activity to give it meaning for the adult with autism. Staff may hope that the individual will gain from the experience of climbing a mountain, feel the exhilaration as he or she reaches the top and enjoys the view, but it may be impossible to offer these as goals to the individual who cannot imagine what has not yet been experienced. In such cases it may be wise to revert to strategies that might be used with children, to offer, for example, mint cake or chocolate to those reaching the top. Park (1986) shows how mechanistic rewards can nevertheless lead to greater understanding and an eventual ability to use other more intrinsic motivation for actions. In the same way she describes (Park 1992) how her daughter did not develop her profitable, and now seemingly enjoyable, pastime of painting until she was offered money for a picture and could then paint in order to see the numbers in her bank account grow – a not unusual source of motivation for those with or without autism.

TEACHING UNDERSTANDING AND AWARENESS

Attending to relevant meanings

What has been said above might lead the reader to suppose we are advocating a Behavioural approach with adults with autism, but that is far from the case. Behaviourism is a useful tool in the education of those with autism in teaching everyday skills and habits where the performance of those skills in an automatic way is beneficial. Thus, there is nothing wrong with learning to wash one's hands after a visit to the toilet as a matter of routine, without needing to understand about the nature of germs or the finer details of hygiene. It can lead to difficulties in some situations, e.g. on outings or on holiday, where conditions may be more primitive and washing facilities unavailable, but often the situation is so unlike the 'normal' one that the changed routine is accepted. In any case, the benefits of establishing a functional routine, that is followed as a matter of course rather than requiring continual monitoring and prompting, outweigh the occasional problems encountered in unusual situations.

The idea that adults somehow have the 'right' to choose not to wash their hands or clean their teeth at night simply because many of the 'normal' adult population make such choices is a naive one. Such a 'right' is (like choice) only meaningful if the adult is fully aware of the consequences of his or her actions and has chosen that course of action in spite of such awareness; this would be a difficult case to make in most cases of adults with autism.

Nevertheless, if the only teaching approach used with autism is that of Behaviourism, then this is likely to make for less rather than more flexibility in thinking and behaviour. Teaching one step at a time does nothing to help the individual see the overall purpose of his or her actions and the concentration on rewarding performance does nothing to educate the cognitive strategies that are needed for such flexibility. So, while the use of behaviourist techniques may have their place in the overall approach to working with those with autism, there is a need to recognise the underlying learning style in autism and work towards remediating that, as well as accommodating it with particular structures. Individuals with autism need to be shown explicitly the overall purpose of a task and have the limits of that task delineated in the way described above.

A cognitive approach to everyday problems means that the staff member will help the individual develop cognitive strategies rather than just behavioural ones, and, most importantly, become aware of those strategies and be better able to access them on future occasions. In this approach adults with autism will be encouraged to develop their own structure rather than to rely on a staff-generated one. At the first step, this means involving clients in planning for activities. They need to be taught to make choices about what to do and when, in appropriate circumstances, and they need to decide on what they will need to complete the task. Of course, this cannot be managed all at once and each of these processes will need to be broken down into steps. For example, when being asked to wipe the tables in preparation for lunch, the adult might be offered a cloth, a bucket, cleaning fluid (all necessary for the task) and then an irrelevant item such as a broom for the floor. Even without language, in such ways, the adult can come to develop ways of attending to task relevance, by discarding the broom, in this case.

Note that the task is simplified but the steps are not meaningless ones, with each one needing to be chained to the next in an automatic way, as is the case in a Behavioural programme. Rather, the individual's attention is drawn to the overall meaning of the task at each step. In the example above, the nature of the task of cleaning the table needs to be considered in order to discard the broom as irrelevant. Increasing the difficulty of the task by adding other irrelevant items still keeps the focus on this meaning. Once the adults have learnt to discard irrelevant items, they can be taught to pay attention to the relevant aspects of the cleaning process by accepting relevant equivalents, so that either a sponge or a cloth is acceptable whereas a comb is not; in the same way they can be taught to accept a bucket or a bowl of different colours and dimensions, all of which focus on the functional attributes of the items rather than on their look, feel or smell, which the person with autism, left to him or herself, might select as the focus of attention.

Developing memory strategies

To aid the development of useful memory (as opposed to rote memory of skills or knowledge that depends on prompting or cueing to become available), individuals with autism need to become aware of their own strategies for learning and they need to be consciously aware of the tasks they are undertaking and the experiences they are undergoing, and, where possible, to be emotionally engaged with those tasks and experiences. Those who are able to understand and use spoken language can be encouraged to talk about what they are doing as they are doing it and to notice when they are enjoying something and when they are finding it difficult and frustrating. These same prompts that are used to direct attention to these experiential aspects of their learning can be used later as cues for recall of the task and the adult's role in it.

For those without spoken language, the task is harder to overcome. We have achieved some success through the use of instant photographs of the individual at key stages of the task, which direct attention at the time and can be used as later cues for memory (Powell and Jordan 1991). Access to a still video would be even more advantageous (in that it would be more flexible) and would also be a fraction of the running costs. For those with very severe learning and language difficulties, it may still be possible to increase understanding, and aid later recall of a task, through the use of strategies that help the focus on that individual's experience at the time. This can be done by performing tasks alongside the adult with autism, emphasising the key points in an exaggerated and explicit way, and drawing the individual's attention to their own expression of emotion (intense interest, enjoyment, frustration or even anger), by modelling and by using a mirror to capture the expression at the time (as well as the photograph for later recall). Even just being able to use an object of reference (a shopping bag to 'stand for' a shopping trip, for example) to recall a past event and to plan a forthcoming event not only adds to communication, but enables the individual to exercise some choice and to remember some key aspect of the event (its nature as a shopping activity, in this case) rather than just be tied to particular meaningless chunks of memory (as in only remembering one of the items purchased) or some isolated salient (perhaps idiosyncratically so) aspect of the event.

Developing choice

A mere ability to protest does not necessarily mean that the individual can exercise meaningful choice, which involves holding more than one possibility in mind while deciding between them. Of course, the most basic level of exercising choice would involve teaching the individual to refuse items or activities not wanted and to accept those that are. The barriers to doing this effectively are that it can sometimes be difficult to be sure of what the individual does or does not want or like (even when they have speech, since they may simply say what they have been taught to say in answer to a question or invitation) and, from the adult with autism's perspective, it can be difficult to know what is wanted and what choice means.

As an example, it would seem sensible to start with clearly expressed preferences as in the case of a young lady who would throw a temper tantrum (and the pudding concerned) if an unsuspecting staff member offered her a pudding after her meal, when, in fact, she loved to eat apples. Having been guided, then, to say (or in her case, sign) 'yes' to an offer of an apple, and 'no' to a pudding, the prompts were eventually withdrawn and all went well until she made a mistake and signed 'yes' for a pudding. Staff prepared for the onslaught as she was given the pudding, and prepared to intervene and prompt 'no', remove the pudding, offer an apple and prompt 'yes'. None of this carefully worked out programme could be put into operation, however, as she accepted the pudding and ate it, eating puddings thereafter. If staff had wanted her to eat puddings, this might be regarded as a success, but clearly there is little point in training unhealthy eating habits at the expense of healthy ones, and, as a programme to teach about choice, it was a failure.

This example shows the difficulty in teaching concepts without ensuring understanding. In this case, it seems obvious that, not understanding what a choice meant, the girl simply assumed that this was one more conforming behaviour that she had to adopt without understanding. To overcome this problem, it is necessary to concentrate on and teach the meaning of choice right from the start. This is difficult in most situations of working with adults, since they will often have come from educational situations that stressed conformity to externally imposed (and little understood) rules. In this case it would have been better to introduce a separate stage of choice involving pictures (or words, if they are understood) before the point of selection of the items themselves. Thus, she would simply learn to associate the pictures with the items and then to select her own menu for her meal before going to 'ask' for it.

Similar choices could be introduced into all (or nearly all) aspects of the day until the idea of making decisions and evaluating alternatives is understood. Many adults with autism may never be able to do this mentally (even Temple Grandin, Grandin 1992, finds this impossible), but can be helped to make effective choices by using lists, pictures, symbols or even objects of reference. It is important in the latter case to establish first that objects of reference are understood and that the making of the choice is not confused with the point of choice as in the apple/pudding example above. If that individual had needed recourse to objects of reference to express choice, she would needed to have first learnt an object to 'stand for' fruit (a pretend apple perhaps, or a fruit bowl in which the fruit is usually presented) and one to 'stand for' pudding (an empty pudding bowl, for example). Otherwise, it is difficult for her to focus on the process of making a choice and she is liable instead to react to the actual items being presented.

Teaching more flexible and creative behaviour

We have stressed the teaching of understanding first, because there is, as we pointed out earlier, a danger that just teaching behaviour will only substitute one set of rigid behaviours for another, without doing anything to address the fundamental difficulties involved. Nevertheless, the most obvious manifestation of the poverty of imagination and the lack of flexibility in adults with autism lies in their repetitive and often stereotyped behaviour. Again, we need to try to work out the 'meaning' of that particular behaviour for the individual concerned, before we can do anything effective to alter that behaviour. It is not just a question of effectiveness, either, but also of ethics. As Sinclair (1992) notes, people with autism do not necessarily want to change their behaviour, they may just want to understand ours. Donna Williams (cited in Matthews 1993, p.3) also objects to the notion that her behaviour should be altered in the pursuit of, 'acting normal without regard for whether the autistic person understands the behaviour they have been taught to perform'.

So, the course of a programme to develop more flexible and creative behaviour in adults with autism would need to have several parallel fronts. There would need to be careful and insightful observation, trying to determine the meaning and function of the existing behaviour for the adult with autism. Then there would need to be further observation and more hypotheses testing to determine which aspects of the more flexible and creative behaviour that we would like to develop are an enigma to that person with autism, and, furthermore, what functions could be served by the new behaviours that would have meaning for the individual with autism and that would add to that individual's quality of life. If no such meanings or value can be determined then we would need to question whether we should be developing the programme at all. The next step is to try to teach that understanding which would overcome the difficulties in seeing the meaning and purpose of the 'more desirable' behaviour. Only after this would it be productive to try to teach the behavioural forms.

The above statements form the general principles on which to operate. However, there are some exceptions where there may be a value in teaching behavioural form as a way through to teaching understanding. This particularly applies to social behaviours where it is virtually impossible to teach the meaning of the behaviour unless the individual can experience that meaning for him or herself. Again, Park's (1986) example, of teaching her daughter the meaning of social greeting and praise through the mechanical means of getting her to reward herself with a point on a golf counter, is a good case in point. The reward of changing the number on the counter made sense to her and enabled her to improve her social adaptability and thus her quality of life, but it also enabled her to reach an understanding of what these social signals meant, and for the first time they were salient to her. Thus, if it is difficult for us to emphasise the meaning of events in a way that makes them meaningful to the person with autism, it may be better to use his or her own meanings and attach them to the behaviour that is to be encouraged. If this can be done in such a way that it does not just reinforce particular behaviour patterns, but also makes key aspects of the events salient, then this will also further that individual's understanding and make their behaviour more adaptable in turn.

CONCLUSION

Individuals with autism do not behave in inflexible, repetitive ways because such behaviours as such are part of the biology of autism. It is true that some forms of perseverative behaviour do follow from particular aspects of brain damage, but the real difficulty is in being aware of one's own thinking and behaviour and thus having the ability to plan actions, monitor them, adapt them according to their effectiveness in pursuing a particular goal and remember and apply them in new situations.

We are not dealing with wilful stubborn behaviour (although it can sometimes appear like that), but with a core difficulty in having access to and reflecting on one's own thinking. It is seldom a matter of motivation but more that they cannot do what you want them to do, and they often cannot even do (or at least plan to do) what they want to do themselves, because they do not understand what is wanted or how to evaluate the situation, including their own behaviour, to see what is required. We need to respect the fact that, as Option (Jordan 1990) says, they are doing the best they can within their own understanding and the resources available to them.

BIBLIOGRAPHY

Boucher, J. and Lewis, V. (1989). Memory impairments and communication in relatively able autistic children. *Journal of Child Psychology and Psychiatry*, **30**, 99–122.

Frith, U. (1989). *Autism: Explaining the Enigma*. Oxford, Blackwells.

Grandin, T. (1992). An inside view of autism. In E. Schopler and G. Mesibov (eds.) *High-Functioning Individuals with Autism*. New York, Plenum Press.

Halliday, M.A.K. (1975). *Learning to Mean: Explorations in the Development of Language*. London, Edward Arnold.

Hobson, R.P. (1993). *Autism and the Development of Mind*. London, Erlbaum.

Jordan, R.R. (1990). *An Observer's Report on the Option Approach to Autism*. London, National Autistic Society.

Jordan, R.R. and Powell, S.D. (1990). *The Special Curricular Needs of Autistic Children: Learning and Thinking Skills*. London, Association of Heads and Teachers of Adults and Children with Autism.

Kanner, L. (1943). Autistic disturbances of affective contact. *Nervous Child,* **2,** 217–250.

Matthews, P. (1993). Preamble to the presentation: investigating the autism enigma. In G. Linfoot, D. Savery and P. Shattock (eds.) *Biological Perspectives in Autism.* Sunderland, University of Sunderland Autism Research Unit, and London, National Autistic Society.

Park, C. (1986). Social growth in autism: a parent's perspective. In E. Schopler and G. Mesibov (eds.) *Social Behaviour in Autism.* New York, Plenum Press.

Park, C. (1992). Autism into art: a handicap transfigured. In E. Schopler and G. Mesibov (eds.) *High-Functioning Individuals with Autism.* New York, Plenum Press.

Powell, S.D and Jordan, R.R. (1991). A psychological perspective on identifying and meeting the needs of exceptional pupils. *School Psychology International,* **12,** 315–327.

Powell, S.D and Jordan, R.R. (1993a). Being subjective about autistic thinking and learning how to learn. *Educational Psychology,* **13,** 359–370.

Powell, S.D. and Jordan, R.R. (1993b). Diagnosis, intuition and autism. *British Journal of Special Education,* **20,** 26–29.

Sinclair, J. (1992). Bridging the gaps: an inside-out view of autism (or do you know what I don't know?). In E. Schopler and G. Mesibov (eds.) *High-Functioning Individuals with Autism.* New York, Plenum Press.

Wing, L. (1988). The autistic continuum. In L. Wing (ed.) *Aspects of Autism: Biological Research.* London, National Autistic Society.

5

Attachment and loss: a focus on transition and bereavement

Hugh Morgan

THIS CHAPTER explores the significance of attachment and loss for adults with autism. Using research into bereavement and psychosocial transitions as reference points, a model of attachment and loss for adults with autism is presented, with particular reference to the transition from child to adulthood and from one home to another. The process of bereavement for adults with autism is then explored and support strategies recommended.

It will be proposed that the third aspect of the Triad of Impairments – a lack of imagination (Wing and Gould 1979) – directly and adversely influences any process of change for people with autism. This inflexibility of thought may mean that the attachment that the person with autism holds to their assumptive world tends to be fixed and static so that a transition, requiring a reshaping of expectations, is likely to be extremely traumatising. In the past, literature looking at attachment and loss has focused on people whose cognitive capacities have not been impaired by an inflexibility of thought, but even so it can be seen that the process of loss of an attachment, i.e. an attachment that has been security-fostering for the person with autism, is likely to follow a path not dissimilar to the grieving reactions of others following a bereavement. The process of psychosocial transition, particularly the maturational change from child to adulthood which, for people with autism, is so often accompanied by situational change, i.e. from one home to another, can introduce extreme anxiety into the life of the young adult with autism, for they can lose the capacity to predict their environment. The person with autism is likely to start the transition from one state to another with a lower capacity for adapting to change than others who go through a psychosocial transition. This will occur because the psychological and emotional foundations upon which people with autism make sense of their world are restricted as a consequence of the widespread nature of their imaginative, social and communicative deficits. Because transitions for people with autism are often less easily identified than the more commonly accepted changes (arising from bereavement for example), then supporting and coping strategies are unlikely to be in place.

The implications for practitioners are that when previously well established attachments are broken, new attachments will then need to be developed. The key to assisting adults with autism to successfully make the transition from one setting to another will depend upon the capacity of the practitioner to identify these attachments and to understand the reasons for their significance to the person with autism. The focus of attention should therefore be upon the practitioners who work with adults with autism to help them to make sense of the changes. The rationale employed and the language used will be dependent upon the individual situation, as will the duration of the process.

ATTACHMENT
Introduction

Most research looking at attachment and loss has focused on the nature of relationships between people. Bowlby (1960, 1969, 1973, 1980) describes the critical characteristics of attachment and loss between children and adults, which Parkes (1972) extends by saying that the attachment relationships of adults resemble those of children or rather that attachment relationships of adults are profoundly affected by their experiences as children (Parkes 1988). Much research in this area has targeted bereavement, where the physiological reactions to bereavement and the phenomenology of grief are frequently explored, assessed and measured (see Irwin and Pike 1993; Shuchter and Zisook 1993; Stroebe and Stroebe 1987).

Sigman *et al.* (1986) demonstrated positive social responsiveness by young children with autism, aged two to five years, to their mothers, suggesting that they were able to differentiate between familiar and unfamiliar figures and to form attachments with significant others.

Other studies, for example Rogers *et al.* (1991), have also provided evidence of children with autism being securely attached to their care-givers. Hobson (1993) though, cautions against the application of attachment theory for he says that as yet, we do not understand the reasons for the care-giver's significance for the child with autism, nor can we measure the quality of the attachment, and assess the long-term implications. The basis of the attachment might differ in that it might depend on the predictability of behaviour. This chapter is concerned with looking at the practical implications of attachment and loss for adults with autism.

Attachment and adults with autism

For Weiss (1993), the basis of relationships of attachment is that they are security-fostering and the loss of these relationships will result in persistent grief. In autism it is as if the 'security-fostering' referred to by Weiss may not be solely confined to significant others, but may be associated to a 'precious' item such as a cotton reel, or a piece of string. O'Gorman (1970), who sharpened the earlier work on diagnostic criteria by Mildred Creak (1961) noted that children with autism had a pathological attachment to the same surroundings, equipment, toys and people (albeit the relationship with the person was likely to be purely mechanical and emotionally empty), and that severe anger, terror, or increased withdrawal occurred when the sameness of their environment was threatened.

Tinbergen and Tinbergen (1983) have suggested that people with autism very much wish to form attachments with others, the misdirection of these attachments being the consequence of the inhibition of the normal social response. Wing and Gould (1979) reported their findings from a study of a populace in Camberwell, which led them to believe that abnormal social interactions occurred across the full range of autistic spectrum disorders, which could be divided into three groups: the socially aloof, passive, and active but odd.

Should people with autism be encouraged to develop and increase their attachments with others? By looking briefly at socialisation, one of the three components in the 'Triad of Impairments' identified by Wing and Gould (1979) this question may be considered further. Tinbergen and Tinbergen (1972) initially argued that the child with autism should not be forced into social interactions with others for fear of increased withdrawal. By contrast, Howlin and Rutter (1989) took the alternate stance, arguing that when children with autism are encouraged to participate in social or constructive activities, so their social responsiveness increases whilst obsessional and ritualistic behaviours decrease.[1] This debate is somewhat complicated in relation to adults who have not received such encouragement. Their many years of ingrained non-social behaviour are compounded by the increased expectations of the wider community, which, while it may tolerate anti-social behaviour in children, is far less accepting of this behaviour, and even of asocial behaviour, from adults. Even so, practitioners working with adults with autism in residential settings often report that these adults seek to form consistent contacts with staff rather than with peers, and this has been also been shown to be true of adolescents with autism (Volkmar 1987). It may be that attachments can be formed with others, but it is suggested that their likely basis is in the functional use that the 'other' person has to the adult with autism.

---

1 In fact in later years Tinbergen and Tinbergen altered their stance and by 1983 had come to say that carers should attack 'approach/avoidance' conditions (which they say is the case in autism) either by low intrusion or by high intrusion such as forcing attachment, witnessed by their endorsement of 'Holding Therapy'.

LOSS

Security-fostering attachments

It is impossible, though, to generalise about the type of loss which will affect an individual with autism, for each person will have their own idiosyncratic attachments to objects, people, personal space and so on. Likewise, we can observe that for adults with autism, reactions to, and expressions of, loss can take many highly idiosyncratic forms, but seem to stem from an underlying anxiety. The reason for this heightened anxiety may arise from the removal of something predictable in the world of the adult with autism, thus introducing uncertainty into their lives. Our inability to recognise that a loss has occurred and to empathise with the individual concerned results in a failure in our role as practitioners to offer adequate management and support.

Weiss (1993) points out that when we feel secure in our attachment relationships, we tend not to display attachment feeling and behaviours. It is when there is a threat to the attachment relationship that an increase in attachment behaviour will be produced. In autism, this is not necessarily so, and we can often see that attachment behaviours are displayed even when there is no apparent immediate threat to the object of the attachment, an indication perhaps of the individual's desire to cling on to, and retain, some predictability and control over their lives. So far we have looked at attachment to individuals and at attachment to objects, but a further attachment often displayed by people with autism is to routine and to predicted outcomes as will be seen in the following vignette:

VIGNETTE 5.1

A 25-year old man with Asperger syndrome had a particular and possibly 'expert' knowledge of the local bus service and had known some of the drivers who had been with the bus company since his childhood, but most of the other drivers were fairly transient. None the less, he counted them all as his friends. It had been noticed that there were four key situations, although very unlikely to occur, the mere thought of which would trigger attachment behaviours, and the young man would become extremely anxious, shouting and asking repeated questions of others, all designed to seek reassurance that the bus drivers would be back the next day. The four situations were: bus strikes, bad weather forcing the buses off the road, bank holidays when no buses could operate (Christmas day only), and congested buses which failed to stop to pick him up. Over the years, strategies were developed to help him to accept more appropriately such rare situations, but he has remained fearful of the buses being unable to pick him up, constantly seeking reassurance from others.

Loss of attachments

The types of behaviours displayed when the loss of an attachment occurs have been described by scholars for many years. Bowlby (1980) identified four phases of recovery from loss before a return to previous levels of ordinary functioning: shock, protest, despair followed by a long interval of adaptation. He was, of course, referring to the attachment relationships formed between children and their parents, but, for adults with autism, it is helpful to apply such delineation to loss in their attachment situations.

It may be useful to look at examples of losses which are apparently trivial, but to the adults with autism themselves, they are extremely disturbing. The displays of shock and protest are clearly seen, but the period of adaptation is less clearly definable. In each case the period of adaptation, lasting days, weeks or months, was characterised by a complete desynchronisation of every facet of the individual's routine of daily life. The loss of attachment in each practical situation significantly affected the life of the individual both in the short term and sometimes also extending to the long term. Each loss was identified by the application of a functional analysis of behaviour, i.e. the antecedent, behaviour and consequence of the behaviour, but the ongoing strategies for management moved away from strictly behavioural approaches. In each case, the loss appeared to catch the person with autism off-guard, and with their limited problem-solving capacity (Powell *et al.* 1994), propelled them into bizarre or stereotypical reactions.

VIGNETTE 5.2

SHOCK, PROTEST, PERIOD OF ADAPTATION: SEVERAL WEEKS

Every weekend, a 29-year-old man with autism and a moderate learning disability was collected by his father from the residential unit in which he lived. His father would always turn up in a blue car. On one occasion his father was unable to collect him so the unit offered to take the man home in the unit's own transport. As the usual time came for the father to collect his son, so he stood by a window in the house looking out for the blue car. The practitioner who was to drive the man explained that she would be driving him home and encouraged him to move away and to follow her to the rear of the unit where the transport was waiting. As they went outside, so the man became extremely anxious and began shouting and repeating, 'blue car, blue car,' and rocking back and forth. Although he had been out in the unit's vehicle on many occasions, his expectation was that each time he went home, the blue car would collect him. Sadly, the practitioner received a broken nose, the result of a head-butt, despite her calm, kind and careful words of reassurance. Whether this young man had an attachment to the blue car or to the broader expectations of the situation, i.e. that his father would arrive, that they would take the same route as usual and so on, his distress at the loss of sameness caused him considerable anxiety and led to his protest. For several weeks, he remained extremely anxious, seeking an inordinate amount of reassurance from practitioners that other components of his life would remain the same.

VIGNETTE 5.3

SHOCK, PROTEST, SHORT PERIOD OF ADAPTATION AFFECTING ALL ASPECTS OF HIS DAILY LIFE

A 23-year-old man with autism and a severe learning disability was dressing one morning when he discovered that a button was missing from his shirt. His reaction was to initially engage in wrist-biting and other self-injurious behaviour prior to three days and nights of extremely ritualistic behaviour, including standing outside his bedroom for five hours at a time, not letting anybody pass up or down the corridor, and avoiding taking meals. Gradually he became secure again within his environment and reverted to more socially appropriate behaviour. Although, the protest at the loss of the button was relatively brief, for three days all aspects of his daily life were invaded by this loss.

VIGNETTE 5.4

SHOCK, PROTEST, AND LONG PERIOD OF ADAPTATION

A 19-year-old man with autism and a severe learning disability lived in a residential unit with 19 other adults, who, unlike himself, had no diagnosis of autism. During the day he would attend a social education centre (SEC) also for people with learning disabilities, which closed for three weeks during the summer. During the break, the day room in which he spent much of his time had been modernised and redecorated. On his first day back to the SEC following the summer break, he began, within only 30 minutes of being in the redecorated room, severely punching himself on the head. This behaviour had not been seen before by the SEC staff who were alarmed and he was returned to the residential unit where he soon appeared to calm down. The following day the same behaviour erupted and he was kept off from the SEC until the following week, by which time he again appeared relaxed enough to return to the SEC. Within a few minutes of arrival the self-injurious behaviour re-emerged and on this occasion when he returned to the residential unit the behaviour continued and did not decrease in frequency for several weeks, by which time he had broken every knuckle in both hands and removed large portions of his hair, creating frighteningly large lesions in his scalp. Behavioural approaches to his self-injurious behaviour were singularly unsuccessful (used under the guidance of the Principal Clinical Psychologist), producing an extension of the adverse reactions, and it was only when pressure to conform to the expectations of behaviours of the others with learning disabilities in the home (i.e. by staff focusing upon the way in which they responded to him, in terms of tone of voice and the messages that were given, and by helping him to organise his day in a non-pressured way – by developing a routine in which he felt confident) did his behaviour improve. It was clear that the young man had found his unexpected 'new' environment at the SEC to be unsettling, triggering his reaction which in the end became self-perpetuating. His attachment to the old scheme of the room had not been recognised by anybody working with him.

TRANSITION: ONE EXAMPLE OF ATTACHMENT AND LOSS IN AUTISM

Introduction

Longitudinal research, retrospective studies, short-term investigations and the re-analyses of contemporary data have been important methodological tools for identifying and exploring childhood factors which predict and influence outcomes in later life (Maughan and Champion 1990). Economic deprivation in childhood (Elder 1979), lack of parental support (Crook and Eliot 1980), and the effects of institutionalised upbringing (Rutter et al.1990), are examples of targets for researchers in this area. The risk and protective mechanisms involved have been reviewed by Masten and Garmezy (1985) and particular attention has been paid to the associated issues of vulnerability, stress and resilience (Rutter 1985). The transition from child to adulthood, i.e. 'rites of passage' a stage of development so favoured by Hollywood as a subject for cinema, has also occupied the efforts of many researchers.

Defining adult status

The developmental tasks involved in the transition from child to adulthood have been identified by many writers (Erickson 1965; Havighurst 1953, 1972; Levinson et al. 1978), and in proposing developmental tasks, they have found common agreement (Maughan and Champion 1990). Havighurst's (1953) stage model of psychosocial development included the following tasks: achievement of emotional independence from parents and other adults, a greater maturity of relations with peers, the development of a masculine or feminine social role, desiring and achieving socially responsible behaviour and acquiring a set of values and an ethical system as a guide to behaviours.

The Office of Economic and Community Development (OECD)/ Centre for Research and Innovation (CERI) (1986) study set out the main indicators of adult status which has since received international recognition and widespread acceptance as a definition. The OECD/CERI study identified certain key goals at four different stages in life which were based on normative notions of what constituted adult status in present day society. The key goals included:

Personal autonomy, leading towards responsibility for one's own life, and, obtained through making choices and decisions, building up self-esteem and developing relationships with others.

Useful employment leading to economic self-sufficiency. This would involve ensuring that opportunities for work experience (supported or otherwise) lead on to full employment.

Social interactions and community participation through recreational and leisure activities.

Adult role within the family and the opportunities to contribute to the home and to develop relationships leading to marriage, with the establishment of one's own home (OECD 1988)

Maughan and Champion (1990) took into account such research in their investigation of the specific transitional period from child to adulthood. Included in their suggestions for future investigation into this important developmental period were the need to identify the interactive relationship between inner resources for the individual and outer experiences providing a gauge of risk and protective factors. They recommend that there should be a close look at the timing, sequencing and synchronisation of the transition, the implications and nature of the support systems that are available, and whether there are gender differences which influence all stages in the process.

Transition in autism

Whereas previous research exploring the process of transition has focused upon groups with assumed intellectual abilities within normal ranges, comparatively little research has looked at developmental transition for young adults with intellectual disabilities and specifically for those with pervasive developmental disorders. For the person with autism, the developmental transition from child to adulthood, and indeed any other significant transition (not necessarily or exclusively transitions involving a biological change), is likely to involve the cutting of old attachments. Whilst transition can be a developmental process, it may also be situational, i.e. from school to work, from home to residential care, one residential unit to another, and so on. As will be seen, transition sometimes can be simultaneously maturational and situational and these changes from one state to another can provoke extreme anxiety in the individual with autism and, indeed, in their families.

The individual with autism may well have two hurdles to leap when making a transition, the first arising from their autism and the second, in many cases, from an associated learning disability. A prominent characteristic of autism is an inflexibility of thought leading to a difficulty in adapting to changes in the environment, which impacts upon the individual's capacity to integrate easily into new settings and with new people. The situation will be compounded because many people with autism will also have a learning disability and, often because of a lack of understanding, reasoning and insight, the transition will be felt by the person with autism as a loss, rather than a positive move towards greater autonomy. There are many occasions in the life of a person with autism when she/he has to transfer from one state to another. Attachments previously well established in one setting will be broken and new attachments will then need to be developed in another. The key to assisting adults with autism to make the transition from one setting to another successfully will depend upon the capacity of the practitioner to identify these attachments and to understand the reasons for their significance to the person with autism. In terms of devising a framework for understanding the process of transition for people with autism, it is helpful to continue with the theme of attachment and loss.

Theoretical framework

We all have an internalised, assumptive model of the world enabling us to predict the actions of others with a degree of confidence and certainty, but, when major change occurs, particularly when it has occurred without warning, our expectations and our ingrained habits of thought and behaviour are severely challenged. In this painful and often confidence-sapping process, anxiety may inhibit our capacity to make sense of what has occurred, indeed to resist change, and thus delay our ability to create a new internalised schema of the world.

Parkes (1993) talks of this process as being a psychosocial transition (PST) that is defined by three critical characteristics that: (1) require people to undertake a major revision of their assumptions of the world, (2) have lasting rather than transient implications, and (3) take place over a short period of time, thus restricting the opportunity for preparation. He is careful to say that PSTs exclude events that do not result in any lasting change and that gradual processes of transition, for example maturational change, do not constitute a PST.

For people with autism, the process of change from one state to another is inextricably linked to an inflexibility of thinking; consequently, attachment to their assumptive world is fixed and static so that a transition requiring a reshaping of expectations is likely to be extremely traumatising. Resistance to change is often observed in people with autism and is also a component in a PST. The focus of attention should therefore be upon the practitioners who work with adults with autism to help them to make sense of the changes. But here a distinction needs to be made against the concept of PSTs. The person with autism is likely to start the transition from one state to another with a lower capacity for adapting to change than others who go through a PST. This will occur because the psychological and emotional foundations upon which people with autism make sense of their world are restricted as a consequence of the widespread nature of their imaginative, social and communicative deficits. People with autism will experience many of the life changes that others undergo, but these changes will often be traumatic for them because of their autism. For other people these changes will be recognised as transitions because they do not find them threatening. It follows that transitions for people with autism are likely to occur more frequently, but, because they are often less easily identified than the more commonly accepted changes (arising from bereavement for example), then supporting and coping strategies are not in place.

Parkes (1993) acknowledges that outcomes from PSTs can be improved by observation of the initial reaction to the event and by knowledge of risk factors. Anticipation, where preparation for an event takes place, can reduce the risk involved in a PST. He recognises that in cases of terminal illness, preparation can positively influence the outcome, and the work of the Hospice movement epitomises the role that psychosocial medicine has in these situations. But for adults with autism, we have to look at individual situations and transitions that sometimes occur more frequently and arise from the person with autisms' predilection for routine and sameness. Two key areas of transition which have been identified as problematic for some people with autism are the transition from adolescence to adulthood and from one home to another. We will call the first maturational transition and the second situational transition.

Maturational transition

The psychological and biological changes which take place through puberty, adolescence and into adulthood are an inevitable part of human development and centre around the need for greater independence and the development of sexual drives and needs. Parkes (1993) says that maturational changes do not constitute PSTs, but, for certain individuals with autism, the profile may be different. It has been recognised that for people with autism and their carers, the transitional process from child to adulthood can be the most difficult of the developmental stages (Adams and Sheslow 1983). The OECD/CERI (1986) study was outlined earlier, in the section entitled, 'Defining adult status' as was Havighurst's (1953) stage model of psychosocial development, which identified tasks to be surmounted as children discard their childhood attachments and cross the social divide to adulthood, and upon which Adams and Sheslow based their evaluation for people with autism. Adams and Sheslow (1983) argue that the social, emotional and communicative deficits that define the syndrome of autism in childhood continue, with some qualitative alteration in the impact upon the adolescent, to such a degree as to block or impede the 'rites of passage' as detailed by Havighurst. They point out also that the expectations of the community can be more accepting of the 'odd' behaviour of the child with autism, whereas when the child becomes an adult, the tolerance of the community towards the 'odd' behaviour decreases and more socially acceptable behaviour is expected.

There is of course the danger that without carefully planned approaches an 'eternal child' situation will occur, negating the opportunity to ensure that a quality of adult life can be achieved (Open University 1988). By adhering too closely to the goals set by the traditional and conformist OECD/CERI model or by Havighurst's 'rites of passage', there is a risk of denying adult status to many adults with autism. It may be better to seek ways of reclassifying the definition of adult status so that the individual with autism will be able to achieve adult status in a way which is meaningful to them and which affords dignity and respect from others. Jordan and Edwards (1995) provide an interesting example of the way in which this can apply. A goal of the OECD study was to ascribe adult status, which can be achieved only as part of a family in which relationships are equated with marriage and having a family. Jordan and Edwards identify that for many people with autism this would not be a preference, never mind an aim, in their lives. They ask, why should not adult status be compatible with living by oneself, either completely independently, or with the support or understanding of others ?

It has been suggested that the move to adulthood for people with autism may be characterised by a slowing down in the capacity to learn (Baron-Cohen and Bolton 1993) and that high-class education can be undone by a lack of stimulation in adulthood. But such a suggestion fails to recognise that children and adults with autism are: (1) extremely poor at transferring skills learned in one setting to another and (2) that the process of transition from school to adult settings often fails to acknowledge the attachments of people with autism to their 'old' setting and their need to develop new attachments in 'new' settings in accordance with their individual needs.

Organisational structures often fail to enable the person with autism to make the transition from child to adulthood successfully by means of a gradual replacement of old attachments with new. Within the UK, the wide chasm in responsibilities and funding between Education and Social Services Departments restricts the opportunities for life-time planning for the person with autism. The belief that education is synonymous with schooling and that care practice is the main function of adult provision, rather than the view that education is 'for life', inhibits the opportunities for adults with autism to gain access to the education and training necessary to equip them with the skills to undertake adult roles. Historically, liaison and communication between workers in both sectors is not good, but this was recently acknowledged in the 1993 Education Act (Department for

Education 1993) and the subsequent Code of Practice (1994). The Code of Practice instructs local authorities to include a 'Transitional Plan' for every young person from the age of 14 and during every annual review of need until they leave school. The purpose of the 'Transitional Plan' will be to draw together information from a range of individuals within and beyond school, so as to plan coherently for the young person's transition into adult life. Within the USA, however, life-time planning becomes a more likely scenario in some States, as programmes such as those operated by TEACCH (who coined the phrase 'seamless service', now also adopted by the National Autistic Society in the UK), strive to provide the life-long consistency which autistic people require.

As will be seen in the following vignettes, individuals with autism can react to the change from one setting to another in ways which were not anticipated by those working most closely with them, and this illustrates how apparent competence in one situation can mask permanent underlying deficits. Both examples involve situational transition, the transition from child to adulthood being inevitable, although incidental.

VIGNETTE 5.5

A 19-year-old man with a diagnosis of Asperger syndrome had been a pupil at a residential school for children with autism for ten years. When he reached school leaving age, he transferred to a residential unit for adults with autism. Articulate and popular with teaching staff, it was thought that only a short period of introduction to the new unit would be necessary. The first weeks following the move appeared to go smoothly and the young man impressed the practitioners in the adult unit with his command of language and apparent ability to 'fit in'. Gradually, however, his behaviour began to deteriorate, becoming obsessional and displaying aggression to himself and others. Increasingly, he talked anxiously of his days at school, of staff and pupils, of incidents, and of local events. Despite having initially appeared to settle in to his new surroundings, his behaviour, coupled with the content of his language, gave a strong indication that he felt frustration, distress, perhaps also anger and helplessness at the loss of his previous home. Within 12 months, the home felt that they could no longer manage his overtly aggressive behaviour and his local authority arranged admission to a local psychiatric hospital. He clearly had not been given the opportunity to develop a concrete concept of his new home, to make the attachments at his own pace and had not had the opportunity to make his goodbyes to his old home. A further factor which may have contributed to his disorientation was that he had not been involved in the process of identifying the most appropriate resource for him to go to after leaving school. It is impossible to reach anything other than the conclusion that this man was let down badly by his practitioners who had not fully acknowledged his underlying impairment, the importance of his old attachments, and his need to establish new attachments before and during the process of attachment.

Contrast this example with vignette 5.6 which illustrates a greater awareness of autistic learning by practitioners.

VIGNETTE 5.6

A 19-year-old woman with a diagnosis of autism and a severe learning disability had spent many years in a residential school for children with autism prior to moving to a unit for adults with autism. Funding was agreed at an early stage and a programme of gradual introduction to the adult community was co-operatively developed between the young woman's key workers in the school and in the adult unit. Her parents were involved and approved of the plan. The introductions were paced to meet her capacity to adapt to the change, commencing with cups of tea, building up to meals, day centre activities, overnight stays and so on. Gradually the woman developed a concrete knowledge of the place that she was moving to, her bedroom, her new peers, her new carers and the structure of the day and evening. The practitioners in the new unit began also to develop their own knowledge of the woman whilst she was herself able to make her goodbyes to her former school.

Situational transition

Less predictable are the circumstances leading to situational transition, i.e. from one place to another, which can of course occur at any time of life. Changes in life circumstances may rest upon the availability of appropriate support services for the family and also the accessibility of residential or day centre care at any given point in time. Elderly or infirm parents who have kept their autistic son or daughter at home may be suddenly forced into a position, through illness or bereavement, of urgently needing to place their son or daughter in residential care. Without adequate preparation of the adult with autism, and indeed the parent, the effects of this transition can be devastating for both the person with autism and his or her family. For practitioners who have to pick up the pieces of such circumstances, the situation can also be most distressing and extremely challenging to the care systems that they work in. Too often, families and practitioners who have experienced such a situation reflect, with the benefit of hindsight, that the requirement of an effective life-time plan or regime would have made all the difference. Clearly, a number of factors will be of significance which will include emotional issues, such as loss of significant persons, of possessions and of environment. Transition for people with autism can therefore mean a complete loss of contact with people close to them, with a lack of control over the decisions made to determine the outcome of the transition. The loss of attachments with no opportunity for understanding and assimilating the reasons for the change, and regardless of acquiescence to the change, is likely to bring despair and havoc into the life of the adult with autism.

Even so, each situation must be approached on an individual basis. The ways in which transitions are planned and undertaken should be based upon an understanding of the means by which adults with autism make sense of their environment and also of their individual circumstances. It will be seen in vignette 5.7 that the loss of a family home for a young man living in a residential community for adults with autism could have had devastating effects, but, instead, he was helped to understand and to rationalise in such a way that he was able to transfer his attachments from his old home to his new home.

VIGNETTE 5.7

SITUATIONAL

Planning

Careful planning enabled a 37-year-old man with autism and moderate learning disabilities, who lived in a specialist community for adults with autism, to accept the sale of the family home in London and his mother's transfer of home to a small flat in another city. Previously, when for any reason, a planned home visit had to be cancelled, he exhibited extreme anxiety, often accompanied by challenging behaviour and could be consoled only by being given a firm date for his next visit. Because of his characteristic high anxiety level, it was agreed in discussion between his mother and the practitioners caring for him that he should be given no advance notice of the move. This policy was endorsed in consultation with a clinical psychologist, highly knowledgeable and experienced in the field of autism.

What he was told

On the day of the move he was told that his London home was 'all gone' and he was given the complete address of his new home and the date on which he would visit it with his key worker. He was then encouraged to write a letter to his mother at the new home, in which he said 'Welcome to mine and your new home', stated that the old home was gone (referring to it by the address) and wrote out the new address in full.

First visit

He was brought by his key worker and his mother showed him round the flat in which many items familiar to him had been retained, especially in his bedroom – bed, bedspread, rug, fur animals and his clothes in the wardrobe, which were pointed out to him.

Conclusion

He accepted his new home at once. However, the fact that he had always referred to home visits by the home address (no mention of 'mummy' or 'home') had misled his mother and practitioners into believing that the primary attachment was to the location. On reflection, it was concluded that this attachment was to the caring function provided by his mother, and the continuity of this function needed to be guaranteed by a fixed location. This has implications for bereavement in the future.

SUMMARY

We have seen in this section that traditional theory of attachment and loss has some relevance for people with autism. Adults with autism are particularly vulnerable to idiosyncratic losses, for their attachments are less easily identified by carers, and their psychosocial transitions (Parkes 1993) may occur more frequently. Displays of recovery from loss broadly follow the path laid down by Bowlby (1980), i.e. shock, protest, and varying periods of adaptation.

The practical implications for transition for adults with autism are clear: practitioners need to understand the reasons how and why attachments are formed, and to plan the timing, sequencing and synchronisation of transitions based upon an understanding of these attachments and of the individual circumstances. Based upon this underlying knowledge, practitioners can anticipate the problems that may occur. This will impact upon the delivery of services where transition is likely to occur, i.e. from school to adult units, home to day centres, and to colleges of further education.

BEREAVEMENT

This section looks at a further example of attachment and loss in autism, by investigating the specific issue of bereavement and identifying several salient features required in order to provide support for adults with autism undergoing a bereavement. It is important to emphasise that reactions to bereavement are uniquely felt by all of us and it is also true that the adult with autism will react in a way that is meaningful to him or her. As practitioners, we can help to determine the quality of the acceptance and recovery process and the tasks that are outlined – as are the pressures that practitioners face. The section begins with vignette 5.8 followed by descriptions of reactions by adults with autism to bereavement

VIGNETTE 5.8

Beth is a 23-year-old woman with a diagnosis of autism and severe learning disability. She has lived in residential care since childhood and is highly dependent upon others, requiring considerable supervision. She has verbal but echolalic language. Beth sometimes displays high levels of anxiety and lability of mood which often precede challenging behaviour.

At the time of her father's death Beth lived in a residential unit for adults with autism. Two members of staff informed Beth of the death of her father, who had died suddenly from a heart attack. She was advised of this fact in a simple but factual way, but gave no immediate indication or awareness of the loss, asking only for a pot of tea. Over the following weeks, Beth displayed disruptive behaviour, losing interest in food, crying and howling and spending long periods of time in the toilet with a towel over her head. At first, when Beth was asked if she knew where her father was she would reply 'shopping or in the house'.

VISITS HOME:
THE CONTINUATION OF FAMILY ATTACHMENTS

Until her father's death, Beth would return home every two to three weeks, for a weekend stay, but after he died, Beth's mother, who now lived alone, was less certain of being able to cope, as her husband had taken the lead role in supporting Beth when at home. It was clear that visits home were to be very important for the maintenance of contact between Beth and her mother.

Beth's first visit home was only for a few hours, supported by a member of staff. These visits were gradually increased. After four months, Beth's mother felt less vulnerable and more confident and Beth spent her first weekend at home alone with her mother. However, it quickly became clear that the pace of introduction of these longer visits had been too rapid, and perhaps no longer appropriate now Beth's father was not around. It was agreed to reduce the periods at home to one overnight stay, once a month. This arrangement appeared to produce greater benefits giving Beth time to be at home with her mother and also allowing time for her mother to grieve.

AFTER THE FUNERAL: HELPING BETH TO SAY 'GOODBYE'

Although staff support was offered, Beth did not attend the funeral. This was a decision taken by Beth's family. However, it was recognised that Beth would need to be encouraged and supported to accept the loss and to say goodbye to her Dad. Supported by her key worker, Beth visited the cemetery on a regular basis and initially as a matter of routine. She was not coerced into making any input to the visits except that she clearly looked forward to going to McDonalds afterwards. Whilst at the cemetery, flowers were placed against a tree and within several weeks she seemed to recognise the tree where her flowers were to be placed at each visit. Truthful and concise explanations were given to Beth by the supporting key worker.

Within four weeks, Beth appeared to recognise the surroundings while being driven to the cemetery. She volunteered that it was 'sad'. When Beth was asked why she was there, she said, 'for Dad'. When asked what she would like to say to her 'Dad' she said 'be happy'. When asked how she felt about her Dad she said, 'you do miss him'.

Shortly before Christmas, while approaching the cemetery, Beth was asked if she knew where she was going. She replied, 'flowers for Dad'. Beth was asked if she knew where her Dad was. Beth said, 'he is dead'. When asked by staff where to put the flowers, Beth said, 'by the tree'. Beth got out of the minibus without any prompting and walked to the tree to lay the flowers and said 'Happy Christmas Dad'. Beth was very calm and relaxed and did not then ask to go to McDonalds.

Bereavement is individually experienced

As with normalisation, sexuality and challenging behaviour, approaches to working with people with learning disabilities who suffer bereavement are becoming increasingly 'trendy'. There is thus a danger that practitioners will adhere to one, single, approach to bereavement, and, by so doing, will forget that the impact of bereavement for the person with autism will be individually experienced (as it is for all of us) and that their grieving process may fall outside a 'fixed' theory of grief.

It has already been seen that people with autism are especially vulnerable to changes from one state to another due to the idiosyncratic attachments that are developed. Children with autism are well able to recognise the difference between familiar and unfamiliar individuals (Frith 1989) and the same is undoubtably true for adults with autism. Whilst it has been observed that people with autism have great difficulty in appreciating the thoughts and feelings of others, and often show qualitatively different types of attachments, the disappearance of a person close and precious to them can have a profound effect. The most obvious examples are when a close relative dies or a personal 'key' worker leaves for another job. People with autism, like any of us, will react individually to their experience of bereavement. Furthermore, it is likely that the grieving process of people with autism will be affected profoundly by their cognitive disabilities, and the vast intellectual differences that can be found across autistic spectrum disorders serve only to compound the difficulty of making a single approach to support individuals with autism who have suffered a bereavement.

Reactions to bereavement by adults with autism

Worden (1983) says that a continuous relationship exists between 'normal' and 'abnormal' grief, but that difficulties are usually reflected in the intensity and/or duration of the reaction. He proposed that grief could be separated into 'normal' (uncomplicated) and 'abnormal' (complicated) grief. 'Normal' grief will involve a wide range of feelings/behaviours, the intensity of which will decrease and disappear over time. Feelings will include sadness, anger, shock and guilt; physical reactions may occur; the bereaved may be confused and disbelieving; and patterns of behaviour may include crying, loss of sleep and so on. Worden identified four types of 'abnormal' grief: chronic grief; delayed grief; exaggerated grief; and masked grief.

Whilst it is clear that a limited intellectual capacity does not imply a limited emotional capacity (Sireling and Hollins 1985), it is also clear that the emotional perception of people with autism may be qualitatively different to those of people with other disabilities yet, as will be seen, their reactions to bereavement are wide-ranging and may well fall under the two headings of 'normal' and 'abnormal' grief described by Worden (1983).

Vignettes of patterns of bereavement identified in adolescents and adults with autism were collated and analysed by Allison (1993). Immediate and long-term reactions were detailed and brief extracts are summarised here and in Appendix 5.1, in order to present evidence of the unique way in which adults with autism can respond to bereavement. Immediate reactions included:

Ran round the room with grief.

She wanted to know when it had happened, and at what time. Was angry because her brother had left her.

No emotion. Put soup spoon down and said, 'Are you alright, Mum? Why can't Charles (foster brother) come home and head this family? I don't want to be a step-father.' (Appeared to...) understand loss immediately. Reacted by fulfilling father's tasks such as coal carrying, walking the dog and cleaning the car.

Accepted the news calmly.

Screamed on evening of funeral. Not long after funeral was humming parts of *Beethoven's Ninth Symphony*, one of his grandfather's favourites.

Disbelief.... anxious about (*his father*) not really being dead, saying 'Promise me he is really dead'. Soon afterwards sought reassurance about his mother's health. When told of his mother's death, he said 'Oh, really?' It took two or three days for him to (*appear to*) realise that he had suffered a loss. He then said, 'I miss her'.

Subsequent reactions included:

Frequently expressed a sense of loss, became very withdrawn on the first Mothers' Day after his mother's death when he realised there was no point in sending a card. He began to be very dependent on staff.

Seemed to be in pain. Prone to infections, anxiety, hyperactivity.

Later she wrote, 'We are sad to think of Grandpa in his coffin'. Many times said that Grandpa was in his house and would come back.

Said, 'I am not going home because Daddy has gone to heaven', without appearing upset.

Unresponsive, 'personality change'. Concerned about mother's health. Tried to hurry past end of road where grandmother lived. Did not wish to visit her house again.

Supporting adults with autism through the bereavement process

Vignette 5.8 given at the beginning of this section illustrated the need for an individual approach to the issue of bereavement, based upon a knowledge of the factors contributing to the bereavement and of the individual character of the bereaved. These factors will determine how the news of the death should be conveyed to the bereaved and the nature of the support which should be given. This support will include acknowledging and respecting the grief of the bereaved, recognising rather than excluding the memory of the deceased, and helping the bereaved to come to terms with death (Allison 1993).

Within a service, the adult with autism may be directly affected by the death of a relative, peer, staff member, or acquaintance, and may even be distressed by the knowledge that someone known to them has lost somebody close. Practitioners have an important role in helping an adult with autism come to terms with a bereavement.

The role that practitioners can play in bereavement

Death is unavoidable and the deceased irreplaceable. As parents and perhaps also other close relatives become elderly, there is an increasing likelihood that the adult with autism will have to face the loss of a person close to him/her. Many adults with autism still live at home with their families when the death of a parent occurs, yet they will often enter a residential setting, perhaps for the first time, as a consequence of this bereavement. During this critical period, adults with autism are particularly vulnerable, for the individual, like others in society, can display a wide range of grieving behaviours, several of which may lead to them being referred to a specialist service. The loss of attachments, of familiar environments and maybe also of 'precious' things, is likely to exacerbate the vulnerability and sense of loss that a person with autism will have at the time of the bereavement. There is thus a danger of 'pathological' behaviour leading to inappropriate decisions being made (Oswin 1985).

It is proposed that there should be two approaches to bereavement for adults with autism. The first needs to be a structural approach from service planners who must identify the increasing risk of bereavement to adults with autism within defined geographical areas and age ranges. Service planners must deliver edicts to local managers and to community teams to develop individual profiles which include details of the individual's attachments, previous reactions to change (where these are known), and the types and quality of support services that will be required when a bereavement occurs. Service planners must also be aware that a person with autism will require stability and the opportunity to become secure and confident with a new environment and with new people for some time to come after a bereavement. This should automatically rule out placement for assessment purposes only during the short term, and ideally not in the two years following a bereavement. Likewise, changes of unit for any other reason are ill-advised.

The second strategy that will need to be implemented will be the hands-on support to help the individual through the grieving process. Practitioners have several important roles to play in the grieving process affecting adults with autism.

In the case of the terminal illness of a parent/carer, practitioners can influence preparatory making arrangements, perhaps by arrangements for visiting, assisting with the organisation of the arrangements, by talking through with the client that illness will lead to death and ensuring that both the client and the parent/carer will be as reassured as possible that, when the death has occurred, the person with autism will be supported as much as possible.

It will be reassuring to other family members that their relation with autism will be supported through this difficult period and, in time, the key worker can encourage the family members or an advocate to develop meaningful contacts with the client, so that the loss of one important person does not leave a void never to be filled. The task of the practitioner is to enable the bereaved individual to accept that the loss has occurred and, whilst old attachments will alter, new ones can be made.

Tasks

Pitching the level of explanation

The National Autistic Society report (Allison 1993) made the following recommendations. Those with Asperger syndrome may require detailed explanations and be afforded opportunities to explore their own concepts of death and after-life beliefs. Those with autism and moderate learning disabilities may derive most comfort from simple, factual and direct language. People with autism and severe/profound learning disabilities may become confused by anything other than the minimum amount of information. Even so, these should be seen as only very general suggestions and the implications are that practitioners need to be flexible in their approach to individual situations.

Funeral arrangements

Adults with autism should not automatically be excluded from attending the funeral because others feel that they will not understand, or get upset by the process. Nobody should assume that they cannot understand the bereavement and they, of course, have the right to get upset just like any other mourners, and staff should offer to go along to offer support as suggested by Oswin (1991). But it is not a simple issue about the rights of the individual, for practitioners should be receptive to the views of other bereaved members of the family who, due to their own emotional state, feel unable to cope with the additional stress of their autistic relative being present. In these circumstances this author believes that it should not be for the practitioner to take responsibility for the decision being made, if the person with autism cannot make the decision themselves, rather that the practitioner should plan the means of other support to enable the person with autism to accept the bereavement.

Working through the process of bereavement

Each adult with autism will respond to the bereavement in their own way and the task of the practitioner will be to create opportunities for the individual to work through the process of bereavement. The development of practical opportunities to enable the adult with autism to develop a concrete understanding of what has happened to their deceased relative will be particularly important. A good example of a concrete approach was seen in the vignette of Beth (vignette 5.8), where she was enabled to attend the cemetery on regular basis, to lay flowers and given opportunities to talk about her late father. The key worker can help the bereaved person to develop a folder of memories consisting of photographs, letters, cards and so on.

Understanding the carers

Carers will be concerned about the physical and emotional well-being of the individual, they will be personally very distressed themselves to see such pain within the person for whom they care, have initial doubts about the best way to offer support to ease the pain, but also, in the case of bereavement, may themselves be distressed at the death of the same person. The key to practitioners' confidence to deal with bereavement will depend largely upon the quality of the training that they will have received in both the field of autism and the bereavement process, and the support systems that are in place. A further significant factor may be if they have themselves experienced bereavement.

This training will need to be reviewed periodically (Allison 1993). A useful resource for the development of a bereavement policy and the practical approaches which follow from it is the literature concerning the impact of bereavement on children and on people with learning disabilities (for example see Oswin 1991). Critical features will include the formation of bereavement support groups, composed of experienced practitioners who, after the initial period of training, will need to respond when bereavements or potential bereavements occur.

Bereavement support groups

Bereavement support groups in services for adults with autism can serve many purposes: the group can provide support for the bereaved person with autism. The group can provide training and supervising support for practitioners who themselves support the person with autism. The bereavement support group can have a broad picture of the members of the family by maintaining a record of significant facts on file, e.g. the name used by the client for significant people in their lives, details of any previous losses which can influence subsequent bereavements (Allison 1993). It can play an important role in ensuring that clients are supported during their grieving process by designated members of staff who understand the grieving process. The group can also play a key role in informing and reassuring other practitioners working with a bereaved client so that consistency of approach is established and maintained and conflicting messages are not picked up by the client, who is already likely to be in an emotionally vulnerable state.

CHAPTER SUMMARY

In this chapter it has been suggested that the traditional theory of attachment and loss has some relevance for people with autism. Adults with autism are particularly vulnerable to idiosyncratic losses, for their attachments are less easily identified by carers, and their psychosocial transitions (Parkes 1993) may occur more frequently. Displays of recovery from loss broadly follow the path laid down by Bowlby (1980), i.e. shock, protest, despair and varying periods of adaptation. The practical implications for transition for adults with autism are clear: practitioners need to understand how and why attachments are formed, to plan the timing, sequencing, synchronisation of transitions based upon this understanding and that of the individual circumstances, and to anticipate the problems that may occur based upon this underlying knowledge. This will impact upon the delivery of services where transition is likely to occur, i.e. from school to adult units, home to day centres and colleges of further education. It was seen in the final section, 'Bereavement', that the reactions of adults with autism to bereavement are individual while being profoundly influenced by their disabilities, and that the outcome will be determined by the knowledge and skill base of practitioners. In addition to the hands-on approach by practitioners, service planners need to develop a strategic approach for those adults with autism living in vulnerable situations who are likely to suffer a bereavement of their main care-giver.

ACKNOWLEDGEMENTS

Helen Green-Allison, National Autistic Society. The Library of the Kings Fund Centre, London. Pat Lee, West Midlands Autistic Society.

APPENDIX 5.1

Identified reactions to bereavement by people with autism. Adapted from Allison (1993) cited in Reynolds and Atkins (1995).

1. Failure to grieve after loss. Should not be interpreted as signalling a lack of emotion, for they may be grieving in ways in which practitioners do not understand.

2. Delayed reaction to loss. Kitching (1987) identified that grief is often delayed for people with learning disabilities, who may not initially understand the loss, but come to do so later, and then enter a typical grieving process.

3. Apparent failure to understand the irreversibility of death. For people with autism, repeated questioning as to the return of the deceased may reflect a difficulty with language rather than comprehension. Repeated questioning may be a means of seeking verification that the death has occurred or demonstrating a need for comfort and reassurance.

4. Uncertain responses and inappropriate responses to bereavement. For example, giggling at the funeral. May indicate difficulties in verbal expression, or anxiety at a new or rare experience.

5. Limited means of expressing grief. Grief counselling can involve intense, long-term interactions, which may be unsettling to the person with autism, thus emphasising the need for an individual and sensitive approach to the bereaved.

6. Limited number of relationships. People with autism often have a very limited number of close relationships and the loss of one of these may be catastrophic. It may be difficult for the person with autism to withdraw from the deceased and form new attachments with others.

7. Inability to seek activities which may help in the grieving process. People with autism may not have the insight, self-awareness, self-confidence, motivation or experience to seek activities which may help them through the grieving process.

8. Introduction of undesirable habits or obsessions. In seeking to replace the loss of an attachment, people with autism may develop habits or obsessions considered by others to be inappropriate. These may persist after the grieving period to the detriment of the client, if they are not sensitively tackled.

9. Inability to predict future change. People with autism are unlikely to have an expectation that the pain they are experiencing will end. They, therefore, lack a source of comfort. It is useful to explain the grieving process, bearing in mind that the intensity and duration of their reactions must be determined by the bereaved.

BIBLIOGRAPHY

Adams, W.V. and Sheslow, D.V. (1983). A developmental perspective of adolescence. In E. Shopler and G.B. Mesibov (eds.) *Autism in Adolescence and Adults*. New York, Plenum Press.

Allison, H. (1993). *The Management of Bereavement in Services for People with Autism*. London, National Autistic Society.

Baron-Cohen, S. and Bolton, P. (1993). *Autism: the Facts*. Oxford, Oxford University Press.

Bowlby, J. (1960). Separation anxiety. Internation Journal of Psychoanalysis, **41**, 89–113.

Bowlby, J. (1969). *Attachment and Loss*, Volume 1, *Attachment*. London, Hogarth.

Bowlby, J. (1973). *Attachment and Loss*, Volume 2, *Separation: Anxiety and Anger*. London, Hogarth.

Bowlby, J. (1980). *Attachment and Loss*, Volume 3, *Loss: Sadness and Depression*. Harmondsworth, Penguin Books.

Creak, M. (1961). The schizophrenic syndrome in childhood. Progress of a working party. *British Medical Journal*, **2**, 889–900.

Crook, T. and Eliot, J. (1980). Parental death during childhood and adult depressive disorders: a review. *Psychological Bulletin*, **87**, 252–259.

Department For Education (1993). *The Education Act*. London, HMSO.

Department For Education (1994). *Code of Practice on the Identification and Assessment of Special Educational Needs*. London, HMSO.

Elder, G.H. Jr (1979). Historical change in life patterns and personality. In P.B. Baltes and O.G. Brim (eds.) *Life Span Development and Behaviour*, Volume 2. New York, Academic Press, pp. 159–188.

Erickson, E.H. (1965). *Childhood and Society* (Norton USA 1950). Harmondsworth, Penguin Books.

Frith, U. (1989). *Autism: Explaining the Enigma*. Oxford, Blackwell Ltd.

Havighurst, R.J. (1953). *Human Development and Education*. New York, Longmans, Green.

Havighurst, R.J. (1972). *Development Tasks and Education*. New York, David MacKay.

Hobson, R.P. (1993). *Autism and the Development of Mind*. Hove, Lawrence Erlbaum Associates.

Howlin, P. and Rutter, M. (1989). *Treatment of Autistic Children*. London, John Wiley and Sons Ltd.

Irwin, M. and Pike, J. (1993). Bereavement, depressive symptoms, and immune function. In M.S. Stroebe, W. Stroebe and R.O. Hansson (eds.) *Handbook of Bereavement*. Cambridge, Cambridge University Press.

Jordan, R.R. and Edwards, G. (1995). Educational Approaches to Adults with Autism. Unit 3. Module 1, Distance Education Course in Autism (Adults). Birmingham, University of Birmingham, School of Education.

Kitching, N. (1987). Helping people with mental handicaps cope with bereavement: a case study with discussion. *Mental Handicap*, **15**, 60–65.

Levinson, D.J., Darrow, D.N., Klein, E.B., Levinson, M.H. and McKee, B. (1978). *The Seasons of a Man's Life*. New York, A.A. Knopf.

Masten, A.S. and Garmezy, N. (1985). Risk, vulnerability and protective factors in developmental psychopathology. In B.B. Lahey and A.E. Kazdin (eds.) *Advances in Clinical Child Psychology*, Volume 8. New York. Plenum Press, pp. 1–52.

Maughan, B. and Champion, L. (1990). Transition to young adulthood. In P.B. Baltes and M.M. Baltes. *Successful Aging Perspectives from the Behavioural Sciences.* Cambridge, Cambridge University Press.

Office of Economic and Community Development (1988). *Young People with Handicaps: the Road to Adulthood.* Paris, OECD.

Office of Economic and Community Development and the Centre for Research and Innovation (1986). *Adult Status.* Paris, OECD/CERI.

O'Gorman, G. (1970). *The Nature of Childhood Autism.* London, Butterworth.

Open University Patterns for Living Training Pack (1988). Milton Keynes, Open University.

Oswin, M. (1985). Bereavement. In M.Craft, J. Bicknell and S. Hollins (eds.) *Mental Handicap: a Multidisciplinary Approach.* London. Billiere Tindall.

Oswin, M. (1991). *Am I Allowed To Cry?* London, Souvenir Press Ltd.

Parkes, C.M. (1972). *Bereavement.* London, Tavistock Publications.

Parkes, C.M. (1988). *Bereavement: Studies of Grief in Adult Life,* 2nd edition. New York, International Universities Press.

Parkes, C.M. (1993). Bereavement as a psychosocial transition: process of adaptation to change. In M.S. Stroebe, W. Stroebe and R.O. Hansson (eds.) *Handbook of Bereavement.* Cambridge, Cambridge University Press.

Powell, S.D., Matthews, E. and Morgan, S.H. (1994). Flexibility in Thinking and Behaviour. Unit 4. Module 1, Distance Education Course in Autism (Adults). Birmingham, University of Birmingham, School of Education.

Reynolds, R. and Atkins, C. (1995). Promoting Social and Emotional Well-Being. Unit 2. Module 2, Distance Education Course in Autism (Adults). Birmingham, University of Birmingham, School of Education.

Rogers, S.J., Ozonoff, S. and Maslin-Cole, C. (1991). A comparative study of attachment behaviour in young children with autism or other psychiatric disorders. *Journal of the American Academy of Child and Adolescent Psychiatry,* **30,** 483–488.

Rutter, M. (1985). Resilience in the face of adversity: protective factors and resistance to psychiatric disorder. *British Journal of Psychiatry,* **147,** 598–611.

Rutter, M., Quinton, D. and Hill, J. (1990). Adult outcomes of institution reared children: males and females compared. In L. Robins and M. Rutter (eds.) *Straight and Devious Pathways from Childhood to Adulthood.* Cambridge, Cambridge University Press.

Shuchter, S.R. and Zisook, S. (1993). The normal course of grief. In M.S. Stroebe, W. Stroebe and R.O. Hansson (eds.) *Handbook of Bereavement.* Cambridge, Cambridge University Press.

Sigman, M., Mundy, P., Sherman, T. and Ungerer, J. (1986). Social interactions of autistic, mentally retarded, and normal children and their caregivers. *Journal of Child Psychology and Psychiatry,* **27,** 657–69.

Sireling, F. and Hollins, S. (1985). Cited in Oswin, M. (1991). *Am I Allowed to Cry?* London, Souvenir Press Ltd.

Stroebe, W. and Stroebe, M. (1987). *Bereavement and Health.* New York, Cambridge University Press.

Tinbergen, E.A. and Tinbergen, N. (1972). *Early Childhood Autism: an Ethological Approach.* Berlin, Paul Parey Verlag.

Tinbergen, N. and Tinbergen, E. (1983). *Autistic Children. New Hope for a Cure.* London, Allen and Unwin.

Volkmar, F.R. (1987). Social development. In D.J. Cohen and A. Donnellen. *Handbook of Autism and Pervasive Developmental Disorders.* New York, Wiley.

Weiss, R.S. (1993). In M.S. Stroebe, W. Stroebe and R.O. Hansson (eds.) *Handbook of Bereavement*. Cambridge, Cambridge University Press.

Wing, L. and Gould, J. (1979). Severe impairments of social interaction and associated abnormalities in children: epidemiology and classification. *Journal of Autism and Developmental Disorders*, **9**, 11–29.

Worden, J.W. (1983). *Grief Counselling and Grief Therapy*. London, Tavistock/Routledge.

6

The significance of age, status and gender to adults with autism

Eve Matthews

INTRODUCTION

THIS CHAPTER describes one example of how hands-on practitioners can contribute to the evolving knowledge of working with adults with autism. A summary is presented of a research thesis that was successfully submitted for the award of the Master of Medical Science degree by Eve Matthews. Eve, who is Residential Services Manager in a specialist service for adults with autism, undertook this research, in addition to her 'normal' duties, from 1990 to 1994.

Consider what happens when we meet someone for the very first time: it would seem that in the first encounter there are particular processes that automatically take place, and these will, with some certainty, shape the interactions which are likely to occur. Much of our communication is non-verbal, and indicators such as clothing, a particular sort of hairstyle or other items may be the very first clues which will enable us to make some very preliminary judgments with regard to the nature of the sort of social interaction which is likely to follow. As a consequence of our observations of the sometimes very subtle differences between people, there will be a modification of our behaviour so that we can take into account the status, age and gender of the other person.

Let us now consider the individual with autism, who will inevitably experience difficulties in communication, social interaction and imagination. Do these 'visual clues' hold any meaning or significance for them, or could the non-recognition of these very important elements in non-verbal communication further impede the possibility of successful communication and interaction? Jordan and Powell (1994) suggest that usually humans are very sensitive to social situations, in that they have an in-built ability to respond both abstractly and directly. Abstract responses are brought about through imagination and particular conceptualisations, based on prior experience, whereas direct responses involve the preconscious, which can include things such as smells and movement. However, it would appear that those with autism experience difficulties through a failure to interpret social signals in

115

the usual manner. This is clearly described by Tantam (1988) in the following ways.

People who are not autistic modify their vocabulary, their tone of voice and the amount they speak to accommodate the listener. Adjustments are made, without thinking, for the listener's age, social status, sex and emotional state.......Unfortunately social situations almost always demand an adequate understanding of these subtle clues and no explicit set of rules could possibly be drawn up to cover every contingency.

(Tantam 1988, p. 5)

and,

......autistic people have a diminished understanding of the kind of things which are unique to people and they may not be able to behave or respond to the behaviour which is unique to social situations.

(Tantam 1988, p. 20)

The key concepts described by Tantam are contained in his recognition that there are 'subtle clues', where there is no explicit set of rules governing social interaction. Powell *et al.* (1994) suggest that because those with autism do not have the benefit of this intuitive understanding and are unable to think in a flexible manner, it will mean they are unable to cope with the ever-changing social scenarios that most of us take for granted.

CHAPTER OUTLINE

It is within this chapter, drawing upon some of these concepts, that there is an attempt to explore the hypothesis that adults with autism have a specific failure to recognise the messages which are implicit in the way others present themselves. Two types of methodologies are used, i.e. case studies and a controlled experiment, in an attempt to demonstrate the extent of this deficit among adults with autism. It is emphasised that there may well be other factors responsible for the sometimes very odd interactions of adults with autism, in that the research which follows represents just one attempt to increase the awareness of a specific disability in autism. It would seem that, very often, behaviour, which is accepted in childhood as being simply naive, becomes far more problematic with impending adult status, and this lack of social understanding may lead to 'social blunders' and a distinct lack of fine tuning within the interactions which do take place.

This chapter will begin by briefly considering psychological theories of autism which propose that the features of autism occur as the result of one underlying deficit. The research project will then be described, beginning with four case studies from which we can draw some rudimentary conclusions about the significance of age, status and gender to adults with autism. The experimental research will then be described and evaluated, particularly in relation to the psychological theories of autism.

DIFFERENT WAYS OF EXPLAINING THE TRIAD OF IMPAIRMENTS IN AUTISM

Affective Theory

Autism can be explained in terms of a failure of interpersonal reciprocity

This theory, known as Affective Theory, suggests that individuals with autism have social and communication problems, but that these are secondary to a primary deficit which is affective in nature. The basis of this theory is that those with autism have difficulty in being able to perceive other people's mental states as reflected in their bodily expressions. It suggests that the difficulty for those with autism is that this emotional deficit means that they are unable to perceive necessary interpersonal experiences, and therefore cannot develop the cognitive structures which are needed for social understanding. It is through this lack of perceptual-affective ability that the person with autism is unable to engage in personal relatedness with others.

A body of evidence for this theory has been provided by Peter Hobson and his colleagues, who showed, in a series of experiments, that individuals with autism were impaired in their ability to recognise different expressions of emotion. For example, Hobson and Weeks (1987) found in one experiment that, compared to control groups, children with autism matched pairs of photographs according to the type of hat worn, whereas other groups gave priority to sorting the photographs according to people's facial expression. In another study Hobson (1986) found that children with autism found it difficult to associate different expressions of emotion with different situational events.

Hobson (1987) has also found, from his research, that a person with autism may have difficulty in differentiating adults from children and males from females.

Although Powell and Jordan (1993) do not argue directly from this perspective, there are similarities in their notion that a key problem in autism is that the individual fails to develop a sense of 'experiencing self'. This would lead to a fragmentation of experiences because there would be no sense of 'self' to link these experiences.

Conative or Motivational Theory

Autism can be explained as being a motivational problem

This theory is associated mainly with the research which has looked at the play of children with autism. It suggests that some of the behaviours which those with autism display is a direct result of them not wanting, rather than not knowing how, to join in with the social, communicative and imaginative areas of human life. Studies which have looked at play have found that the play of children with autism tends to have a very sterile and ritualistic quality with very little play being produced of a symbolic quality (DeMyer 1967; Wing *et al.* 1977).

However, in fairly recent research, Lewis and Boucher (1988) found that under the specific play conditions which they formulated, children with autism produced as much symbolic play as control groups. What they did was to compare play in spontaneous and elicited conditions using junk objects and conventional toys. In the elicited condition, the child was given either a junk pair or a toy pair of objects and was then asked, 'what can these do?'. Under these specific conditions they found that as much symbolic play was produced as by control groups. However, in the spontaneous play condition, less functional play was produced by the children with autism, and hardly any of a symbolic nature. Hence the essence of their proposal is that deficits in play were due to conative (motivational) abnormalities.

Theory of Mind

Autism as a lack of theory of mind

A cognitive approach to understanding autism and the Triad of Impairments was developed in the 1980s by Frith, Leslie, and Baron-Cohen while working at the Medical Research Council (MRC) Cognitive Development Unit in London. The main propositions of this theory are that social and communicative abnormalities are due to a fundamental inability to 'read the minds of others'. This fault, i.e. 'mind blindness', would inevitably lead to an abnormal pattern of development which then results in the behaviours of those who are autistic.

The development of a theory of mind in normal children appears to emerge very early in life. Leslie (1987) has suggested that this could be present even before the age of one year. He argues that the ability needed for a child to use pretence is very complex and it could cause confusion, but this is made possible by the child having two types of representation which prevent the interference between pretence and real world knowledge. For example, a child may want to use pretence to use a cardboard box as a car. According to Leslie, this provides evidence that a child has 'primary representations' in which things can be seen as they are in the real world, i.e. it is a cardboard box, and 'metarepresentations', i.e. the cardboard box is a car. Leslie's proposal is that individuals with autism have a specific impairment in that they do not have this capacity to form metarepresentations. What is important is that metarepresentations are essential not only to allow a capacity for pretence, but they are also vital for representing other information or propositional attitudes (mental states) such as the ability to think, hope, intend, wish and believe.

Over the last few years a whole series of experiments have been carried out to test the theory of mind hypothesis (for example, Baron-Cohen *et al.* 1985; Perner *et al.* 1987, 1989).

These three theories will be returned to later on in this chapter in an attempt to relate them to the Visual Clues Experiment.

So far in this chapter, the difficulties which adults with autism have in relation to non-verbal communication and social interaction have only been very briefly described, giving some indication of the nature of the 'problem' in autism. However, the research which follows was prompted by personal observations of the adults with whom I worked, in that they appeared to fail to make the necessary adjustments in order to take into account the age, gender and status of other people. The following four case studies may be helpful in providing the reader with a more graphic illustration of the way in which autism manifests itself and the types of interactions which are likely to take place. The following were compiled using case notes written by parents and practitioners, and reports which had been written with a view to the individual being offered a place at a specialist Residential and Day Care Provision for adults with autism.

CASE STUDY ONE: ROBERT

Robert is a 21-year-old man with a diagnosis of Asperger syndrome. Robert seems to understand language at the concrete level, by both responding to the spoken word and by initiating conversation. However, it is after more prolonged contact with Robert that communication becomes more difficult. Initially, conversation will begin conventionally, and usual topics might include recent events in the news, and the weather forecast. Very quickly, the conversation will frequently deviate into the realms of fantasy and the focus of interest will revolve around the subjects of horse racing and Dr Who. These subjects will be talked about at great length by Robert, with his tone of voice often being very flat and in a monotone. He appears to be unaware that others may find the conversation uninteresting and there is no apparent reaction to the non-verbal messages that others give to him which indicate that they are bored. Robert's case notes make reference to these dialogues and it would appear that there is very little account taken with regard to at whom the conversation is directed, i.e. the listener might be someone who Robert knows well, or, it may have been a chance meeting in a local shop with a complete stranger.

Robert's communication often reflects his very limited interests and these have a tendency to be obsessive, in that they impinge upon all areas of his daily life. In his free time, Robert will frequently watch recorded episodes of Dr Who and will act out the roles of different characters as he is watching them. Whole scripts can sometimes be repeated verbatim. On occasions there are attempts to include others in these role-playing games, despite their obvious reluctance to become part of the proceedings.

It might appear that Robert has a capacity to form relationships with others in that he actively seeks out company. However, these interactions are unusual. For example practitioners report that he can often be very affectionate towards others, but this can often be inappropriate to the context. It has been observed that even upon meeting completely new people he can appear 'over friendly', both physically and conversationally, to both males and females. In essence, it appears that he is unaware of the conventions which govern social interaction and does not appear to respond to the non-verbal signals that his attentions may not be required. Despite his interest in making friends, there appears to be far more difficulty in keeping them. It has been observed that strangers are often surprised at a first meeting to be bombarded with information about the Grand National and Dr Who while at the same time being affectionately patted and hugged.

CASE STUDY TWO: DAVID

David is a 25-year-old man with autism, who would appear to be very able. He enjoys meeting and talking to people and has wide social networks. He is both literate and numerate and is fluent in two languages and he is able to travel unaccompanied, using public transport, around a very busy city. As in the previous case study, David's behaviour will now be described with particular reference to the Triad of Impairments in autism.

David comprehends the spoken word well, although his own speech has a tendency to be very repetitive and this frequently revolves around his main interest of the Regional Bus Service. It has been noted that David will lapse into monologues and there is a marked difficulty in being able to sustain a meaningful conversation about subjects other than buses. He will talk repetitively, focusing on bus routes, numbers, destinations, etc. I have known David on a daily basis for six years yet, each day, he will ask me which bus I caught, despite this being unchanged for the period of time that I have known him. Repetitive questioning can frequently be directed at individuals with whom he has had little contact, or who he is meeting for the very first time.

David's interests would seem to be very restricted, indicating poverty of imagination which is characteristic of those affected by autism. David also has difficulties in social interaction. On numerous occasions it has been noted that his initial contacts usually follow a similar pattern. Very often individuals will be bombarded with the same questions, which might be considered quite personal. He might ask their age, the ages of family members, marital status, birth dates, the particular bus routes that they live on, etc. The dialogue is very one sided, with there being very little opportunity to have a reciprocal conversation. These types of interaction can often follow the same pattern despite it being a chance meeting.

CASE STUDY THREE: SAM

Sam is a 35-year-old man with autism. Sam can read and write and he keeps a regular diary. He also has above average artistic ability and attends a local art class, which he has done for the last six years. Although Sam has a very wide vocabulary, his speech is observably abnormal in its delivery. His voice has a tendency to be very loud with the rate and rhythm of his voice being very slow and deliberate. He frequently reverses pronouns, e.g. using the word 'you' instead of 'I'. Historically, it would seem that Sam appears to prefer his own company to that of others and if an individual does initiate conversation it tends to quickly become very much on Sam's terms. Sam will either ignore individuals who are attempting to communicate with him, or, in no uncertain terms, he will tell them to, 'go away !'.

Sam does have some interests. He enjoys reading and watching videos, but the nature of the subject matter is often very factual. For example, he will read books on electrical appliances, trains, the history of particular areas in Birmingham, do-it-yourself, etc. The information that is read by Sam is not normally disclosed to anyone else and any questions related to these subjects directed to Sam by others is usually unwelcome.

Sam appears to be impaired in his ability to reciprocate social interactions. He can, on occasions, appear very irritated if there are others around him engaged in conversation. Social gatherings will only be tolerated for very short periods of time and he will often withdraw from such situations, since it would appear that they make him very anxious. He appears to be unaware of the existence of the feelings of others and he will declare outright if he has taken a dislike to a particular person. It has been observed that Sam will barge past people without an apology and will often interrupt the conversations of others.

CASE STUDY FOUR: RACHEL

Rachel is a 21-year-old woman with autism who has lived at a Residential and Day Care Provision for adults with autism for a number of years. When carrying out particular tasks, it sometimes seems as if Rachel is in slow motion, although she has fairly good independence skills in terms of self-care. She seems to enjoy domestic tasks, sewing and music. She experiences difficulties in communication in that, although she is able to use speech, her vocabulary appears to be limited. Parents and practitioners report that she appears to understand all that is said to her, although she may choose to disregard any demands that are made of her. One of the characteristics of her communication is that her speech is echolalic. Rachel frequently will repeat the last few words of conversation that are either directed at her or someone else. Also responses to questions will either be one word or very short sentences. Rachel's voice, particularly when she is anxious, will sometimes be very loud, with there being very little alteration to its pitch or tone to indicate emotion. Volume is usually the main indicator of her underlying emotional state. Pronoun reversal has also been noted as characteristic of her speech. Rachel does not tend to initiate speech and in social situations will often look directly ahead of her, with little or no eye contact with others. There also appears to be a lack of flexibility in her thinking and this is demonstrated by her preference for routine, with any deviations to this routine causing her much distress. There appears to be an absence of reciprocal social interaction, and, in the five years that I have known Rachel, she has never spontaneously said, 'hello', or spoken my name. However, she will always respond if she is greeted.

What can these case studies tell us about the significance of age, status and gender to adults with autism?

The case studies which have been provided show the diversity of autism and its various manifestations. However, all of these individuals show behaviours which are identifiable as being characteristic of the Triad of Impairments in autism. In relation to communication, all were able to use verbal communication, but of an unusual pattern. The main similarity between all four being that communication was extremely one sided and often characterised by lengthy monologues. All but Rachel initiated conversation, but to sustain or change the direction of conversation was very difficult. All appeared to have difficulties with the interpretation of non-verbal communication, and any signs of boredom, disinterest, etc., on the part of the listener were frequently ignored. There were differences between these individuals in terms of the number of approaches made and their main topics of conversation - but the underlying similarity still remained that there was a difficulty in being able to communicate effectively.

Similarities also existed in relation to the imagination element of the Triad of Impairments. Although there were variances in the type of limiting, and sometimes obsessive, imaginative activities, there still remained the underlying similarity that their chosen and preferred interests had become very fixed and they were resistant to attempts to introduce new ones. A further corresponding characteristic was inflexibility of thinking, in terms of a dislike for change, which could often provoke anxiety and a preference for routine.

The social impairment was also notable in all four case studies. All experienced difficulties in reciprocal two-way interaction despite the fact that social approaches were often made to others. Robert, David and Sam frequently sought out the company of others, but the tendency was for these interactions to fall short of what might be considered usual. They were all capable of bombarding others with questions, or, at other times, directing monologues at people with little response to non-verbal signals of boredom or lack of interest on the part of the listener. Rachel appeared to make few spontaneous approaches to others, demonstrating a qualitatively different deficit in social interaction.

WHAT ARE THE IMPLICATIONS FOR THE EXPERIMENTAL RESEARCH?

From these case studies, which are based upon the observations of parents and practitioners, a picture begins to emerge which might suggest that those with autism may not attach the same value to indicators of age, status and gender. Visual clues would normally influence the type of approaches we make towards others, but the case studies would seem to suggest that for the adult with autism they do not have the same significance, in that their interactions with others usually followed a similar, but very unusual, pattern.

Using this evidence alone would be insufficient to suggest that age, gender and status did not have any significance to adults with autism. It was therefore necessary to carry out a further investigation in order to test empirically the significance of age, gender and status to adults with autism.

THE VISUAL CLUES EXPERIMENT

The Visual Clues Experiment was an experiment to test the hypothesis that adults with autism fail to recognise visual indicators of age, status and gender.

The case studies outlined above have already provided a good illustration of the problems of inflexibility that adults with autism seem to experience in communicating and interacting successfully with others, but this does not provide enough evidence for this very specific deficit which is being suggested. To explore this very intriguing area of difficulty, the aim of the experimental study was to consider two main areas. These were

1. To look at the abilities of adults with autism in being able to make an association between various visual clues, including a specific type of hat with a specific 'character'. These included: old man, old woman, rich man, rich woman, young boy, young girl, scary/evil person.
2. The ability of autistic adults to recognise gender.

Who took part in the experiment?

Three groups of individuals took part in the study in order that comparisons could be made of the performance of those who had been diagnosed as having autism/Asperger syndrome. The autistic participants all lived in a specialist unit for adults with autism, four of whom were used as case study illustrations of the deficit which is being hypothesised. A total of 12 adults with autism took part in the Visual Clues Experiment. All 12 were judged to be of varying ability by the author, based upon the knowledge of working with them for the previous five years. The inclusion criteria for this group was that they all appeared willing and able to co-operate in the initial tests that were carried out to identify both verbal and non-verbal mental age. All of the 12 people with autism had previously been diagnosed as being autistic according to established criteria, since this was one part of the Oakfield House admissions policy statement. Also they had all been tested using the Handicapped Skills and Behaviour Schedules (Medical Research Council 1980).

It was to ensure that the results of the experiment were not primarily due to general learning disability that two control groups were used. One of these groups was drawn from a local infants school, which is also situated in Birmingham. This school accommodates children who have followed a normal developmental pattern. The second control group was drawn from a school for children with learning disabilities which, again, was located in Birmingham. This school provides education for young people who have disabilities which range from moderate to severe.

How were these groups matched?

For the experiment to produce valid results, the two control groups needed to be of the same mental age as the group of 12 people with autism and so two tests were used to establish this. The tests selected were the British Picture Vocabulary Scale (BPVS) (Dunn and Dunn 1982) and the Raven's Progressive Matrices (RPM). With the use of these tests the groups were matched in the following way. The selection of the group with autism, which was the starting point for matching the three groups, has already been

Table 6.1. *Means, standard deviations and ranges of chronological and mental age*

Diagnostic group	No.	Parameter	Chronological age	Non-verbal mental age Raven's Progressive Matrices	Verbal mental age British Picture Vocabulary Scale
Autistic	12	Mean	22:6	24	6:9
		Standard deviation	4:9	7:4	2:2
		Range	(18:8)–(33:7) 14:9	(13)–(36) 23	(4:0)–(10:3) 6:3
Learning disabilities	12	Mean	16:5	19	6:5
		Standard deviation	1:9	5:4	2:8
		Range	(12:10)–(19:1) 6:3	(11)–(27) 16	(2:10)–(10:3) 7:4
Normal	12	Mean	6:11	18	5:10
		Standard deviation	0:5	4:2	1:5
		Range	(6:5)–(7:4) 0:9	(13)–(27) 14	(4:5)–(8:8) 4:3

described, and so the next task was to test this group using the BPVS and the RPM. They were all tested at Oakfield House, adhering closely to the rules for the administration of these tests, as set out in the accompanying manuals. When all of the 12 adults with autism had been tested, the scores were then calculated for both tests. Following this, the group with autism were then matched, in terms of their performance in the tests, with children who had followed a normal developmental pattern and young people with learning disabilities.

From Table 6.1 it can be seen that the three groups were very closely matched with the only real difference being that there were more males than females in the group with autism (not shown in the table). This reflects the unequal gender distribution among those who have autism. Apart from this, the three groups were well matched in terms of verbal and non-verbal mental age.

What materials were used in the Visual Clues Experiment ?

The materials used in the experiment were based upon the representation of the following seven characters: an old man, an old woman, a rich man, a rich woman, a young boy, a young girl and an evil/scary person.

Each of these seven characters were then represented by a mask, a hat and three additional items. The following is a list of the items which were used.

Old man

Old-man mask
Hat – checked trilby
Walking stick
Grey beard
Pipe

Old woman

Old-woman mask
Hat – green silk
Ball of wool and knitting needles
Brown wig
Brown handbag

Rich man

Rich-man mask
Hat – crown
Gold chains
Box of gold coins
Silver bow tie

Rich woman

Rich-woman mask
Hat – crown
Gold chains
Box of gold coins
Gold handbag

Young boy

Young-boy mask
Baseball cap
Toy car
Ball
Boy's toy doll

Young girl

Young-girl mask
Hat – straw boater
Doll
Straw bag
Skipping rope

Evil/scary person

Evil/scary mask
Black hat covered with rubber spiders
Spiky black wig
Rubber snake
Leopard skin glove with claws attached

Initially all of these items were selected by the author as being judged to be representative of the seven characters, but in order to avoid any bias it was deemed necessary for them to be independently rated.

Firstly, all of the items were rated in terms of gender by an individual who had no real involvement in this study. All of the items were presented and they were then asked to rate them in terms of whether they believed them to be male items (M), female items (F) or, whether they judged them to be non-gender specific (NGS). Subsequently, items were rated in the following way:

Old-man mask (M)
Checked trilby hat (M)
Walking stick (NGS)
Grey beard (M)
Pipe (M)
Old-woman mask (F)
Green silk hat (F)
Ball of wool and knitting needles (F)
Brown wig (F)

Brown handbag (F)
Rich-man mask (M)
Crown (NGS)
Gold chains (F)
Box of gold coins (NGS)
Silver bow tie (M)
Rich-woman mask (F)
Gold handbag (F)
Young-boy mask (M)
Baseball cap (M)
Toy car (M)
Ball (NGS)
Boy's toy doll (NGS)
Young-girl mask (F)
Straw boater (F)
Doll (F)
Straw bag (F)
Skipping rope (F)
Evil/scary mask (M)
Black hat covered with rubber spiders (M)
Spiky black wig (M)
Rubber snake (NGS)
Leopard skin glove with claws (NGS)

Secondly, these items were then rated in terms of the character that these items were supposed to represent. Beforehand, the independent rater was advised that it was permissible to select items as being suitable for more than one character, the only provision being that not less than three items could be selected for each of the three characters. A list of the seven characters was presented and they were then asked to:

1 Select the most suitable hat to go with each of the seven masks;
2 Select three additional items from the materials on display to go with each of the characters.

This independent rating was carried out to ensure that it was possible to pair each of the character masks with one of the hats and to ensure that there were at least three additional items which represented each character.

Following these ratings, all masks were indicated as being symbolic of the character that they were supposed to represent and these were then correctly paired with the appropriate hat. The rater also selected three additional items which had previously been judged as being symbolic of a particular character.

What was the procedure used in the Visual Clues Experiment?

The Visual Clues Experiment was carried out in June and July 1992, with all of the 36 who had been selected to take part being tested in an environment which was familiar to them, i.e. their school or home. For all three groups the very same procedure was followed. Firstly all the masks were laid out on the floor in a row in a random order. Then all hats and additional props were randomly arranged on the floor next to the masks. A video camera was set up in the corner of the room to record each subject's performance. At the end of each session all of these items were rearranged, again in a random order.

All of the subjects in each diagnostic group were tested individually and selected at random. Upon entering the room, I sat with each individual and explained to them the task which had to be carried out using standardised instructions which had been memorised. Following this, each individual was given up to five minutes to examine the items. The list of seven characters was then read out to them and they were asked to choose one of these and find the correct mask, a hat and three other things which corresponded to that character. If an individual did not immediately choose one of the seven characters then some very gentle encouragement would be given. For example, 'would you like me to choose a person for you?', and a character would then be selected at random by myself. Throughout the Visual Clues Experiment, only very simple language was used to guard against confusion or misinterpretation.

This procedure was followed three times with each of those who took part in the study. There was no time limit imposed, and individuals either indicated by gesture which items they believed were representative of a character, or, on some occasions, individuals actually preferred to wear the items.

What was the method of scoring in the Visual Clues Experiment?

From the video recordings which were made, a transcript was made of each individual's performance, noting the character chosen, mask, hat and additional items. These selections were then scored in a very specific way. A score of one was given for each item chosen which corresponded with the judgment of the independent rater. For example, if an individual selected the walking stick as being representative of an old man then they were given a score of one. Individuals were then scored in terms of any 'gender mistakes', in that a score of one was given if any selections were made that did not correspond with the gender of the character which had been selected based upon the independent rater's judgment. For example, if the character selected was that of an old man, and a handbag was selected as being representative of this character, then they would be given a score of one. Hence for all 36 subjects a calculation was made for:

1 the total number of correct selections made by each individual in respect of the characters they had selected;
2 the total number of selections made which were incorrect in respect of the gender of the character they had chosen.

What were the findings of the Visual Clues Experiment?

The results of the Visual Clues Experiment with regard to the first of these calculations, i.e. correct choices of items, were that for the group with autism, out of a possible score of 180, a total score of 66 was achieved for all 12 individuals who took part. For the group who had learning disabilities a total of 114 correct choices of items were made, and for the 12 children who had followed a normal developmental pattern, a total score of 130 was achieved.

From an initial observation of the findings of the Visual Clues Experiment, it would appear that the scores of the 24 non-autistic subjects were far higher than the group of individuals who had been diagnosed as having autism. However, it was important that an empirical analysis was applied to the results of this experiment.

Firstly, a descriptive analysis was used, by applying two measures of central tendency, i.e. the mean and the median.

From Table 6.2 it can be seen that, quite clearly, when calculated in respect of mean scores, the non-autistic groups selected an increased number of correct items appertaining to their character selections. Whereas the group with autism only achieved a mean score of 5.5, the learning disabilities group scored 9.5 and the group who had followed a normal pattern of development scored 10.8. The median score was also calculated, and again it was found that the scores of the non-autistic group were far higher than that of the group with autism. This was an important calculation, since it would show that the results were not due purely to either very high or very low scores in each diagnostic group.

The results of the Visual Clues Experiment are also shown visually in the form of a frequency distribution histogram in Figure 6.1.

From this histogram it can be seen that class intervals of 0-3, 8-12 and 12-15 were used to show the distribution of the scores. This showed that only the group with autism was represented in the lowest class interval of scores 0-3, and, although they were represented at the top end of the frequency distribution, only one subject's score fell into this category. The histogram shows, in fact, that both control groups had an equal number of

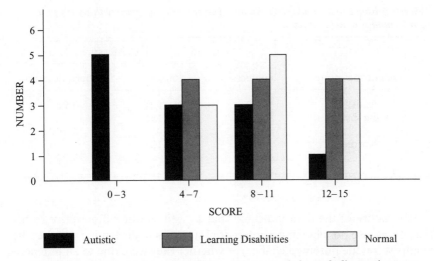

Figure 6.1 *Total score, i.e. correct choices of items made by each diagnostic group.*

Table 6.2. *Mean and median scores for each group with regard to the correct number of items selected*

Diagnostic group	No. of subjects	Measure	
		Mean	Median
Autistic	12	5.5	5
Learning disabilities	12	9.5	11
Normal	12	10.8	10.5

subjects whose scores fell into this category, i.e. four subjects in each group. In the 4-7 class interval, the autistic group and normal children were represented by equal numbers, while there was one more subject represented in this class interval with regard to the learning disabilities group. The final observation which can be made relating to this frequency histogram is that, in the 8-11 class interval, there were fewer autistic subjects represented. Three autistic subjects fell into this category, four with learning disabilities and five children who had followed a normal developmental pattern.

Finally, two measures of variation were used to give an indication of the spread of the scores around the mean, in order that this would give some idea of how representative the average was. Both the range and standard deviations were calculated for each diagnostic group and these are shown in Table 6.3.

Table 6.3 *Range and standard deviations of scores for each group with regard to the correct number of items selected*

Diagnostic group	No. of subjects	Measure	
		Range	Standard deviation
Autistic	12	(0)–(12)	3.92
Learning disabilities	12	(5)–(13)	
		8	3.29
Normal	12	(5)–(15)	
		10	3.29

The nature of the data indicated that as well as using descriptive statistics, it was also possible to use inferential statistics to determine whether the results were due purely to chance, or whether they were due to an independent variable. A parametric test was selected to see if there was a significant difference between the performances of each diagnostic group, or whether this was due purely to sampling error. In other words, if another group of autistic individuals was selected, would they in fact achieve scores comparable with the control groups. An independent t-test was used on the data obtained from the three groups. When this test was used to analyse the differences between the data obtained from the learning disabilities group and the group with autism, the value of t was calculated to be -2.71. With 22 degrees of freedom, the probability of this value of t occurring by chance was found to be 0.013, therefore there was a significant difference between the two groups at the 5% level. There was also found to be a significant difference between the scores of the group with autism and the scores of the children who had followed a normal pattern of development. In this case, the t value was calculated to be 3.17. With 22 degrees of freedom, the probability of this occurring by chance was 0.0048, therefore there was a strongly significant difference between these two groups at the 5% level. Analysis of the data from the children who had followed a normal pattern of development compared to those with learning disabilities resulted in a t value of -0.45. With 22 degrees of freedom, the probability of this occurring by chance was 0.66, therefore there was no significant difference between the two groups at the 5% level.

The second part of the analysis was concerned with gender mistakes, based upon the total number of items selected which did not match the gender of the character that had been chosen previously. Use was made of the gender ratings which have been referred to previously. From Table 6.4 it can be seen that each time a 'gender mistake' was made, this was noted

Table 6.4. *Full list of the items used in the experiment and their gender ratings*

| | | Items chosen which were unrelated to the chosen character | | |
| | | Diagnostic group | | |
Rating	Items used	Autistic	Normal	Learning disabilities
	Masks:	✔		
F	Old woman			
M	Old man			
F	Young girl	✔		
M	Young boy			
M	Scary/evil (person)			
M	Rich man			
F	Rich woman	✔		
	Hats:			
NGS	Gold crown			
M	Checked trilby hat	✔		
F	Green silk hat	✔✔✔✔		✔
NGS	Straw boater decorated with a ribbon			
M	Blue baseball cap	✔		✔
M	Black hat covered in rubber spiders	✔		✔
	Additional props:			
M	Pipe	✔		
NGS	Walking stick			
M	Grey beard			
F	Woman's brown wig	✔	✔	
NGS	Rubber snake			
F	Gold chains	✔		✔✔
NGS	Box of gold coins			
NGS	Ball			
M	Toy car			
NGS	Toy doll (Dennis the Menace)			
F	Doll	✔✔		
F	Straw handbag	✔		
F	Large brown handbag	✔		
NGS	Glove (leopard skin fabric with claws)			
M	Spiky black wig			
F	Ball of wool with knitting needles	✔✔		
F	Small gold bag			✔
F	Skipping rope			✔
M	Silver bow tie			✔✔
	Total of incorrect gender choices	19	1	9

M=Male F=Female NGS=Non Gender Specific.

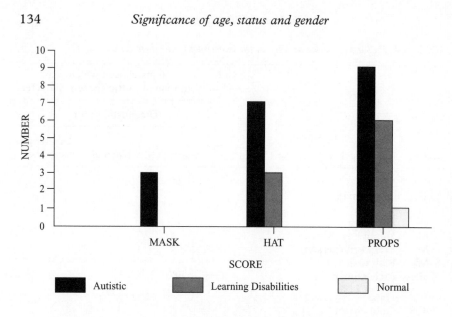

Figure 6.2 *Total score categorised by diagnostic group for 'gender mistakes'*

and it can be seen that there appeared to be far more gender mistakes made by the group with autism in comparison with the two control groups. Nineteen 'mistakes' were made in total by this group. In the learning disabilities group, a total of nine mistakes were made, and in the group of children who had followed a normal pattern of development, only one item was selected which was not appropriate to the gender of the character which had been chosen.

Using a frequency distribution histogram, the results can be seen more clearly.

From this histogram it can be observed that these data were divided into class intervals with regard to gender mistakes made with hats and those made with other props. It can be seen that there appear to be differences between the diagnostic groups in respect of choosing items not appropriate to the gender of the character they selected. Only the autistic group selected masks which were not appropriate to the gender of their character, a mistake which was made.

Even more mistakes were made with regard to the hat selection. The learning difficulties group also made three gender mistakes, but the autistic group selected a total of seven items which were inappropriate with regard to the gender of their chosen character. Finally, it appears that the autistic group was again found to make gender mistakes with regard to selecting additional items, i.e. props, to go with their chosen character.

Again more individuals in the group with autism selected inappropriate items. A total of nine mistakes was made by this group, only one mistake being made by a child from the group who had followed a normal developmental pattern, and six mistakes being made by the group who had learning disabilities.

SUMMARY OF THE RESEARCH

The primary aim of this research was to test the hypothesis that those with autism may experience difficulties in the recognition of the difference between people on the basis of visual clues. This hypothesis was then explored using two very different types of methodology, i.e. case studies and a Visual Clues Experiment. The case studies provide a vivid illustration of the types of behaviours which are found amongst adults with autism and Asperger syndrome. Purely at a descriptive level, it would appear that adults with autism fail to respond to visual clues, i.e. non-verbal indicators, which would normally play a role in successful communication and social interaction. The case studies merely set out to present a picture and it would appear that the hypothesis that adults with autism experience 'problems' in this area would be confirmed.

It was by using the second type of methodology that the hypothesis was more rigorously tested in the form of the Visual Clues Experiment. In this experiment there were two aspects of visual clues which were explored. Firstly, the experiment aimed to discover whether adults with autism could make an association between various visual clues, such as a specific type of hat with a particular character, e.g. old man, rich woman, etc. The results of the Visual Clues Experiment confirmed that, compared to control groups, i.e. children who had followed a normal pattern of development and young people with learning disabilities, significantly fewer correct selections of items were made by adults with autism in respect of the character they had chosen. This was shown quite clearly by both a descriptive and inferential analysis of the data. The second aspect of the hypothesis, which was explored using the Visual Clues Experiment, focused specifically upon whether or not adults with autism were impaired in their ability to recognise gender in others. This hypothesis was also confirmed since it was found that more 'gender mistakes' were made by the group with autism compared to the two control groups.

What are the implications of the findings from this research in relation to current psychological theories?

The findings of this research have implications for some of the proposed psychological theories which attempt to explain the underlying deficit in autism. These have already been referred to in the section entitled 'Different ways of explaining the Triad of Impairments in autism' earlier on in this chapter and it is now possible to reconsider these theories in the light of the evidence of the Visual Clues Experiment.

Do these results provide more evidence to support these theories, or does it show inherent weaknesses in them?

Firstly, Affective Theory, i.e. that autism can be seen in terms of a failure of interpersonal reciprocity. This suggests that although people with autism have social and communicative problems, this is only secondary to a primary deficit which is affective in nature, i.e. that there is a dysfunction in being able to perceive other people's mental states as reflected in their bodily expressions. The main support for this theory has come from Hobson and his colleagues, who produced a body of evidence which, they suggest, provides an explanation for behaviours found among those with autism. The research carried out by Hobson is undoubtedly important and the recognition of emotion in others is clearly very problematic for those with autism. However, it does not really provide a satisfactory explanation for the findings of the Visual Clues Experiment, since the requirements of the task in this experiment did not necessitate any emotion recognition. All that was required was for individuals to find objects which did not have any emotional component.

Another 'problem' with this theory is that it does not appear to take into account how important clothing is as an indicator of age, gender and status. Although autism is seen as a failure of interpersonal reciprocity, it does not consider the valuable information that clothes communicate in interpersonal relationships in terms of non-verbal information (the importance of which has already been outlined). Taking this into account it would seem that Affective Theory would not be able to provide an answer for the results of the Visual Clues Experiment as to why fewer correct items were selected. Additionally, Affective Theory fails to provide an explanation as to why the 12 adults with autism made more 'gender mistakes' compared to control groups. An interesting point of note arises from the analysis of the Visual Clues Experiment in relation to the visual recognition of gender. The data showed that on only three (out of a possible 36) occasions was a mistake made when those in the group with autism were asked to select a mask to match their chosen character. This implies that, in autism, perceiving gender and age is not as problematic when looking at a face as it is when looking at other items on display. Contrary to this, Hobson (1987), in his research, found that those with autism had difficulty in differentiating between adults and children and between males and females.

To conclude, Affective Theory does provide an insight into what is obviously a notable deficit, but from the evidence of the Visual Clues Experiment, it would appear that a great deal more 'goes on' within social interactions than the non-recognition of emotion. There are other factors which are important. Mental states, as reflected in bodily expressions, are evidently not the only variable that we need to consider. An impression of another individual as a whole is important and this will be affected by additional variables such as the immediate environment and past experiences, not just what is observed at a particular time.

The problem with this theory is that it is extremely difficult to 'prove' or 'disprove' it, since it is impossible to establish causal priorities. From Hobsons' perspective, it could be argued that, although he recognised that those with autism have deficits in the social understanding (e.g. visual clues) of the way others present themselves, this is only secondary to the primary emotional impairment. In other words, the results of the Visual Clues Experiment are in fact an extension of this deficit, in that the affective deficit means that those with autism are unable to learn about the special qualities of clothes with regard to their specific 'clues' about age, gender and status.

The second theory which was proposed to explain the underlying deficit in autism was that of it being a Conative or Motivational explanation. This has been associated largely with the studies carried out which have looked at the nature of play among autistic children, in that the quality of it tends to be sterile and ritualistic. The Conative hypothesis suggests that it is not that children with autism do not know how to play in an imaginative way, it is that they do not want to. Following this it would suggest that those with autism display behaviours, i.e. poor communication and deficits in social interaction, as a direct result of them not wanting to join in with the social communicative and imaginative areas of life, rather than them being unable to do so.

In the light of the results of the Visual Clues Experiment, however, this theory fails to explain why the group with autism performed badly when doing the set task, even though they not only agreed to take part, they actively did so. All individuals were asked if they wanted to take part and they did so willingly, yet they still performed less well. Instructions were also very specific with regard to what the requirements of the set task were, yet many more incorrect selections of items were made compared to control groups. Lewis and Boucher (1988) found that symbolic play could actually be elicited under specific experimental conditions - yet it did not appear that this was possible, although this was not specifically tested in the Visual Clues Experiment. It did not appear to be a case of not wanting to select items, but of being unaware of the special qualities that particular items implied. Finally it could be argued that, from the picture which was presented in the case studies, it does not appear that individuals were not motivated to make approaches to others. Frequently, spontaneous approaches were made to others, although very often these approaches were not of the nature which could be considered usual.

The final psychological explanation to be considered at the start of this chapter was the Theory of Mind explanation. This suggests that social and communicative abnormalities are due to a fundamental inability to 'read the minds of others'. This theory argues that there is specific impairment in the ability to read mental states, such as beliefs, desires and intentions to themselves or others. If this lack of a metarepresentational capacity is viewed in relation to the Visual Clues Experiment, it is possible that it does provide an explanation with regard to the poor performance of the group with autism. Could it be that a possible reason for their performance was because the research materials, i.e. hats, items of clothing, etc., and the requirement to match them with particular characters necessitated that they made a second order or metarepresentation? Hence it could be argued that their poor performance was due to the research materials having implied qualities. If these were not acknowledged it would mean the group would experience difficulties in the set task because age, gender and status were only implied. When 'clues' were more obvious, i.e. had little symbolic element, such as selecting a mask as corresponding with the chosen character, there were far fewer incorrect selections made. However, when additional items needed to be selected this appeared to present more difficulties, which was possibly because an increased number of metarepresentations needed to be made to make the correct selections. It could be concluded then that one possible explanation for the results of the Visual Clues Experiment is that adults with autism have an impaired symbolic capacity.

The Theory of Mind hypothesis suggests that a metarepresentational capacity is necessary for propositional attitudes such as to think, hope, wish and believe. Having these abilities then allows us to make predictions about another's behaviour. It could be argued that being unable to make even the most preliminary judgments about others based upon clothing clues will seriously impair the type of interaction which is likely to take place, and will further reduce the possibility of those with autism being able to form metarepresentations with regard to such things as intentions and beliefs.

SOME CONCLUDING THOUGHTS

Within this chapter there has been an attempt to explore the hypothesis that adults with autism, due to perceptual and processing difficulties, may have a specific difficulty in being able to recognise the 'special qualities' that others have on the basis of visual clues. The absence of recognition of indicators of age, gender and status would not allow there to be an intuitive assessment of situations, in order that communication and social interaction can be modified accordingly.

The hypothesis was explored using two types of methodology. Firstly, four case studies provided illustrations of the nature of some of the communication and social interaction behaviours which are sometimes shown among adults with autism. The behaviours of these adults all appeared to correspond closely to the Triad of Impairments in autism (Wing and Gould 1979), and purely at the level of observation it did not appear that the same value was attached to visual indicators of age, status and gender. Secondly, an experiment to test the Visual Clues hypothesis was reported. In this experiment 12 adults with autism were asked to select from the research materials presented to them, i.e. hats, masks, items of clothing, etc., items which they believed were representative of different characters. Compared to control groups, it was found that the group with autism selected significantly fewer correct items corresponding to each character. It was also found that the group with autism selected more items which were incorrect in respect of the gender of their chosen character.

These findings cannot be seen in isolation from theories which have attempted to explain the features of autism as the result of one underlying deficit. It was concluded that the results of the Visual Clues Experiment were more likely to be due to apparent difficulties in being able to make second order representations, rather that it being due to a conative or affective abnormality.

What are the practical implications of the results of the Visual Clues Experiment?

It would appear that this study has highlighted a difficulty that those with autism have in being able to recognise symbols of age, status and gender purely on the basis of visual clues. Although this may only be a very small contribution to our knowledge with regard to what is known about autism, it is important in the sense that the more accurately we can define what the nature of the 'problems' are in autism, the more effective both diagnosis and 'treatment' can be.

Education may be a key area whereby attempts can be made to overcome this deficit. For example, services for adults with autism can now use very creative approaches in education which may facilitate improved communication and social interaction, particularly for the more able with autism. Lord and O'Neill (1983), for example, suggest that it is possible to use social skills training programmes which are based upon 'real life' problem solving. This stresses the importance of discussing alternative ways of dealing with social situations. Due to the problems that individuals have with generalising experiences, role play is also suggested in order that situations can be made more concrete for individuals. Wing (1983) further suggests the teaching of concrete rules in social situations and the use of video-taped interactions. Such approaches are advocated by a number of authors (for example, Howlin and Rutter 1987; Baron-Cohen and Bolton 1993).

However, teaching approaches such as this are not always as straight forward as they might at first appear, and they often need to be used with caution. For example, due to the problems of rigidity of thought which adults with autism often experience, it may mean that rules are applied inappropriately, since it is impossible to plan for an endless number of social situations. There are also problems of generalisation. Jordan and Powell (1994) also make the interesting point that it may be that we cannot teach the fundamental, perceptual awareness of social meaning which then allows social understanding to develop. Social skills training, in their view, is extremely difficult because people with autism are having to learn what most of us feel at the perceptual intuitive level from the outside.

At Oakfield House Autistic Community in Birmingham the approach tends to be used whereby an individual is introduced to areas of daily life in a more 'natural' way in order for them to become as involved as possible in all areas of social life. For example, some individuals are currently taking part in education courses at local colleges. These courses are undertaken with the support of a 'college coach' and pointing out 'social blunders' in situations would usually be carried out tactfully in the context in which it occurred. Another important consideration has been to focus on training college staff with regard to the specific problems which those with autism experience.

As a final point, it is evident that this lack of understanding of the subtle rules which govern social interaction and communication needs further investigation, since the case studies which were presented earlier in this chapter clearly demonstrate that adults with autism often want to develop relationships with others. The move towards accessing community-based facilities for adults with autism will inevitably create an increased number of social situations for which social understanding is required. It is hoped that further research will define the nature of the 'problem' more accurately, in order that practitioners can have an enhanced level of understanding about the difficulties faced by adults with autism and the interventions which are needed.

BIBLIOGRAPHY

Baron-Cohen, S. and Bolton, P. (1993). *Autism: the Facts*. Oxford, Oxford University Press.

Baron-Cohen, S., Leslie, A.M. and Frith, U. (1985). Does the autistic child have Theory of Mind? *Cognition*, 21, 37–46.

DeMyer, M. (1967). Toy-playing behaviour and use of body language by autistic and normal children as reported by mothers. *Psychological Reports*, 21, 973–981.

Dunn, L. and Dunn, L. (1982). *The British Picture Vocabulary Test*. Windsor, NFER - Nelson.

Hobson, R.P. (1986). The autistic child's appraisal of expressions of emotion. *Journal of Child Psychology and Psychiatry*, 27, 321–342.

Hobson, R.P. (1987). The autistic child's recognition of age and sex related characteristics of people. *Journal of Autism and Developmental Disorders*, 17(1), 63–79.

Hobson, P. and Weeks, S.J. (1987). The salience of facial expression for autistic children. *Journal of Child Psychology and Psychiatry*, 28(1), 137–152.

Howlin, P. and Rutter, M. (1987). *Treatment of Autistic Children*. Chichester, John Wiley and Sons.

Jordan, R.R. and Powell, S. (1994). Distance Education Course: Adults the Implications of Autism. Module 1. Unit 3, Distance Education Course Autism (Adults). Social Skills and Interaction. Birmingham, The University of Birmingham, School of Education.

Leslie, A.M. (1987). Pretence and representation: the origins of 'Theory of Mind'. *Psychological Review*, 94, 412–426.

Lewis, V. and Boucher, J. (1988). Spontaneous, instructed and elicited play in relatively able autistic children. *British Journal of Developmental Psychology*, 6, 325–339.

Lord, C. and O'Neill, P. (1983). Language and communication needs of adolescents with autism. In Schopler, E. and Mesibov, G. (eds.) *Autism in Adolescents and Adults*. New York, Plenum Press.

Matthews, E. (1994). On the basis of visual clues, is the recognition of the differences between individuals possible for autistic adults? (Master of Medical Science Thesis, University of Birmingham.)

Perner, J., Leekam, S.R. and Wimmer, H. (1987). Three year old's difficulty with false belief: the case for a conceptual deficit. *British Journal of Developmental Psychology*, 5, 125–137.

Perner, J., Frith, U., Leslie. A.M. and Leekam, S.R. (1989). Exploration of the autistic child's theory of mind: knowledge, belief and communication. *Child Development*, 60, 689–700.

Powell, S.D. and Jordan, R.R. (1993). Being objective about autistic thinking and learning to learn. *Educational Psychology*, 13, 359–370.

Powell, S.D., Matthews, E. and Morgan, H. (1994). Flexibility in Thinking and Behaviour. Module 1. Unit 4, Distance Education Course in Autism (Adults). Birmingham, University of Birmingham, School of Education.

Raven, J.C. (1956). *Coloured Progressive Matrices*. Royal Dumfries, The Crichton.

Tantam, D. (1988). *A Mind of One's Own*. London, National Autistic Society.

Wing, L. (1980). The Medical Research Council Handicap, Behaviour and Skills (HBS) schedule. In E. Strong, S. Ongren, A. Dupont and J. Nielsen (eds.) Epidemiological research as a basis for the organisation of extra-mural psychiatry. *Acta Psychiatrica Scandinavica*, **62**, (supplement 285), 241–247.

Wing, L., Gould, J.,Yeates, J. and Brierly, L. (1977). Symbolic play in severely mentally retarded and in autistic children. *American Journal of Child Psychology and Psychiatry*, **18**, 167–178.

Wing, L. (1983). Manifestations of social problems in high-functioning autistic people. In Schopler, E. and Mesibov, G. (eds.) *High-Functioning Individuals with Autism*. New York, Plenum Press.

Wing, L. and Gould, J. (1979). Severe impairments of social interaction and associated abnormalities in children: epidemiology and classification. *Journal of Autism and Developmental Disorders*, **9**, 1–29.

7

Developing a support model, within a further education college, for adults with autism

Hugh Morgan, Gwenn Edwards
and Lynn Mason

THE OPPORTUNITIES for adults with autism to gain access into further education have been extremely limited in the past. Recent changes in legislation and funding arrangements may lead to increased opportunities for people with learning difficulties and/or autism seeking to attend colleges of further education. The aim of the project described in this chapter was to identify the additional support systems necessary in order to place two adults with autism successfully in mainstream courses within one further education college. The basis for the development of support systems, which included a staff development programme, was the close link between the college and the home of the two adults with autism. It was found that, with appropriate support, the two students were able to increase the length of attendance at college. It was also observed that college staff achieved a greater awareness of the specific difficulties of autism. The importance of collaborative links which enabled the sharing of information to take place on a regular and consistent basis was demonstrated.

POLITICAL BACKCLOTH

Analysis of the lack of provision for adults with autism within the further and higher education sector should be set against a backcloth of political and economic changes directly affecting the provision of education to the adult population in general (Corbett and Barton 1992). During the 1980s there was a rapid rise in the volume of courses being set up for people with learning difficulties in colleges of further education, as opposed to colleges of higher education. This may have resulted from a perception that the role of further education is changing, but perhaps also from the impact of equal opportunity rhetoric and legislation. Certainly the impact of normalisation theory, to obtain 'an existence as close to normal as possible' (Nirje 1969, p. 181), has assisted in propelling forward the opportunities for adults with learning difficulties so that they may obtain access into areas, including further education, which previously would have been unavailable to them.

However, the focus of further educational opportunities for people with learning difficulties has shifted in emphasis over the past few years and has become more vocational in orientation. This shift has reflected the lack of employment opportunities available to young people generally, and specifically to school leavers with learning difficulties. To be perceived as 'normal' in society, whether in the UK, other EEC countries, or in North America, one must be employed (Borsay 1986) and young people not in employment are usually considered to be on the periphery of society. Courses in colleges of further education tend to concentrate on pre-employment training skills and may be perceived as offering a compensatory education. Courses such as community living skills will often provide a curriculum designed to develop competence in areas including shopping, personal hygiene, budgeting, etc. However helpful these courses are to the individual with learning difficulties, without pre-planning for post-course educational or work-based activities, the value of such courses as preparation for future employment is debatable. Indeed, such courses also emphasise the fact that people with learning difficulties have to negotiate more hurdles than most in order to be successful in the job market (Corbett and Barton 1992).

THE VALUE OF EDUCATION FOR ADULTS WITH AUTISM

There is often an association made between education and schooling so that services for adults are contrasted with 'educational' services for children. This gives a false picture of any services for adults with learning difficulties but it is particularly unfortunate when considering services for adults with autism where the need for life-long education is paramount. The association of education with schooling not only has the effect of denying adults with autism access to formal educational opportunities through which their lives could have been enriched, but also has a pernicious effect on the way in which services are 'delivered' and the needs of the individual addressed.

(Jordan and Edwards, 1995, p. 3)

In Chapter Two, it was seen that evidence for the value of education for adults with learning disabilities had been demonstrated by many studies dating back to the early eighteenth century. Over past three decades, many studies have demonstrated that children and adults with severe learning disabilities (no doubt including many with autism), who were previously living in long-stay hospitals, could make significant progress when provided with education. Heaton-Ward (1975) said that the aim of education and training for 'the mentally subnormal patient' was to enable him/her to live outside the hospital environment, either completely independently or with varying degrees of supervision.

For adults with autism specifically, Elliot (1990) conveyed that continuing education for people with autism can assist in the management of behaviour and in the development of communication and life skills. Often, adults with autism need continuing education throughout adult life to enable them to catch up on the basic knowledge and skills that eluded them during their school years. Education in adult life can also help individuals with autism to develop leisure interests, enabling them to occupy and enjoy their 'free time', thus compensating for a lack of imagination. As Jordan and Edwards (1995) say, adults with autism, like any other adults in society, have the right to continuing education.

ADULTS WITH AUTISM IN FURTHER EDUCATION

Where access to further education has been achieved, adults with autism have been provided with a general service for people with additional learning needs, rather than an autism-specific service, and the educational infrastructure and support necessary for successful placement has often been lacking. This has resulted in failed opportunities for people with autism, and, in some cases, will have had profoundly damaging effects as the individuals become frustrated at their inability to impose regularity on what for them, is an often unpredictable environment (Powell *et al.* 1994).

There is currently a paucity of literature available concerning the integration of adults with autism into the further education system within the UK. One of the few examples, a development project sponsored by the City of Birmingham Continuing Education Department, sought to identify how colleges could best address the needs of adults with autism. Gray (1993) reported on

1 the current usage and need for further education for adults with autism
2 good practice elsewhere
3 barriers to access
4 positive steps that should be taken.

The outcomes of this study confirmed that there was very little provision within the further education sector for this group of adults. The study highlighted that people with autism often were placed in classes for people with learning difficulties which were not appropriate and did not meet their specific needs.

RECENT CHANGES IN FUNDING OF FURTHER EDUCATION COLLEGES

In recent years in England and Wales there have been two significant changes in legislation which may help to underpin an increase in opportunities for adults with autism seeking placements in colleges of further and higher education. These acts are the *Further and Higher Education Act 1992* and the *Education Act 1993*.

The *Further and Higher Education Act 1992* has been the first Act to make any recommendations concerning further education for people with learning difficulties. The responsibility for further education falls to the Further Education Funding Council (FEFC) who have a duty to provide

1 sufficient full-time education for all 16- to 18-year-olds
2 adequate part-time education for students aged 16 years and over
3 adequate full-time education for students over 18 years.

The FEFC (1993) will only fund courses that fall within Schedule 2 of the Act, i.e. courses that carry a qualification. This Act was followed by the *Education Act 1993* and the subsequent Code of Practice. Within the Code of Practice there is the requirement for starting the transition process at the age of 14 years. Each pupil will have a Transition Plan which will be reviewed annually. This will be a multi-agency plan to which each individual contributes, which implies that young people with autism should have the same opportunities as other young people to move into further education. The FEFC so far has shown a commitment to students with disabilities and/or learning difficulties and this is reflected in the establishment of the Tomlinson Committee which is looking at definitions, assessment, planning, the role of specialist colleges, funding and support, collaboration and quality, as well as giving everyone involved an opportunity to voice their concerns through the FEFC '*Call for Evidence*' (1994).

WHY HAVE COLLEGES OF FURTHER EDUCATION FAILED ADULTS WITH AUTISM?

Both the formal agenda of the college, i.e. the content of the curriculum and the way in which it is taught, and the informal agenda, i.e. the travelling to and from college, meal breaks and free periods, can present the adult with autism with challenges which they are ill-equipped to manage. There are, therefore, a number of variables in the further educational system which the adult with autism can find anxiety provoking, and these are summarised below.

1 The content of the curriculum, e.g. concentrating on the means of communication rather than teaching, *about* communication, academic skills taught out of context with their use.
2 The methods of teaching, i.e. it is difficult for many students with autism when spoken language (and especially formal lectures) is the main medium of instruction.

3 The context of the teaching environment, i.e. large groups of students in large, noisy rooms.

4 Out of class activities, e.g. travelling to and from college and between classes, meal breaks, free periods.

5 Relationships with staff. Both learning support and mainstream college staff often fail to understand autism and are therefore liable to misunderstand and misinterpret behaviour. This sometimes leads to disruptive and difficult behaviour by the adult with autism leading to subsequent exclusion from courses.

6 Relationships with peers, e.g. misunderstandings on both sides can lead to victimisation of the young adult with autism.

7 The induction period is often too short to allow proper acclimatisation by the student with autism to his peers and vice-versa.

8 The structure of sessions, e.g. many support sessions tend to be very flexible with students virtually 'dropping in' throughout the session, which makes it difficult for the student with autism to concentrate or to relax.

In conclusion, it is clear that most of these points provide evidence to support the proposal that further education has not yet really addressed the need for differentiation, at least as far as those with autism are concerned.

FORMAL AGENDA

Crucially, within the formal agenda of a college, lecturers often have a misunderstanding of, or lack of knowledge about, autism. As a result the teaching staff may feel some conflict, as the kind of responses and techniques they would employ for people with learning disabilities are inappropriate for adults with autism (NoRSACA undated). Gray (1993) emphasised that often course structure failed to allow an appropriately paced introduction period. The adult with autism can also be ill-prepared to make choices in vocational and educational programmes, and a curriculum emphasising independence and decision-making may trigger anxiety.

Grandin (Grandin and Scariano 1986), herself with a diagnosis of autism, emphasises that the teaching of people with autism should take place in an intense and highly structured environment. Whilst Grandin's assertion may not be practical or even necessarily desirable for all people with autism, it is clear that the design of educational programmes should take account of the fact that people with autism have major cognitive deficits. A significant example is in the area of sex education where approaches to sex education, for people with 'general' learning difficulties may be inappropriate for people with autism. In this case, training procedures often involve enabling the individual to recognise when they feel uncomfortable and to express this recognition, but for people with autism who have difficulties in recognising their own emotions, there are likely to be problems in identifying, reflecting and telling another person about them. All this highlights the need for differentiation within the curriculum - an area that further education has yet to address successfully .

INFORMAL AGENDA

The lack of support for the person with autism in the informal agenda of a college can itself destroy a placement, however appropriate the class teaching. Meal breaks in often crowded and noisy college canteens can be very frightening to the unprepared and unsupported person with autism. Choosing a meal from a wide range of foods and then finding a table at which to eat the meal can be immensely anxiety-provoking to people who, through cognitive imbalance, find it difficult to make choices. The journey to and from college requires a sufficiently high level of social competence, a skill area in which the person with autism may well be deficient and which can require tremendously specialised and individualised support and training to remedy.

APPROACHES TO FURTHER EDUCATION FOR ADULTS WITH AUTISM

Evidence is very limited. Based on the TEACCH programme, Life Education for Autistic People (LEAP) centres were established by the National Autistic Society in the UK to provide structured teaching approaches, including further education, to prepare young adults with autism for their lives ahead. A fine example of innovative practice is the joint project between the Nottingham Regional Society for Autistic Children and Adults (NoRSACA) and the North Nottinghamshire College of Further Education. Known as the Highfield House Project, it offers an alternative model for integration to a college of further education to the one described in this chapter. This project is therefore summarised in Appendix 7.1 in order to permit the reader with the opportunity to consider alternate ways of working.

A different example has been provided, since 1989, by the West Midlands Autistic Society, which has placed 14 students with autism on courses provided by two colleges of further education within Birmingham. These students have entered the colleges on sessional and individual bases, taking part in mainstream as well as discrete courses.

The project which will be described now is an attempt to identify and evaluate the opportunities and support required for two adults with autism, who have additional moderate learning difficulties, to participate in a college of further education. The project also attempts to demonstrate a structure which may be pursued by colleges, parents and carers when seeking a placement in a college of further education for a person with autism.

THE OAKFIELD HOUSE/MATTHEW BOULTON COLLEGE PROJECT

Background and method

The study reported in this chapter takes the information from the East Birmingham College Study (Gray 1993) as a starting point and aims to further the information base, by linking a local college and an autistic community and placing two young people onto Schedule 2 courses (i.e. courses carrying a qualification) with on-going support. The support model was taken from the previously successful Birmingham project of 'job coaching', which supported young people with learning difficulties into work placements.

With grant-aided support from the City of Birmingham a short-term research project was carried out to assess the levels of support that young people with autism require in order to access pre-vocational training at a local further education college. The project was planned for two academic terms. The college selected to be involved in this project had no previously recorded experience of working with adults with autism, and was chosen initially because of its close proximity to the home of the adults with autism. This meant that the participants could get there by travelling by just one bus. The project was to be a joint venture between Oakfield House and Matthew Boulton College.

Settings/location

Matthew Boulton College, Birmingham, is situated only two miles from Oakfield House. The formal teaching location was provided in an annex to the main college, the Community Access Centre, just three hundred yards from the main campus building. The college lacks a history of 'encouraging' the attendance of students with disabilities, tending to focus in the past on academic and vocational activities. However, skilled and enthusiastic teaching staff brought into the college over recent years sought to increase and improve the opportunities available to students with learning difficulties.

Procedure

A Steering Group was established with representation from Oakfield House, Matthew Boulton College and the sponsoring Education Department. The group met initially to select the young people and the courses to be involved, as well as to decide upon the initial levels of support required. Also discussed were the development needs of the teaching staff at the college, and the role of the supporter, who was also to record exactly what happened in every session – information which would contribute to a final report. The Steering Group met on a monthly basis to monitor progress and discuss any changes that might be required.

Preparation for enrolment was carried out during a preliminary visit to the college by Oakfield House staff in order to consider appropriate options to offer the two individuals from the 200+ courses offered by Matthew Boulton College. Being able to select from a wide range of options was a skill that the two young people were unable to cope with, therefore the Oakfield House staff decided to reduce the options to numeracy, literacy and information technology, as both had already demonstrated a preference for these options back in the familiar environment of Oakfield House. It was agreed that they should attend separately and, preferably, on different days.

A 'key' member of staff was identified by Oakfield House to provide on-going support to the two students, Gary and Kate, throughout the duration of the project. The support worker appointed had been employed by Oakfield House for over three years prior to the project and had developed a good 'working' relationship with both Kate and Gary. This support worker was to plan, in advance, each college attendance. This entailed identifying bus routes, organising money for tickets and meals at college, support of the individual student in the lecture room, providing feedback time to lecturers and college assistants, de-briefing of the students on their return to Oakfield House and finally, writing-up.

Visits to the Community Access Centre were then arranged for the individuals so that they could decide which course to follow. During this initial visit, concerns of the college staff were observed which were alleviated initially by the knowledge that a member of the Oakfield House staff would be attending all the sessions with the young people. These issues would also be addressed by the planned staff development sessions.

Participants

The two adults with autism, Gary and Kate, were 21 and 23 years of age respectively at the start of the project. Gary has a diagnosis of childhood autism and moderate learning difficulty, identified according to the

International Classification of Diseases (ICD-10, World Health Organisation 1993). Kate has also the same diagnosis, and neither has additional medical conditions. The following brief case vignettes are derived from HBS assessments (Wing 1980) and focus on the 'Triad of Impairments' (Wing and Gould 1979) of autism spectrum disorders, that is, the communication, socialisation and imaginative restrictions of the individuals.

VIGNETTE 7.1

Observations over several years have led to the judgment that Gary has little expressive speech but good receptive language. His speech is used to meet his direct needs through requests, although is often indistinct and the listener has to attend closely to what he attempts to say. Fewer problems in interpreting his speech are found when Gary is distressed, usually if he believes that an 'attachment' is under threat. In such situations he is observed to leap up and down, shouting 'No' and swearing. Although difficult to measure empirically, Gary appears to dislike loud noises or noisy environments and is believed to be hypersensitive to noise.

Gary is very much a loner, only interacting with staff or with peers when he requires his needs to be met. Whilst Gary does not use money appropriately and does not appear to know dates, months or years, nor is he able to tell the time by the clock, he has a reasonable 'body clock' type of understanding of the concept of time. He appears to enjoy art and craft activities and is observed to be relatively competent in most arts and crafts. He also appears to enjoy writing and always attempts to make his work look neat and tidy. However, he does not appear to understand the written word and has not developed reading skills. There is no real evidence that Gary engages in imaginative and spontaneous activities.

VIGNETTE 7.2

Kate has been able to understand instructions involving decisions. Kate can use verbal speech to form sentences and has occasionally asked questions of others. However the content of her speech has seemed rather odd to strangers. Her conversation can be fairly repetitive, although, on occasions, it can be varied and appropriate to the context of the situation. Kate has appeared able to understand complex social gestures. She can make requests in words. Kate will spontaneously share her personal interests with staff but not with peers. She has been observed to take part in leisure activities with peers, but these are usually motivated by staff. She will make social approaches to others, but these can be rather bizarre and one sided, i.e. on her own terms.

Introduction to the college

Kate and Gary's first visit to the Community Access Centre involved visiting the various teaching areas and observing students in literacy and numeracy groups. They also met two or three members of staff and used the canteen and drinks machine.

Information-giving and meeting people was kept to a minimum to avoid causing any anxiety. Gary appeared happy, he smiled and chatted to himself, but did not or could not indicate whether he would like to come to college again.

Kate reacted very differently. Initially her response to any question was a loud and impatient, 'I don't know,' but when the attention was turned away from her and directed at Gary or the key worker, she would interrupt, pull and tug at the members of staff, demanding attention. She shot off several times on her own into rooms and disturbed activities going on. She insisted that someone accompany her to the toilet, and then talked incessantly and loudly to make sure that someone was still close by. Staff reaction to this initial visit was generally one of concern and apprehension. Kate appeared uncontrollable at times, and staff questioned whether she would have a disruptive effect on other students and the groups she may join. It was always going to be difficult to assess Gary and plan work for him because of his lack of communication skills. Staff were concerned about how much he had actually understood during the visit.

It was quickly recognised that staff would need more information about Kate and Gary and about autism in general. Staff also talked to the other students about Gary and Kate and explained that both might feel anxious, even threatened by joining the group and it was hoped the group would be supportive.

Beginning the project

Initially, Gary and Kate joined a basic skills workshop, attending for one hour of a three-hour workshop. Normally, students would drop in to workshops on an informal basis and would generally work on improving their literacy and numeracy skills by working on their own, at their own pace, using paper-based materials. The role of the teacher in this setting was to be on hand to offer help and advice.

Gary and Kate encountered a number of difficulties in this setting. Firstly the needs of the group were varied and diverse, and, with only one member of staff available, there was little opportunity for individual support. The drop-in policy meant that there was often disruption caused by people arriving and leaving at different times, and the group could become too large on occasions. The major difficulty, however, was that there was no formal structure to these sessions and little opportunity for Kate and Gary to get to know the group and join in the activities. These issues were raised at the Steering Group meeting and a number of significant changes were made.

Changes made

Additional staff were employed and this resulted in a reduction in group size. The general workshops were withdrawn and specific groups were set up to develop particular skills. Gary joined a literacy group and Kate joined a spelling and basic mathematics group, and more structured modes of learning were introduced. Individual learning plans were agreed, and learning goals set, by discussion between college lecturers, the support worker, the Steering Group and also by gauging Gary and Kate's views, through the observation of their preferences to tasks. Finally there was a move from paper-based to practical learning activities. Kate was given tasks to use money and receive change, rather than concentrate on addition and subtraction exercises.

Findings

A total of 172 hours was allocated to the project over the two terms. These hours consisted of:

Classroom support	55 hours
Coffee and dinner support	33 hours
Travel to and from college	22 hours
Research and writing-up of project	62 hours

Therefore, it can be seen that around one-third of the total time allocated for the project was spent in the teaching situation, whereas two-thirds was necessary for preparation, travel, support during college meal breaks, and report writing. Additionally, Steering Group meetings consumed a further 20 hours over the two terms.

Throughout the duration of the course, teaching staff recorded their observations of the two. Gary joined six other students in a basic literacy group, but initially appeared to be reluctant to take part in activities and would become agitated if asked to join in. Slowly he settled into the group. He liked to look at the work of others in his group and listened to group discussions. Gradually he began to say, 'hello' to the other students unprompted and became less agitated in response to questions asked of him. Gary enjoyed the paper-based activities, but he liked to be able to select what he wanted to do. He gradually became more confident and relaxed, and would respond well to praise and encouragement. By the end of the programme he tried hard to please, would answer simple questions and became more tolerant of others.

Kate very much required one-to-one support. She experienced great difficulties concentrating for any length of time. Her mood swings very much affected her progress. Some days she would be unco-operative and disruptive, constantly demanding attention and reassurance and, when encouraged, could become withdrawn.

The teaching staff had difficulty deciding what level of teaching materials to use with Kate. They started with basic letter formation and copy writing to see what she could do, and then gradually realised that she was capable of more when she had become more settled and her concentration improved. The staff learned to ignore her disruptive behaviour and this generally had a calming effect upon her, and she gradually became more co-operative. The other students also ignored Kate's problem behaviour and chatted to her quite willingly. Kate responded well to this and began to interact quite well with the group. She would talk to others and would thank them for letting her join in with them. For Kate this social interaction and contact was more important to her than the learning process; however, as she made friends and settled down, her ability to concentrate and complete her work steadily improved.

Discussion

The Steering Group played a key role in resolving problems that arose during the project, which included: clarification of the role of the support worker as part of the group in the classroom situation, so that the expectations of both they and the teaching staff became clearer. It had been reported at an early stage that the group was too large for both individuals. This changed to the two young people's advantage, as there was restructuring of all the groups, so that they ended up in smaller and separate groups. The monthly Steering Group meetings were invaluable for ironing out any difficulties which arose, before they caused any 'damage'.

Teaching approaches were discussed, recognising the need for directive teaching. During the first few weeks there were a number of staff changes, the effect of which was to disturb the young people with autism. This situation was subsequently improved by the appointment of a member of staff to be attached to the Community and Access Division who had previous experience of working with young people with learning difficulties and young people who displayed challenging behaviour. The Steering Group was also used as a venue for the sharing of information between the two organisations to consider approaches which would stimulate the two individuals in the class situation.

Both Kate and Gary presented behaviours which were seen by the college staff as being 'challenging' and which initially seemed to disturb some of the teaching staff more than their fellow students.

The Steering Group sought to identify methods of dealing with 'bizarre' behaviours shown by Gary and Kate, which included the inappropriate touching of themselves and others.

The 'drop-in' nature of the courses presented problems. Firstly, the classes had, by definition, very little formal structure and every session was seen to be 'different'. Secondly, as a 'drop-in' class, there were no set times, so all students came and went as they wished.

The interchange of information between the two organisations, which was implicit in the staff development programme, was extremely valuable. Staff development took different forms, input from Oakfield House was used to provide college staff with a knowledge base in autism. Informal sessions looked at different styles and approaches. College staff visited Oakfield House to see what the students did there and how the Oakfield House staff interacted with the young people. The knowledge that college staff had of autism, initially stimulated by this project, was extended through attendance at autism-specific conferences. Staff at Oakfield House became more aware of the structure/approaches within the college.

Recommendations

Considerable learning was derived from this project by the students and by the staff from both organisations. Any future project will need to consider the essential role of staff development and the support necessary in order to understand and respond appropriately to the individual needs of the students. From the perspective of the college, this will include provision of training in the field of autism for lecturers, classroom assistants and relevant ancillary staff. Preparation for the initial entrance to college should include a period of familiarisation or pre-access work with the young people before they attend college. The sharing of information between the link organisations was found to be very important, especially during the early days for the college staff, in order to provide them with a basis to develop a starting point. Also important was the decision to stagger the start time of courses to allow the students to settle in gradually. Once in college, there should be consistency of approach and consistency of staffing within the teaching situation. It is also proposed that the support worker should come from the host organisation, where they will already have formed a bond with the person with autism.

A future area in the further education of adults with autism to be investigated will be whether the skills learned by the adult with autism within the formal and informal agenda of the college can be transferred to settings away from the classroom situation. Perhaps a key component of the teaching of people with autism within the further education colleges will be to consider ways in which the teaching situation can be employed to encourage the person to socially empathise with others and to develop social skills. As for further education, employment for adults with autism can be unsuccessful, not through the competence of the individual with autism to appropriately perform the job task, but because of his or her ability to cope with the social context of the employment situation. The teaching of leisure pursuits for people with autism, so lacking imagination and spontaneity, will enable them to begin to achieve a life enrichment not previously encountered. It may be seen that the education of adults with autism needs to be based on an understanding of the condition, with attention directed at the teaching process rather than solely at the award of a qualification at the end of a course. Recommendations from the Oakfield House/Matthew Boulton College Project are summarised.

1 Formations of links between colleges and organisations working on behalf of, and representing the views of, people with autism.
2 Training in autism for all college staff involved, i.e. lecturers, classroom assistants and ancillary staff.
3 Period of familiarisation or pre-access work.
4 Sharing of information between link organisations.
5 Staggering start time of courses to allow gradual entry.
6 Consistency of approach and staffing within the teaching situation.
7 Support worker should initially come from the specialist service then gradually and systematically hand over to college support.
8 Attention needs to be paid to the learning process rather than product, and the social benefits that may accrue through planned contact with others.

CHAPTER SUMMARY

This project has shown that young adults with autism are able to participate in pre-vocational access programmes in a college of further education, but require a high level of support including structured staff development and feedback time. The benefits of this project quite outweighed any initial difficulties that were experienced. The teaching staff at Matthew Boulton College certainly developed an insight and more understanding of autism. The programme of staff development was worthwhile and will continue.

Supporting Kate and Gary in an integrated setting in further education had a profound effect upon service delivery. Kate and Gary highlighted just how important it is to take the needs of the individual adult with autism into account when planning a programme of work. Also highlighted was how very important it is to provide a sense of security and structure to the learning process, and, above all, the importance of preparation and pre-access development before placing the adult with autism into an integrated further education setting. Additionally, this project demonstrated the need for the student with autism, within both the formal and informal aspects of college life, to receive close support from a person experienced and knowledgeable in the field of autism.

The importance of staff development programmes was demonstrated, as was the close support of staff specifically trained to assist the person with autism. These findings, obtained from work with adults, are also consistent with research findings indicating that teachers and ancillary helpers require considerable autism-specific training to assist their teaching of children with autism (Wormald *et al.* 1993). However, it would be of future interest to investigate the implications of this project for the other, non-disabled, students of the college. Also of interest would be to ascertain their reactions to the students with autism, their developing understanding of autism and their potential capacity to play a role in supporting the person with autism in the college environment.

ACKNOWLEDGEMENTS

The authors wish to record their great appreciation to members of the Steering Group Committee, especially Lilleth Gordon, Sue Humpherson, Lorraine Sturmey and Jackie Thronicker, for their high degree of commitment which enabled this innovative project to work so effectively. The authors also wish to express appreciation for the contribution by Fred Parsons which is presented as Appendix 7.1.

APPENDIX 7.1

The Highfield House Project, accessing
further education for adults with autism
in Nottingham

Fred Parsons

The Highfield House Project gained its title because this was the name of
the college building in which the crucial base rooms were located. The function and purpose within these rooms was to access further education for
adults with autism.

BACKGROUND

In late 1987 and early 1988, Whitegates in Worksop, Nottinghamshire, was
in the process of opening as a residential care home with educational day
services for adults with autism, a specialist service governed by the
Nottingham Regional Society for Autistic Children and Adults
(NoRSACA).

Prior to the opening of Whitegates, when considering admissions, it was
abundantly evident that the greatest areas of need in terms of service delivery were in responding to the needs of school leavers. Education, and very
often education of a boarding school nature, is a statutory and more readily
accessible provision, whereas appropriate adult services were, and still are,
insufficient in number to meet demand.

Consequently, the Whitegates Adult Service concentrated upon meeting
the needs of school leavers with autism, which led to the initial resident
group being within the age range of 16 to 20 years. Bearing in mind the age
range, it was, therefore, paramount that an integral and major component
of the Whitegates Adult Service would be a clearly defined commitment to
continuing and further education.

INTRODUCTION TO THE FURTHER EDUCATION
COLLEGE

Back in 1988 the initial contact from Whitegates with North
Nottinghamshire College of Further Education was in connection with the
enrolment of two young resident men, as students. Both students had the
right to access further education, both were academically well matched to
the college course they selected and both, on occasions, presented behavioural difficulties when experiencing social interaction situations, this being
inherent within their autistic condition. In order that these two students,

and latterly others, should succeed in pursuing their studies, it was clearly apparent that a mechanism of support for both the student and the college tutoring staff needed to be put in place.

In the first instance the support mechanism took the form of Whitegates providing staff familiar with the students and possessing expertise in dealing with people with autism. Their function at this stage was often to act as the enabler and interpreter for the student with autism in translating communication, events, environment and circumstances into less anxiety provoking messages.

DEVELOPMENTS LEADING TO THE HIGHFIELD HOUSE PROJECT

The following two years saw Whitegates enrolling more students with autism into the further education college. Both college tutors and Whitegates personnel became more proficient in supporting the increasing number of students through their studies. The courses being accessed were matched to the students abilities and choices. These included:

Word processing (beginners)
Craft – T1
Machine knitting
Screen printing
Beauty and care
Catering
Performing arts (dance/drama/music)
Printing – offset/letterpress (3)
DIY and maintenance
Textiles
Communication
City and Guilds (C and G) numeracy/literacy
Catering club (12–2pm)
Duke of Edinburgh award
Independence skills
Personal development

THE PILOT PROJECT – USING A BASE ROOM IN THE FURTHER EDUCATION COLLEGE

The project that commenced in April 1991 seemed to be a logical development of the programme already under way. The partnership had already established a basis for commonality of approaches, philosophies and working practices, whilst retaining the necessary objectivity of the individual establishments concerned.

At the start of the Highfield Project, several students with autism were integrating into further education on a full-time or sessional basis; three were accessing classes with additional tutor support and four students were quite independent within the college environment. However, what was now envisaged was the creation of a base room within the college that could expand the educational provision for these students and which would also allow access to those students, who, by virtue of their more challenging behaviour, had previously been denied the opportunity. The base room would serve the following purposes:

1 To provide a contact point for those students on full-time courses.
2 To offer 'drop-in' facilities for those students who were unsupported in college session.
3 To supply a college environment for those students attending on a sessional basis to receive the other elements of their educational programmes.
4 To make available a quiet, supportive environment through which students can be introduced into college and further education.

From the base room, integration could be achieved into mainstream further education. The stages in which this took place were:

1 Preparation work to be undertaken with students prior to introduction to college by familiar instructor/key worker/tutor.
2 Introduction to unfamiliar base room and routines by familiar tutor, i.e. Whitegates tutor based in college.
3 Introduction of unfamiliar college staff to students within what has become a familiar base room.
4 Move to the unfamiliar environment of a different classroom to interact with unfamiliar people, i.e. students and staff, whilst supported by familiar Whitegates and college staff.
5 Gradual withdrawal of support by Whitegates staff in order to encourage interaction with college staff.

SOME NOTABLE ACHIEVEMENTS OF WHITEGATES STUDENTS ATTENDING NORTH NOTTINGHAMSHIRE COLLEGE OF FURTHER EDUCATION

Seven years on, and the working partnership between Whitegates (NoRSACA) and North Nottinghamshire College of Further Education continues to flourish. Whitegates now operate from two base rooms in the college. In addition, the organisation now runs its own further education unit, the latter providing further education for students with autism funded by the Further Education Funding Council.

In conclusion, it is believed that the project has worked successfully. Evidence of its efficiency is the following list of student achievements:

Credits towards C and G Wordpower (foundation level)
Pentathletes Award (Bronze)
Newark Agricultural Shop Pottery Award
Credits towards Duke of Edinburgh Award (Bronze)
PVCE Communication Skills
RSA Word Processing
RSA Word Processing Core Skills
BTec National Computer Studies
'A' Level Computer Programming
GCSE English
GCSE Mathematics
GCSE German

It is believed that these student achievements would not have been possible if the Highfield House Project and its support network had not existed.

BIBLIOGRAPHY

Borsay, A. (1986). Personal trouble or public issue ? Towards a model of policy for people with physical and mental disabilities. *Disability, Handicap and Society*, 1(2), 179-196.

Clarke, A.W. and Clarke, D.W. (1974). *Mental Deficiency: the Changing Outlook*, third edition. London, Methuen and Co.

Corbett, J. and Barton, L. (1992). *A Struggle for Choice - Students with Special Needs in Transition to Adulthood*. London, Routledge.

Department of Education (1992). *The Further and Higher Education Act*. London, HMSO.

Department of Education (1993). *The Education Act*. London. HMSO.

Elliot, A. (1990). Adolescence and early adulthood. In K. Ellis (ed.). *Autism: Professional Perspectives and Practice*. London, Chapman and Hall.

Further Education Funding Council (1993). Circular 93/92. *Recurrent Funding Methodology: Tariff Values for 1994-5*. London, FEFC.

Further Education Funding Council (1994). *Call for Evidence*. London, FEFC.

Grandin, T. and Scariano, M.M. (1986). *Emergence Labeled Autistic*. California, Arena Press.

Gray, C. (1993). *Further Education Colleges and Adults with Autism: Report of a Development Project*. Birmingham, City of Birmingham Education Department.

Heaton-Ward, W.A. (1975). *Mental Subnormality: Subnormality and Severe Subnormality*, fourth edition. Bristol, John Wright and Sons Ltd.

Jordan, R.R. and Edwards, G. (1995). Educational Approaches to Adults with Autism. Unit 3. Module 1, Distance Education Course in Autism (Adults). Birmingham, University of Birmingham, School of Education.

Nirje, B. (1969). The normalisation principle and its human management implications. In R. Kugel, and W. Wolfensberger (eds.). *Changing Patterns in Residential Services for the Mentally Retarded.* Washington, DC Presidents Committee on Mental Retardation. Government Printing Office.

NoRSACA and North Nottinghamshire College of Further Education. (undated). *The Highfield House Project: Accessing Further Education for Adults with Autism.* Nottingham. NoRSACA/North Nottinghamshire College of Further Education.

Powell, S.D., Matthews, E. and Morgan, S.H. (1994). Flexibility in Thinking and Behaviour. Unit 4. Module 1. Distance Education Course in Autism (Adults). Birmingham, University of Birmingham, School of Education.

Wing, L. (1980). The Medical Research Council Handicap, Behaviour and Skills (HBS) Schedule. In E. Strong, S. Ongren, A. Dupont and J. Nielsen (eds.) Epidemiological research as a basis for the organisation of extra-mural psychiatry. *Acta Psychiatrica Scandinavica*, **62** (supplement 285), 241–247.

Wing, L. and Gould, J. (1979). Severe impairments of social classification and associated abnormalities in children: epidemiology and classification. *Journal of Autism and Developmental Disorders*, **9**, 11-29.

World Health Organisation (1993). Mental Disorders: a Glossary and Guide to their Classification in Accordance with the 10th Revision of the International Classification (ICD-10). Geneva, World Health Organisation.

Wormald, E., Cleasby, D., Nimmo, C., Price, G., Shaw, M., Taylor, P., Tromans, P. and Williamson, J. (1993). *Speaking Out - Educating Children with Autism. A Survey of Parents' Views.* Birmingham, West Midlands Autistic Society.

8

Employment training and the development of a support model within employment for adults who experience Asperger syndrome and autism: the Gloucestershire Group Homes Model

Alison Matthews

INTRODUCTION

AN INDIVIDUAL who experiences autism or Asperger syndrome has a right to use mainstream training and employment services. However, many people are unable to access such services without support. A specialist employment training service is therefore required to enable successful access to take place by providing adequate training, preparation, support and often co-operation with employers, the employment service, the careers service and mainstream training providers. This service needs to supplement and support mainstream provision.

A specialist service needs to identify the broad spectrum of training needs and work skills of individuals, and provide the necessary support and vocational opportunities to ensure that individuals can successfully participate in their chosen area of work, with the appropriate degree of mainstream integration.

The model developed by the Gloucestershire Group Homes (GGH) Employment Training Unit (ETU) provides a service that recognises the wide variety of vocational needs of adults who experience autism or Asperger syndrome. This is reflected in the diversity of training and vocational opportunities. The aim of the service is to encourage people to pursue their own informed and realistic choice of employment, through training, work experience and continual support. Given the nature of autism, the most successful work options are likely to be ones developed with the autistic individual in mind and where there is some degree of continuous support (Van Bourgondien and Woods 1992).

Competence in a work skill does not necessarily indicate the competence to undertake that work skill in mainstream employment. Having a work skill is often not the problem for a person experiencing Asperger syndrome or autism, but being able to cope with the social interactive aspect of work, in a changing and often unpredictable environment, can be extremely difficult. Problems occur, things go wrong, machines break down, staff change, all these challenge the individual with autism or Asperger syndrome.

The barriers to effective work integration triggered by autism or Asperger syndrome and sometimes an associated psychiatric disorder (depression in particular) are diverse and complex.

GGH has developed a flexible training approach which is based on meeting the needs of the individual and offers a continuum of vocational options in a specialised and supportive environment. Whilst it is entirely appropriate for some individuals to train and develop the necessary skills to access mainstream employment, for others it is not. For these people a sheltered and specialised working environment is required to provide the opportunity to enable them to contribute their work skills and participate in their chosen vocation without the overwhelming demands of a totally integrated mainstream environment.

The employment service structure was influenced partly by the work of the vocational options being developed in North Carolina (see Van Bourgondien and Woods 1992), and partly by the experience gained from other specialised employment training methods, education techniques and work options previously developed by the author at a college of further education.

The North Carolina vocational options include job coach, enclave work, mobile crew, small business models of supported employment and a model where the vocational programme is integrated with the residential programme (Van Bourgondien and Woods 1992). Whilst the GGH Employment Service has some similarity with the North Carolina Model – for example, with the role of the job coach – the interpretation of mobile crews, enclave work and the small business model differ. The service continues to change and develop in accordance with the needs of the trainees. This chapter describes the Gloucestershire Group Homes Model. It illustrates how a model similar to that in North Carolina is being used in the UK to the benefit of adults who experience autism or Asperger syndrome.

THE GLOUCESTERSHIRE GROUP HOMES EMPLOYMENT TRAINING MODEL

GGH provides a specialist service for adults experiencing Asperger syndrome. The service currently provides 16 residential places in four group homes in the community with varying degrees of support. The ETU provision was developed in 1992, by GGH, in response to the growing demands of the residents and the recognition that, in order to access mainstream employment, people who experience autism or Asperger syndrome require a specialist service.

The ETU also currently supports a further five people who experience Asperger syndrome and who live outside the service; either through direct training, or through ETU staff working with social services, disability employment advisors or staff from other training organisations, in order to best meet the specific needs of the individual with Asperger syndrome.

The service provided by GGH specialises in working with people who experience Asperger syndrome, but also works with some people who experience autism. There are differences and similarities in the training needs of these two groups of people; these will be detailed throughout the chapter. The ETUs structure is equally suitable for both groups, as it provides all relevant levels of support and training.

This chapter describes the following:

Key elements of a GGH specialist employment service
Outlining the pathway to employment
Basic Skills Training and Personal Development
Assessment
Career guidance
Enclave work
ETU business model
Mobile Crew Work experience
Work experience with a job coach
Role of job coach supporting an individual in employment
Supportive employment services in the UK.

KEY ELEMENTS OF A SPECIALIST EMPLOYMENT SERVICE

The following is a list of essential objectives for those providing a specialist service:

- to achieve an understanding of autism and Asperger syndrome – trained staff
- to achieve an understanding of how autism or Asperger syndrome affect behaviour
- to address autism or Asperger syndrome and develop areas of personal development affected by disability
- to provide individuals with the necessary skills to be able to meet the basic criteria for integration into employment
- to be aware of potential demands on the individual that work will make, and of how they will cope, given the nature of his/her disability
- to provide the individual with coping strategies for the above-mentioned demands.

- to compensate for the specific skill deficits of an individual (i.e. flexibility and initiative)
- to link the individual's support network together, to provide consistency and a holistic training approach
- to fulfil the duty of enabling the individual to reach his/her potential.

The service has been most successful when it has been able to work directly with the support network (family, key workers and social workers) on a regular basis, and is less successful when there has been limited or no communication with the support network.

Given the nature of autism and Asperger syndrome, it is essential to be aware of any difficulties that may be experienced outside the individual's working day. Frequently, difficulties outside work may affect the individual's ability to participate in a work-based activity. Equally, difficulties experienced at work may only manifest themselves 'away' from the working/training environment in the secure environment of the individual's home. Consistent liaison with the individual's support network is important to ensure that trainers are aware of the individual's ability to cope with the demands of work.

OUTLINING THE PATHWAY TO EMPLOYMENT

A trainee starts in the ETU centre and undergoes basic skills training, then there is a gradual movement towards employment from the ETU base. The service is completely flexible, and a trainee may move from having full support to having less support, then to working in a sheltered environment and on to open employment. Equally, they may move from having no support back to receiving partial or full support, and from open employment, to a more sheltered environment, depending on their ability to cope at any one time.

Figure 8.1 illustrates the progression into employment and the recognition that support from the ETU may be needed on a continual basis.

BASIC SKILLS TRAINING AND PERSONAL DEVELOPMENT

A secure training base is required for basic skills training. Security is established through the trainee's familiarity with the staff and the working environment. In this environment, important relationships are formed between trainee and trainer. A network of trainee, residential key worker/family is set up to ensure consistency and a holistic approach to training and development. ETU-based training involves personal development, the development

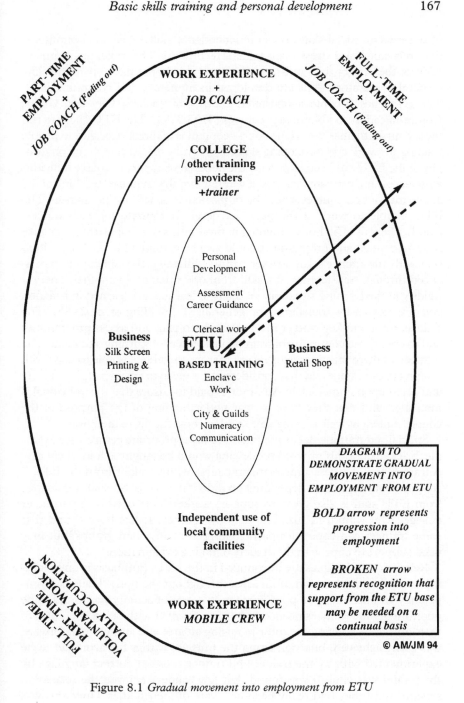

Figure 8.1 *Gradual movement into employment from ETU*

of self-esteem, social skills, social independence skills, skills in communication, relaxation and stress management techniques. The individual learns to address the effects that autism or Asperger syndrome have on his/her life. General preparatory skills are developed in numeracy and communication. The ETU has become a registered centre for teaching City and Guilds Communication and Numeracy courses (3793/3794). The ETU chose to run these courses themselves, as the course content is of direct relevance to people training for work and developing skills in everyday life. Although the philosophy of the ETU has been to provide the necessary support to enable individuals to access mainstream facilities, it was felt that the 'in house' teaching of the above-mentioned courses would be of particular benefit to the trainees. The ETU is able to work at the pace and level appropriate for each trainee. Another benefit of 'in house' training in these courses is that learning can take place in context and programmes could also be continued in the home situation with the trainee's key workers, thus addressing the difficulties experienced through transference of a skill from one situation to another. There is rigidity in the learning situation, i.e. skills, if learned, are learned in isolation and are not easily transferred or generalised (Golding *et al.* 1985). The trainee, tutor and key worker meet regularly to plan and assess programmes and to ensure the continuity of training in a variety of learning situations. The purpose of these meetings is to ensure that the individual is able to cope with training at each stage and that consideration is given to any increase in anxiety and acted upon immediately. Attention is paid to ensure that the individual is motivated and that they have a clear understanding of the purpose of the course content as well as being able to relate it practically to their lives.

Specialised training needs are taught in an appropriate centre – for example, bricklaying skills or word processing would be taught at a local college. A trainee would access a mainstream course with a trainer from the ETU – support would continue depending on individual needs. Specialist guidance from ETU staff is also given to support workers employed by a particular college, who would, in turn, support the trainee. It has been found that some trainees can cope with participating in mainstream groups, but may need support to cope with the anxiety of taking examinations.

Relaxation techniques are introduced in the ETU. Emphasis is on breathing control and relaxation of muscles throughout the body. Trainee's competency and the ability to participate in this type of activity was found to be poor. Firstly the trainees needed to become familiar with being in control of their muscles – copying the tutor in raising an arm and stretching it forward was easily achieved, but 'tightening the muscles within the arm' had to be experimented with by the trainer and trainee – use of correct language by the trainer was vital. It was found that few trainees enjoyed the relaxation sessions until they had really become aware of their bodies. Once this was achieved, however, deep relaxation could take place. Some trainees regularly visit therapists for aromatherapy or reflexology.

Contracts are drawn up between the trainee and the ETU. Contracts are important as they help to focus trainees towards the importance of the discipline involved in work. By attending the ETU, trainees are required, as far as possible, to make a commitment to training and this in turn helps to develop their feelings of purpose, responsibility and involvement in the control of their futures.

ASSESSMENT

ETU individual assessment

In the ETU, an on-going assessment commences, looking in detail at how autism and Asperger syndrome affect each individual. The assessment considers the following:

motivation: what motivates an individual to apply themself to accept and cope with a new situation or set of circumstances?

anxiety: causes and manifestation, and how individual deals with it

boundaries: some individuals have rigid boundaries; self-imposed rigid enforcement of routines and the degree of new experiences he/she can cope with at any given time

level of understanding about self: does individual know what causes anxiety (i.e. routine upset, not understanding social dynamics, not understanding what is being required of them)

constructive 'self-help' mechanism: what sort of behaviours / activities are helpful to individual, things they may need to do to make themselves feel secure, e.g. relaxation techniques

how an adult learns: practical experience, use of visual material (e.g. photographs, diagrams), reading written instruction, difficulties in understanding verbal instructions

additional complications: does individual experience depression, for example, mood swings, patterns of behaviour of which trainer needs to be aware for consistency of ability to apply self to a regular job.

PACT (Placing Assessment and Counselling Team) assessment

It is important to assess the trainee's level of academic ability and practical work skill level, preferably with assistance of the mainstream services. For example, the employment service Placing Assessment and Counselling Team (PACT) provides invaluable assistance in the determination of work skill levels, based on those of normal open employment.

In order to establish a realistic assessment of an individual's work skills, the specialist employment service needs to work with the employment service to ensure that many of the difficulties encountered by an individual are overcome.

The occupational psychologist from the PACT team in Gloucester and the GGH trainers set up a week of testing exclusively for ETU trainees.

Adapting the PACT assessment to people who experience autism or Asperger syndrome

The main barriers of the assessment to overcome were:

- joining a group of up to eight other people, unknown to the individual experiencing autism/Asperger syndrome, undergoing an assessment in the same room
- difficulties in understanding terms /language used in certain tests
- difficulties in understanding purpose/ relevance of a test (particularly for those trainees experiencing autism)
- stress/anxiety caused to the individuals by the need to understand what was being required of them and to perform satisfactorily for the assessor
- performing at an optimum level when having to cope with being in an unfamiliar environment
- difficulty in taking *verbal* instructions.

The ETU trainers were shown all the tests and looked closely at the wording of the instructions. The occupational psychologist, together with the trainers, adapted some instructions to ensure that there would be no misunderstanding. Some trainees needed the instructions to be broken down into shorter two or three element sentences, removing words that may detract from the main semantics of the instruction. It was essential, however, that this was done in such a way that no 'additional' assistance was provided, as this would affect the relevance of the 'norms' for the levels of the assessment. The ETU trainers were also taught how to undertake some tests for those individuals who would find communicating with an unknown person difficult. It was also important, for some individuals, that the test instructions were available for them to read, as some individuals experiencing autism in particular are more able to take instruction from the written word rather than by listening.

The difficulty of understanding the purpose of a test was particularly hard to overcome for some individuals, particularly those who experienced autism, rather than Asperger syndrome. The test itself had to be intrinsically interesting for some individuals in order for them to apply themselves to it.

The occupational psychologist noted that some individuals had worked out their own unique way of doing the test, yet still achieved the required outcome. Some individuals could not appreciate the relevance of time limits, for example, undertaking the instructions was equally important as ensuring that each piece of equipment was thoroughly examined and cleaned before use. Although such action ensured a low score, well below the level required for open employment, due to the lack of speed in completing the test, the test results invariably showed 100% accuracy in task achievement.

The work skills test results were measured in terms of British Standard Institute (BSI) norms and percentiles. The norms related to practical work samples, undertaken by experienced workers in relevant fields. Work sample results can be presented in three forms: time, accuracy and overall performance.

A particular advantage of the trainer working with the psychologists was that the trainer observes very detailed information about the precise nature of a trainee's ability or inability to attend to a certain aspect of a given task. Such information would then be incorporated into a future training programme, or to be taken into account in a work placement.

The PACT assessment was of particular use to the ETU in its infancy; it was felt that we needed detailed information about the actual work skill levels of the group, to substantiate the feelings that we had that the majority of the group could, with appropriate training and support, access mainstream employment, or work in an employment environment that was tailored specifically to the needs of people with autism.

The assessment results did not tell us that an individual could cope in a working environment – this information would be obtained from our own assessments in enclave and mobile crew work. This following vignette illustrates an important observation made through the PACT assessment:

VIGNETTE 8.1

Trainee 'J', who experiences Asperger syndrome, had successfully achieved qualifications at a local college with some support. He had attended mainstream groups and achieved distinctions in RSA qualifications in typing, word processing and audio typing. As we expected 'J' achieved above average (BSI norm) scores in the PACT general clerical test – his accuracy being 20/30% above the level of an experienced worker. Even the time in which he undertook the test was above the score required for open employment.

We observed 'J' throughout the test. He concentrated for 100% of the time but appeared anxious and made his familiar stressful humming sounds. This was 'normal' behaviour for 'J' undertaking this type of work. 'J' used the ETU word processor and spreadsheets, he was highly competent and had worked for various local companies using these skills. 'J' was motivated in clerical work and particularly copy typing by his innate need to have things absolutely correct; any mistake and 'J' would be almost guaranteed to notice it. This ability was therefore developed, 'J' had studied, gained qualifications and started a career path in this area.

However at the PACT assessment 'J' undertook a mechanical simulated assembly task in which he followed a pattern and reproduced a model making a 'Mechano'-like construction. 'J' did well at the test, his work was accurate. The most significant observation made by the trainers was that 'J', for the first time, had undertaken a task with 100% concentration yet had remained completely calm throughout. There were no signs of stress for the full two hours that he spent on the activity. 'J' reported that he had felt calm, completely absorbed and highly interested.

It is sometimes felt that people with autism can hold down jobs that are technologically complex and have little allowance for error (Datlow Smith 1990). Whilst it is evident that many people who experience autism are particularly adept at being accurate in their work, the stress that the need to be accurate causes can be at an unacceptable level for the individual. As Kanner (1943) has observed in his first account of autism, the behaviour of an individual experiencing autism is governed at an early age by an anxiously obsessive desire for the maintenance of sameness . The frequent ability to be good at copy typing and other such precision-requiring activities is often associated with an anxious state. As vignette 8.1 illustrates, 'J' shows outstanding ability in clerical-type work, but the very nature of this type of work confronts his autism and causes him stress.

In an activity such as typing – where an easy mistake can take place every fraction of a second (i.e. a wrong key is touched) – the individual is constantly in danger of having his/her autism challenged. When 'J' undertook a task where he might make a mistake once every one to two minutes (as it took that long to tighten a nut), he was being confronted with the possibility of error less frequently and could deal with it without the high level of stress associated with typing. 'J' was also stressed when the work he was required to type up contained inaccuracies such as spelling mistakes.

The apparent competency of an individual in a given activity needs to be viewed in relation to the amount of stress actually being caused to the individual. This may be compounded by the enthusiasm of the trainer and his or her will for the client to be seen to be achieving, when it is not necessarily in the individual's best interest.

Details of the tests undertaken by the trainees are summarised in Appendix 8.1.

However, we have observed that trainee 'J' is able to use the word processor completely calmly if he is typing out information related to his specialised interests. In this instance he is more able to absorb the otherwise frustrating negative aspects of typing (when mistakes are made or the computer does not perform correctly) with apparent ease.

Temple Grandin is convinced of the importance of directing such interests into constructive channels, working with them, not against them. High-functioning autistic adults, who are able to live independently and keep a job, often have work that is in the same field of interest as their childhood fixations (Grandin and Scariano 1986). Developing known interests is an obvious way to ensure motivation, however, using the specialised interests of an individual who experiences autism or Asperger syndrome has the additional effect of calming the individual and making him/her more tolerant to minor changes/difficulties.

CAREER GUIDANCE

Career guidance is provided in the ETU and throughout training. The ETU ensures that trainees follow their own training programme according to their skills and interests. Many trainees have had little prior experience of work and a limited understanding of what a particular type of work is like. The ETU ensures that the trainee undertakes a variety of work experiences to make an informed choice.

The ETU uses resources such as a comprehensive interactive careers information system (JIIG-CAL Explorer, software, JIIG-CAL Careers Research Centre, Edinburgh University, Edinburgh, UK). Specific careers assessments have been made by the careers service for certain individuals. However the use of such assessments can be limited. Recently a man experiencing Asperger syndrome, who has proved in each work situation he has undertaken that he cannot cope with change or new demands and becomes highly stressed, undertook a careers assessment (questions and answers) which concluded that he should seek work that offers him flexibility, variety and change! Used in isolation, with no practical evidence to support it, such conclusions could be misleading, and inappropriate for the individual. This again illustrates the need for a specialist service in autism to work together with a mainstream service. In the case of an individual who experiences Asperger syndrome accessing support from mainstream services on an 'outreach' basis from the ETU, the ETU is often required to encourage other professionals not to be misled by an individual's ability to articulate and use impressive vocabulary.

Once a trainee has undertaken a variety of work experiences and found a career area that he/she is suited to and that his/her autism can cope with, a career plan would be developed. The trainee may then need to gain the qualifications necessary and undertake appropriate training to achieve his/her aim. The trainee maintains a National Record of Achievement (available from the Department of Employment), which was introduced to provide a single common format to summarise an individual's overall record and to provide a standard presentational style.

ENCLAVE WORK

Before entering work situations in open employment, trainees undertake work in the secure, non-threatening environment of the ETU. The key objectives for enclave work are to:

- develop team work
- develop understanding about the purpose / importance of doing a job of work
- provide a valuable service to local employers
- give opportunity for work skills to be assessed
- provide opportunity to see how trainees respond to the demands of work
- prove to employers the value and quality of work skills of the individual who experiences autism or Asperger syndrome.

The ETU undertakes a wide variety of work to provide the opportunity for trainees to use as broad a range of skills as possible. It is vital to ensure that the trainee understands the relevance of doing a job and trainees are always involved in the complete process of collecting work, undertaking it and returning it to a company. This helps to develop their overall understanding of the purpose of work. Examples of the types of work used in enclave work include: desk top publishing, i.e. designing posters, leaflets, signs, etc.; printing and folding leaflets; enlarging written material for the visually impaired; simple and complex assembly work; clerical work, i.e. photocopying, compiling promotional material, filing, sorting material; and making various components for industry.

Trainees record each job undertaken including information about skills involved, description of how they felt about the work, trainers' comments on competency and observations of stress/anxiety manifested. The ETU enclave work differs from the North Carolina Model, as it undertakes work in the ETU environment. In North Carolina Enclaves (which in their interpretation is a group of up to eight people working with a job coach) work is undertaken in a business or industry.

ETU BUSINESS MODEL

The unit also runs a business involving silk screen printing and a small retail outlet. This facility provides both training and work. Some trainees may move on from their training in the business, others may continue to develop skills and work on a permanent basis. Running an 'in house' business provides trainees with vocational work without the demands of full mainstream integration. It provides meaningful occupation in which the valuable skills of an individual, who would be unable to cope with the social interactive demands of a mainstream setting, can be usefully employed. However such a business is no more isolated from society than any other business – trainees can have contact with customers, suppliers and other related industries if they choose to be involved with that element of running a business. The business is run entirely by itself, there is no reference to autism or Asperger syndrome as far as the public is concerned. The quality of the goods the customer buys is of a high standard and is competitive with other similar businesses.

As far as the general public is concerned, the fact that the people running the business happen to experience autism has no relevance to the goods that they purchase. This is important for the participating trainees, if they are not to be perceived as a different group in society. It also indicates attainment of the objective that the quality of their work is of an acceptable standard for industry.

The business referred to is a Silk Screen Printing Business and a T-Shirt Shop. This facility provides both training and work. The specific work opportunities it provides are listed in Appendix 8.2.

In the T-Shirt Shop, a video camera is used in training to record trainees serving customers. The films are used as training aids and are particularly important for developing the trainee's awareness of his/her communicative abilities. The trainer is also able to watch the trainee serving in the shop on a monitor in a separate room, and thus is able to intervene and support the trainee as soon as he/she requires it.

If a trainee is feeling that he/she requires support at any time whilst serving a customer he/she can ring a buzzer to alert the trainer. Such facilities are essential in providing the trainee with independence but also support when needed.

The following vignette illustrates how an individual with 'marketable' skills can make a realistic contribution to work without having to cope with open employment, it also illustrates the practical use of his specialised interests.

VIGNETTE 8.2

'D' is 27 and experiences autism. He has an obsessional interest in materials – i.e. types of fabric, where the fabric was manufactured, and is attentive to loose threads, marks or holes. 'D' was also interested in computers and was adept at removing programmes and generally enjoyed changing all previously programmed material – in particular changing the fonts. 'D' found it difficult to attend to verbal instruction, preferring to learn from practical experience. He enjoyed doing the opposite of what was asked of him. 'D' chose to isolate himself from others, communicating with them only on his own terms, and only when absolutely necessary. Although he has an extensive vocabulary and can also speak in other languages, he used language infrequently, preferring to type or write questions to others. 'D' had an absolute need for his routine; if this was disrupted, he had, on occasions, shouted or run out of a situation.

The task of the ETU was to develop constructive use of 'D'"s skills and to enable him to co-operate with others so that he could participate in the business.

The starting point for 'D' was use of his obsessional interest with fabric. 'D' was taught or rather he taught himself with written instructions, to inspect the quality of the garments, received from the suppliers, to be sold in the shop or used for printing. 'D' was given explicit written instructions explaining what action to take for every conceivable garment fault that could be found. 'D' learned quickly and adeptly. This fitted into a routine for 'D' that was also acceptable for the business.

'D' was then taught to use the computer constructively. Rather than listen to the trainer, he was shown lists of information and given instructions on how to use a spreadsheet. He was asked to put the information onto a spreadsheet, without being shown precisely how to do it. Because 'D' felt he was in control, he completed the task adeptly. He combined a fixation with fonts with the given task to maintain his interest. 'D' learned to compromise this desire to produce a variety of fonts (Gothic, Grundge, art nouveau, etc.) on business spreadsheets – by changing the text back to Helvetica at the last minute before saving and printing out. Again this was acceptable to both 'D' and to the business. In this way 'D' is now able to keep all business records on computer, to stock-check and to quality-check deliveries. He is required to do this on a regular, routine basis.

Enclave work and training in the business will have provided the trainee with a sample of different types of work and this experience may provide possibilities for future Mobile Crew Work. The trainee will move onto Mobile Crew Work when it is felt that he/she is ready. This will be a joint decision made by the trainee in consultation with trainer, key worker and sometimes parents or a relative. The 'on going' ETU assessment will be considered, as well as any PACT assessments made.

Before integration can take place in the form of the Mobile Crew Work, the trainer needs to satisfy him/herself that there is a degree of predictability about the person's behaviour. Obviously it is impossible to know how a person will react precisely in any new situation, but through the enclave work and ETU-based training, college contact, etc., there should be some pattern of behaviour established. If an individual has excellent work skills, can operate machinery, is precise in their work and so on, yet still has a tendency to throw the nearest object, run into the road or hit someone when faced with a problem, it would be considered too much of a risk for that individual to enter an integrated work setting at this stage.

With training, individuals are encouraged to face and deal with such emotion. Some are able to learn to keep their behaviour under control until they are in an environment where it can be safely expressed and under-stood. This is not to say that they are able to eliminate the feelings of anxi-ety, but rather they are able to put on an immensely brave act for the public, whilst inside themselves the anxiety is still there, until it can be expressed safely. Having the confidence in the trainer's ability to understand their frustration or anxiety, and being able to attribute it to Asperger syndrome helps some individuals to feel more in control of their disability.

The ETU through its understanding of an individual would become aware of specific difficulties that would cause the individual stress, and it is this knowledge that the trainer then takes to the integrated work setting, with the individual, in mobile crew work. It is the responsibility of the trainer to understand what will be required of an individual in work and to look for and deal with potential difficulties.

MOBILE CREW WORK EXPERIENCE

A Mobile Crew is a small group, usually consisting of one or two trainees and a trainer, who go into companies and undertake assignments of work experience as a team. The trainer actually undertakes the work as well as the trainees. The trainer is able to teach trainees within the work place, working through difficulties as they arise, and encouraging the trainee to develop his/her own coping strategies. The trainer encourages trainees to under-stand and use support services within the work place, so that he/she is able to access support from other colleagues without relying on the trainer. This provision of Mobile Crew Work for most trainees will be their first experi-ence of integration into employment. The trainer will have worked with the individual in the ETU and will have developed a working relationship with him/her. The trainer will have an awareness of how the individual's autism/Asperger syndrome affects them.

The key objectives for the Mobile Crew are:

- gradual controlled integration
- training in situ, addressing difficulties as they arise
- security for trainee
- to take the opportunity to prove to employers the value of the trainee's work
- to make a valuable contribution to the company
- for the trainee to gain experience of various types of work to make informed choices for their future
- to assist in providing information to company employees about autism /Asperger syndrome.

GGH Mobile Crews differ from the North Carolina model in that they are most often used for work experience purposes and are on a much smaller scale. However, they are similar in that they both provide excellent opportunities to assess directly the individual's work skills and behaviours, while providing sufficient supervision to ensure that a quality job is performed (Van Bourgondien and Woods 1992). With the ETU model, the trainer also undertakes the work themselves, this not only helps to ensure the job is achieved (providing the trainer has the necessary skills) it relieves the pressure from the trainee to get a job done by a deadline completely by themselves, and it also gives the trainer a comprehensive appreciation of what the job entails and the demands it has upon the individual. The trainer, trainee and employer together draw up a programme teaching the task itself, which also includes skills needed in social interaction, appropriate dress, awareness of health and safety, and so on. The programme is broken down in a task analysis type method and the trainee's performance is recorded each time the skill is used. For some individuals, programmes may include the use of a series of photographic or diagrammatic instructions to assist the individual in understanding specifically what is required of them. The trainee records his/her own performance in consultation with the trainer or employer. Video recording is useful in training, and on occasions the use of video recording through a company's security system has enabled an individual to have the opportunity of using this teaching medium without the camera being intrusive in the work place.

When a trainee is undertaking Mobile Crew Work, it is essential that regular liaisons take place with the trainee's other support network – to ensure that the trainer is made aware of any stress being caused by the work, that may be manifesting itself in the home situation.

When a Mobile Crew first start at a company, the trainer ensures a 'secure' area for the trainee. This may be an empty office, or an infrequently used coffee room, where the trainee can go if they are feeling particularly stressed. When a person first starts in a working environment, there may be unforeseen circumstances that may cause much stress to the individual. At this stage in the training, a 'safe' area within a host company is very useful. This area may also be used for the trainer to address inappropriate incidents with the trainee that have just occurred – away from other employees, thus avoiding embarrassment and more stress. For trainees who experience Asperger syndrome, this is very useful, particularly because of the difficulties many people experience in communication, or in controlling their emotions when presented with an unforeseen situation. An example of this is given in the following vignette:

VIGNETTE 8.3

Trainer Ann and trainee Phil were undertaking Mobile Crew Work experience in a manufacturing company. This was Phil's first work experience. Their task was to work in the office making up packs of promotional material for the company to send abroad by the end of the week. This task involved much photocopying. Phil quickly worked out how to use the photocopier and began to complete the task. The task involved having to photocopy some material and then to compile it, into a set order, in a binder. There were a number of factors to be taken into consideration. None of this caused Phil any problem. The next time Phil had to use the photocopier, there was a small queue. This interrupted Phil's process – he had gone to do the next step as he had been shown, yet was unable to achieve it as the photocopier was not available. Neither the trainer nor the employer had mentioned the possibility of a queue, or what to do if there was one. Phil panicked and started to head for the corridor, beginning to shout. The trainer was able to immediately direct him to the pre-determined 'safe' area. Here she was able to calm him and discuss the incident making Phil see the inappropriateness of his behaviour and provide him with alternative reactions next time he was confronted with a queue. In this way the employee at the photocopier was not aware of the incident, the trainee was made aware of his mistake and taught an appropriate skill to use should the incident reoccur.

One of the objectives of the ETU is to compensate for the specific skill deficits of an individual (i.e. flexibility and initiative). There are few jobs that do not require the worker to show some initiative and degree of flexibility. The trainer needs to anticipate a range of possible variants that may present themselves to the individual related to the work he/she is doing. Having identified these, the trainer then teaches these variants to the trainee, so that he/she can draw upon them when needed. If an individual works at a set speed and has a set order of working, for example washing, drying and putting away glasses in a pub, he/she may need to be taught that when there is a rush on, he/she will only be required to dry the glasses whilst someone else washes. For some individuals, particularly those who experience Asperger syndrome, a basic variation may have to be built into their programme. It can be difficult for the individual to see why there being a rush on should affect the work they have been instructed to do. Gradually, through Mobile Crew Work, the trainer is able to teach the trainee many of the unwritten rules of society, developing their skills in communication – both verbal and non-verbal. Such training must happen in the work situation.

Having completed a number of Mobile Crew Work experiences, and with the experience drawn from these, the trainee has the following options:

to progress to work experience with a job coach (see below)
to develop specific skills at a training college for a chosen career path
to return to enclave work if the stress of integrated work has proven to be insurmountable at this time

if a particular work area has not been identified through the Mobile Crew Work to date, to continue with further Mobile Crew Work.

WORK EXPERIENCE WITH A JOB COACH

The job coach works alongside the trainee in work experience or employment. The job coach does not undertake the work himself (as in the Mobile Crew Model), the role is to assist the trainee in dealing with his/her autism/Asperger syndrome in the work situation. The job coach will have developed a relationship previously with the trainee and will have an awareness of how autism or Asperger syndrome affects the individual before work experience commences.

The key objectives for the job coach are:

* to encourage trainee to develop his/her own coping strategies within the *specific* work environment
* to encourage trainee to develop skills to gain his/her future support from appropriate people within the company (reducing gradually trainer's support)
* to provide and develop trainees own security but not dependency
* to assist other employers in teaching trainee skills of a job
* with the trainee and employer, to assist in assessing placement and progress
* to assist in educating employer and employees about autism/Asperger syndrome.

ROLE OF JOB COACH SUPPORTING AN INDIVIDUAL IN EMPLOYMENT

When a person enters employment, he/she may need a job coach to support him/her through the above-listed objectives. After a period of time the person may feel that he/she does not require full support from the job coach, and such support would be gradually withdrawn. It is essential that the ETU maintains contact with the person and the employer to ensure that the job coach is called in again in the future if required. The person who experiences autism or Asperger syndrome may have learned to cope in a specific working environment – if some elements of this change this may disrupt the 'status quo' of the individual and they may need the job coach back in work for a time to help restore this. There cannot be a time limit or cut off point for this, a significant change may not happen for a period of months or years.

SUPPORTIVE EMPLOYMENT SERVICES IN THE UK

The Disability Employment Advisor, who is part of a team of disability specialists in the PACT, assists a person with a disability by providing:

- enhanced assessment of work skills
- advice on suitable training
- suitable jobs
- current supported employment schemes:
  Supported Placement Scheme
  Job Introduction Scheme
  Access to Work Scheme
- useful specialist equipment
- information on voluntary or private specialist training services.

Further information regarding any of the above can be obtained from the Disability Employment Advisor through the local Job Centre.

A Supported Employment Scheme linked with a specialist employment service, provides comprehensive support for the individual who experiences autism or Asperger syndrome.

Employers themselves are becoming more aware of the importance of integrating people with a disability into employment. The Disability Symbol Campaign is a campaign run by the Employment Service aimed at raising the awareness of employers to the abilities of people with a disability, and encouraging them to make a commitment to them. The disability symbol (with the slogan: 'Positive about Disabled People') has been developed so that people with disabilities will know which employers will be positive about their abilities, and employers can show their commitment to good practice by employing disabled people (Department of Employment 1993).

CHAPTER SUMMARY

A successful specialist employment service needs to understand the specific difficulties a person who experiences autism or Asperger syndrome has in accessing mainstream employment. It must address these needs and provide the individual with the necessary skills and supportive environmental factors to succeed in work. Such a service would benefit from working with other mainstream training and employment services in order to provide comprehensive support, assessment and training for the individual. A service needs to provide a continuum of provision, catering for those people, who, with training, can progress into open employment, yet also provide 'in house' meaningful vocational work for those who would find open employment unsuitable, and require a specialised work environment specifically tailored to their needs. Teaching methods need to reflect the trainers' understanding of the individual, with the emphasis on clear direct unequivocal instruction, often supplemented by visual material – photographs and diagrams. Training needs to be at the pace of the individual, with continual assessment and liaison with the individual's support network. The framework of gradual progression from ETU based training, enclave work, through to Mobile Crew Work experience and then on to work experience with a job coach allows for comprehensive training to take place. There needs to be the flexibility within the system to allow the individual to take steps back when necessary, without this being regarded as failure.

The GGH ETU, now in its third year, continues to develop as the trainees' requirements change. It is currently working on its outreach work with individuals not directly attending the service, but who need support in their established work place or training course.

ACKNOWLEDGEMENTS

The author wishes to record her appreciation to the Manager of GGH, Jackie McCormick, and to colleagues of GGH, in particular Deborah Veal and Adrian Finn; also to the late Judith Frewer for her direction in careers work in the setting up of the service, to Dawn Johansen and Ian Crump for their commitment to working with our service at the PACT office, and to Keith Matthews for his support in the development of the Silk Screen Printing Business. The support of many local employers and of Stroud College of Further Education is gratefully acknowledged. Alison Matthews is the Manager of the ETU, GGH and the Symbol Manager for Gloucestershire Committee for the Employment of People with Disabilities.

APPENDIX 8.1

Details of PACT assessment of work skills

The ETU used ten work samples that assessed the trainee's ability to perform certain types of tasks, suitable for a range of jobs. Outlines of some of the activities undertaken in each task and a few suggestions for the types of jobs that would use these skills are listed below.

Fine finger dexterity, use of small tools for precision work

Suitable for: Appliance Repairer, Electrician, Plumber, Automobile Mechanic, Office Machine Servicer, Vending Machine Repairer, Welder, Assembler

General clerical skills, routine office duties

Suitable for: File Clerk, Library Assistant, Audit Clerk, Parcel-Post Clerk, Telephone Answering Service Operator, Typist, Mail Clerk

Assembly line work

Suitable for: Conveyor Operator, Toy Assembler, Motor Assembler, Machine Feeder, Dry-Cleaner Helper, Farm Hand, General Assembly Line Work

Detailed sorting and classifying

Suitable for: Laboratory Tester, Photographer, Sample Worker, Parking Meter Collector, Sales Agent, Coin-Vending Machine Collector, Shoe Repairer, Hair Stylist, Television Installer

Co-ordination of hand-eye-foot

Suitable for: Sewing Machine Operator, Fork Lift Truck Operator, Laundry Labourer, Off-Set Press Operator

Dawn Johansen, Occupational Psychologist
Gloucester Placing Assessment and Counselling Team

APPENDIX 8.2

Work opportunities provided by GGH ETU business

Training based at the Silk Screen Printing workshop:

practical book keeping, ordering, clerical work
printing, use of printing carousel, tunnel dryer
design work and preparation of art work for printing
screen making, use of vacuum exposure unit
marketing and selling
customer contact and delivery of goods
health and safety
use of communal facilities for employees of other businesses at workshop complex.

Training based at retail outlet:
  training as a shop assistant
  selling, use of cash register
  shelf filling
  stock taking/ordering stock
  book keeping
  appropriate customer care
  health and safety
  personal presentation/appearance.

BIBLIOGRAPHY

Bishop, D.V.M. (1989) Autism, Asperger's syndrome and semantic-pragmatic disorder: where are the boundaries? *British Journal of Disorders of Communication*, **24**, 107–121.

Datlow Smith, M.D. (1990). Autism and Life in the Community: Successful Interventions for Behavioural Challenges. Baltimore, Paul H. Brookes Publishing.

Employment Service (1993). *Employing People with Disabilities*. Department of Employment, London

Employment Service (1994). *Access to Work*. Department of Employment, London.

Employment Service (1994). *Offering Job Opportunities in Supported Placements*. Department of Employment, London.

Employment Service (1994). *The Job Introduction Scheme*. Department of Employment, London.

Golding, M., Graves, E. and Hickling, B. (1985). *The Special Curricular Needs of Autistic Children*. Ealing, The Association of Head Teachers of Autistic Children and Adults.

Grandin, T. and Scariano, M.M. (1986). *Emergence Labelled Autistic*. California, Arena Press.

Kanner, L. (1943). Autistic disturbances of affective contact. *Nervous Child*, **2**, 217-250.

National Record of Achievement. The Employment Department, Sheffield, UK.

Van Bourgondien, M.E. and Woods, A.V. (1992). Vocational possibilities for high functioning adults with autism. In E. Schopler and G.B. Mesibov (eds.) *High Functioning Individuals with Autism*. New York, Plenum Press.

9

Health care of adults with autism

Gillian Wainscott and John Corbett

L ITTLE HAS been written about the special concerns with respect to physical health that affect adults with autism. Certainly they are as much prone to problems and illnesses as the general population. In addition there is known association with numerous other medical conditions (for a detailed account and recent review see Gillberg and Coleman 1995). These include Fragile-X and other chromosomal abnormalities, tuberous sclerosis, neurofibromatosis, hypomelanosis of Ito, Goldenhaar syndrome, Rett syndrome, Moebius syndrome, phenylketonuria, lactic acidosis, hypothyroidism, rubella embryopathy, herpes encephalitis, cytomegalovirus, William's syndrome, and Duchenne muscular dystrophy, all of which bring their own detrimental influences to physical health, affect mortality and may also change the presentation of autism itself. Many of these conditions are diagnosed for the first time in infancy and childhood, but their sequelae are life-long and influence physical well-being throughout life. Gillberg, in his two Gothenburg studies, has documented in detail their incidence and has estimated that if thorough investigations are made of people with autism – and this includes full neurological work-up, X-ray investigation, CT and MRI scanning, metabolic screening of blood and urine, and virological screening, then over one third will be found to have a co-existing medical condition. Whether or not it is helpful for each individual to undergo such a thorough assessment, or whether this in itself can do more harm than good should be debated for each person, depending on the circumstances pertaining for that person at that time. Investigations which are not essential for immediate treatment may be left until the individual concerned is older and better able to co-operate.

In addition to the long, though not exhaustive, list enumerated above, the rate of epilepsy in autism is reported at around 30–50% by adult life. This includes children who have early-onset seizures and those who suffer infantile spasms which are often followed by the development of an autistic syndrome. Many of these have remitted by adulthood, but some people with autism develop epilepsy around the time of puberty. This will be discussed

185

in more detail later in this chapter in the section entitled, 'Epilepsy and autism', but it provides the most important indicator of dysfunction of the brain in people with autistic continuum disorders.

MEDICAL ASSESSMENT

Thus the autistic person has the same health care needs as the general population. In addition they may have special needs associated with any of their co-existing medical conditions. Superimposed on this scenario are the problems related directly to the autism. These will affect the method by which the person with autism obtains the care they may need in adulthood.

Medical care is likely to have been fragmented in childhood, as parents have sought advice and diagnoses from different specialists. By adult life the person may be well known to paediatricians and developmental psychiatrists, and, in later life, to neurologists, physicians and mental health services as well as their own general practitioner, who may have to bring all these opinions together. In addition, because of the presentation in early life, numerous other professionals will be involved, including the members of both clinical and educational teams which the person will come into contact with during their life.

The presence of a new physical illness may be unsuspected initially by carers. Reduced or atypical communication may make it difficult for the person to describe any pain or discomfort arising from different parts of the body, and particularly general malaise. The sudden onset of screaming or temper outbursts, increased restlessness or other disturbed behaviour may indicate physical ailments as diverse as toothache, earache or abdominal pain, while chronic fatigue, menstruation and epileptic disorders lead to even greater problems in diagnosis. Unexpected changes in behaviour should always alert carers to the possibility of physical illness, as it is easy to attribute an increase in behaviour or emotional disturbance to the underlying pervasive developmental disorders of which autism is a part.

Physical examination can present a challenge. It may be difficult to explain the nature of the medical examination which is needed and ensuing resistance or violent reaction may result in a less than thorough evaluation. The examination may have to be repeated if nothing positive is found on the first occasion and symptoms persist. Pain often precedes any localising signs, which may only be picked up later. An example is in the presentation of appendicitis, where the initial symptoms may be generalised abdominal discomfort, anorexia and nausea, which the autistic patient may find difficult to explain and it may be some hours, or even longer, before the pain localises to the right lower abdomen with the characteristic signs found on medical examination.

Laboratory studies, which may involve uncomfortable procedures such as the taking of blood samples, or more simply the collection of urine, may also prove difficult as may sophisticated diagnostic tests such as EEG or brain scanning (CAT, EMR and PET),[1] which involve patient co-operation, and considerable tolerance and help on the part of the patient and their family carers who will need to be present during the examination. Some of the more recent advances in technology may subject an individual to a frightening array of unpleasant experiences which are bad enough for even the best communicators in the world!

It is easy to understand that these experiences will create special problems for people with autism who may be intolerant to some auditory or visual sensations. It is therefore incumbent upon the physician to weigh up more carefully the potential benefit of the investigation to the patient balancing it against the distress it would cause to explain more carefully to patient and carer the precise details of what is involved so that suitable strategies may be devised to lessen the distress.

It must be remembered that difficult or costly investigations should only be carried out in routine clinical practice if there is likely to be direct benefit to the patient. Any procedures demanded by parents, carers or teachers to find a physical cause for the autism, or research procedures to benefit our knowledge of the health problems of autistic people more generally require very careful consideration and preparation.

If admission to hospital is indicated, the distress that may be experienced by the routine-bound autistic child or adult exceeds, both in quality as well as severity, the understandable distress experienced by the general population. It is important that the autistic patient retains links with their own familiar world and this can be achieved by the provision of well-loved favourite objects and by non-anxious reassurance from parents, carers or other friendly people during illness or diagnosis.

PREVENTATIVE MEDICAL CARE

Preventative medical practices include immunisations, sight testing and hearing screening. These may have been overlooked or even avoided during infancy or other vulnerable periods of life, such as puberty or the menopause, because of difficulties that may have been anticipated in their administration, and it may be better to do some investigations during calmer periods.

---

[1] Electroencephalography (EEG) is carried out by Clinical Neurophysiologists, Computerised Axial Tomography (CAT or CT), Electromagnetic Resonance (EMR) and Magnetic Resonance (MRI) imaging, Positron Emission Tomography (PET) are all carried out at hospital radiology or imaging departments.

Immunisations may have been neglected in the autistic child because of the additional concern that a neurologically impaired person is at a higher risk from adverse side effects, though current recommendations, e.g. from the American Academy of Pediatrics, state that children with static neurological disorder (and this encompasses uncomplicated autism), should be immunised. There are undoubtedly a number of autistic adults who have been denied the benefits of this protection and will be at risk of contracting illness in later life. Some viral illnesses such as measles, mumps and rubella (German measles) can be devastating and can also have serious neurological complications of their own.

One of the major problems facing the doctor and audiologist is the assessment of hearing. It is important to exclude deafness as early as possible during childhood, because this can contribute to communication problems, while, conversely, an inappropriate amplification of sound may be very upsetting to the non-deaf autistic child. For reasons of expediency assessment of hearing may have been neglected and its evaluation far from complete, and deafness should always be considered during adult life, whether as an enduring phenomenon which has never been properly evaluated, or as an additional new entity when there is any change in behaviour which might appear to result from an increased difficulty in communication. Careful observation of the person's response to sound can be more important than specialised tests, as these can be difficult to administer. Specialised hearing tests such as evoked-response audiometry, where recording may be made directly of the brain's response and processing of sound, may be advisable and are less dependent on patient co-operation. These will give an indication of the passage of nerve impulses from the ear to various levels in the brain.

PREVENTATIVE DENTAL CARE

Preventative dental care is of particular importance in avoiding the neglect of tooth and gum infections, which will produce considerable discomfort with secondary behavioural and nutritional problems. The autistic adult is at greater risk from both these problems. Because of their communication problems, the rate of congenital dental abnormality is higher in the population with learning disability and autistic problems. The seemingly bizarre behaviours shown by the person with autism include many which affect the mouth, such as grinding of the teeth, the introduction of strange and often dirty objects into the mouth, and biting, both themselves and other people or objects.

Eating habits may not be conducive to good dental health. Food fads or the insistence of sameness in the diet, as well as resulting in nutritional deficiencies, may predispose to gum disease or dental caries, particularly when carbohydrates are involved and this may lead to more general ill health. This situation may be further compounded when carbohydrate-rich foods, e.g. sweets, are used for reward or to reinforce of good behaviour. Thus the scene may have been set in childhood for dental problems and gingival disease in early adult life.

Dental hygiene, such as the regular correct usage of the toothbrush and the process of flossing may be difficult to establish, especially when dental deformity may predispose to the entrapment of food particles between overlapping teeth. The situation may be further compounded by the use of some drugs, such as phenytoin, which can cause gum hypertrophy and gingivitis.

The visit to the dentist, particularly if it occurs as an emergency situation, can cause utter uproar in the surgery which may be prevented by careful dental hygiene and preparation. People with autism tend to be more than usually unco-operative with strangers. Regular contact with the dentist before problems develop will facilitate familiarisation with the unusual appearance of the surroundings and will allow time for the development of trust and confidence. The dentist is also provided with the opportunity to become acquainted with the patient and to evaluate their patterns of behaviour. There are an increasing number of community dental services and practices which provide experienced and empathetic care for the person with a developmental disability including autism.

EPILEPSY AND AUTISM

Epilepsy merits particular mention. In early infantile autism, reported rates vary from a third to a fifth of those with moderate and severe learning disabilities, and, as has been mentioned earlier, epilepsy usually arises before adulthood but may persist and be troublesome later in life.

Epilepsy is not uncommon in people with a mild learning disability and occasional seizures may occur for the first time in adolescence and adult life. Autism is associated with all types of epilepsy and adults who have suffered from infantile spasms in infancy have an increased chance of developing autism or autistic-like behaviour. This is not just related to the associated learning disability which is seen in many children who have suffered this particular form of epilepsy. It occurs typically in the second year of life and is characterised by typical 'salaam' attacks, where the sitting child falls forward rapidly, often many times a day. The EEG in children with infantile spasms is grossly abnormal, even between attacks, and this may give a clue to the cause of autism, as it may occur in previously normal children at a vulnerable phase in the development of communication and interpersonal relationships. Infantile spasms are associated with tuberous sclerosis, which itself is associated with autism, although a small number of people with these two conditions have no history of epilepsy.

Because of communication difficulties, certain types of seizure may be under reported, in particular, complex partial seizures and childhood absence seizures (petit mal). They have also been reported to masquerade as autism when they are very frequent, and may persist in adult life. Children and adolescents may have staring spells which may be difficult to differentiate from posturing and other behaviours which are part of the autism. This dilemma in diagnosis between different forms of epilepsy, autism and other bizarre behaviours requires very careful assessment and this is much aided by the use of ambulatory EEG monitoring, where the person with autism wears a small tape recorder connected to scalp electrodes. Epileptic discharges can then be recorded in everyday life and related to changes in behaviour including lapses in attention.

Generalised tonic-clonic seizures (grand mal) are the most frequent form of epilepsy in the general population. They are relatively common in people with autism, but are associated usually with other kinds of epilepsy and occur as secondary tonic-clonic seizures. Complex partial seizures may lead to abnormal experiences such as hallucinations with feelings of fear and anger which can be very disturbing to the person with autism, particularly during the recovery phase

A number of medical conditions that are associated with autism predispose to fits. If an adolescent or adult starts having seizures, then further more intensive investigations, that might have been deferred at an earlier age for reasons previously discussed (in 'Medical assessment'), may now be indicated, which may include special EEG recordings, various forms of brain scanning (CAT, MRI, PET). During childhood, tuberous sclerosis, neurofibramotosis, and the inborn error of metabolism, such as phenylketonuria, should have been excluded. At a later age Rett syndrome may need to be excluded in girls and Fragile-X syndrome in boys.

Treatment of the associated epilepsy is primarily with anticonvulsants when the seizures are recurrent. The decision to give medication depends on the frequencies of seizures sustained. Treatment is often not started after the first seizure and people with only a few fits separated by relatively long intervals do not usually require any drug treatment. This pattern occurs in about a third of adolescents with autism, and specialist assessment is indicated as the decision not to treat infrequent seizures must be weighed against the recent finding that early treatment may prevent recurrence.

Sodium valproate and carbamazepine are, at present, the drugs of first choice. Newer agents such as lamotrigine and gabapentin show good promise in both being equally effective and, because of their novel modes of action, freer from side effects. It may be that in the future, monotherapy with lamotrigine or gabapentin alone might be the first line of treatment. Other drugs are in development for the control of the yet more intractable forms of epilepsy. Carbamazepine may precipitate tics or Tourette syndrome and for this reason needs to be used with caution in people with autism who are particularly prone to this condition.

It is necessary to monitor both beneficial and adverse effects of treatment. Because of the difficulties in communication inherent in autism, it is more desirable for the person with epilepsy and autism to keep a detailed diary record of his/her seizures in collaboration with or supervised by his/her carers. The diary has the added advantage of being able to facilitate the correlation of other external events with any observed deterioration in fit frequency, severity or duration. The control of anticonvulsant drug dosage, particularly of carbamazepine and to a lesser extent valproate, should include regular estimation of the level in the blood to ensure that a therapeutic dose is being received. Side effects caused by the anticonvulsants are dealt with in detail in Chapter Ten.

AUTISM AND ADOLESCENCE

All ages bring their own problems, with their own effects on physical health, but none more so than adolescence. Puberty occurs in autistic children at the same age and in the same way as in normal children. Because of the lack of imagination of most autistic adolescents, the physical changes that occur are often accepted in a surprisingly matter-of-fact way.

Most autistic girls who have a reasonable level of self-care are able to cope with the practical problems of menstruation with supervision. Resistance to change and insistence on routines can be exploited to good effect to maintain good standards of hygiene. Associated dysmenorrhoea may be severe and especially distressing as an autistic girl may have difficulty in associating this pain with the subsequent menstrual blood flow. Sedatives and analgesics, smooth muscle relaxants or prostaglandin synthetase inhibitors may be helpful as the first line of treatment. If these are not effective, then the oral contraceptive pill will often reduce if not abolish the pain altogether. This treatment has the added advantage of making the menstrual period completely regular and predictable, and thus more acceptable to the routine-bound autistic girl. It may also reduce significantly the amount of blood lost and have beneficial effects on any pre-menstrual syndrome.

Apart from the overt sexual changes, adolescence is a time of change, not to say upheaval, in all bodily systems. It is a time of extremely rapid growth with consequent demand for calorific foods and particular nutrients. The characteristic eating pattern of adolescents is well known to most of their parents, and includes erratic meals at irregular intervals and varied and chaotic choice ranging from junk food and chips to fashionable trendiness encompassing, for example, various types of vegetarianism. Autistic adolescents, by virtue of their liking of sameness and routine, are probably exempt from the complications of intermittent relative fasting and feasting, but, because of their tendency to have very specific food fads, may be at risk of developing specific deficiencies, though these are rarely severe. The most common deficiency encountered is, arguably, iron deficiency, because there is an increased demand for iron with an expanding blood volume and increase in muscle mass, particularly in males. In women there is also loss of iron from the newly established menstrual blood flow. Iron deficiency leads to anaemia, which, whilst rarely profound, can cause tiredness with general malaise and possible behavioural changes. Vitamin deficiencies are rarer these days, perhaps because of the current fashion to 'fortify' all foods, from breakfast cereals to bedtime drinks, with all manner of 'healthy' additives. The autistic adolescent is likely to be taking some medication which might aggravate the risk of developing a specific vitamin deficiency. The best example of this in the past has been the use of phenytoin, prescribed for associated seizure control, which has led to folic acid deficiency and, in some cases, adverse effects on calcium metabolism with subsequent need for vitamin D supplements.

Eating disorders may have started in infancy, but, again, become a major problem in adolescence. Anorexia nervosa usually affects females and autism most commonly affects males, hence the incidence in people with autism is likely to be low, but this combination has been reported in the literature. Stiver and Dobbins (1980) described an autistic girl in her early teenage years who developed a life-threatening condition.

Obesity is more likely to be a problem. In spite of heightened awareness regarding healthy eating, a disappointingly high proportion of the general population are significantly overweight and this pattern often starts in childhood, and persists through adolescence and into adult life. Autistic adolescents start reaping the consequences of the use of food as reinforcers of good behaviour during childhood and though advice has always been to use healthy low-calorie foods, such as raw vegetables, in this way, unfortunately such foods are rarely satisfying and do not produce the desired effect. Thus the scene is set for autistic adolescents to demand more high-calorie foods and the somewhat more sedentary lifestyle will further compound the tendency to obesity. This is further aggravated by drugs which may have been prescribed for behaviour modification, e.g. phenothiazines.

Finally, a small number of people with autism are sensitive to particular foods such as tartrazine (in artificially coloured orange drinks), vanilla and milk products and this allergy may present as disturbed behaviour. The only reliable way to test for this is to avoid each suspected food for a period and then 'challenge' the person with the suspect food.

Other physical problems of adolescence include infections and in particular glandular fever or infectious mononucleosis. Typically this presents as profound fatigue, general malaise, sore throat and generalised lymphadenopathy, usually most marked in the cervical region. More serious complications include splenomegaly. As with all illnesses, the vague initial symptoms may be particularly difficult to evaluate in the autistic person. The diagnosis is usually confirmed on haematological testing, but, as in previous instances, drugs that are frequently prescribed to autistic people, either for associated conditions or for behaviour modification, may interfere both with clinical presentation and with laboratory testing, e.g. carbamazepine (given for epilepsy) and chlorpromazine (possibly given for behaviour problems) might cause leucopenia, thus confusing the diagnosis of a viral infection, and chlorpromazine, in addition, may have an effect on liver function, has been known to cause jaundice and may cause photosensitivity on exposure to sunlight.

The major skin problem affecting adolescents is acne. This is more prevalent in young males and the autistic adolescent is equally prone to this potentially disfiguring problem. Mild cases can be treated by scrupulous cleansing and the use of topical agents, but success depends on regular and careful application. However, the patterns of behaviour seen in autism may facilitate rather than hinder this. More severe cases and where there is superimposed infection may require the administration of systemic antibiotics, still usually tetracyclines and the interaction of some antibiotics with anti-convulsant medication should not be forgotten.

AUTISM IN LATER LIFE

Very little has been written about the physical health problems developing in later life in people with autism. It is well recognised that mortality in the autistic population may be higher, at all ages, than in the general population. This increase is usually in the region of 2% and is associated both with any accompanying learning disability and any co-existing medical condition. As people grow older they are more prone to more physical illnesses, including degenerative conditions, which impede their mobility and this combined with usually an increasing weight makes assessment and treatment more difficult.

EMOTIONAL DISORDERS

Depression

Autism is a very isolating, lonely problem to cope with and each individual sufferer will react differently. It has recently been suggested that there may be a genetic link with severe depressive and manic depressive illness, which will require treatment with antidepressant therapy, including lithium carbonate which is useful in preventing recurrences (see Chapter Ten).

Much sadness, unhappiness and misery seen at vulnerable periods of life (puberty, the menopause and old age) is understandable in the light of the loneliness and communication problems which are part of the autistic condition. This and the bereavement reaction which follows loss of relatives, friends and carers require much understanding on the part of all those caring for people with epilepsy, and individual and group counselling and support are important.

Anxiety

People with autism have particular difficulty in coping with arousal, of which anxiety is the symptom, and particular stressors include environmental changes, specific phobias, high expressed emotion from family, carers and friends. Psychological techniques of stress management, e.g. relaxation, have a particular part to play in the treatment of anxiety in people with autism and is invariably the underlying process in challenging behaviours.

Tics and Tourette syndrome

People with autism very frequently suffer from movement disorders, including various stereotypies (i.e. repetitive movements with no apparent purpose) and tardive dyskinesia, due to sensitivity to psychotropic drugs given to manage behaviour. These movements need to be distinguished from the sudden sharp movements of circumscribed muscle groups, e.g. blinking and facial grimacing and head shaking which are characteristic of tic disorders.

It has recently been recognised that a more severe form of tic disorder, in which there are vocal tics, e.g. grunting and repetitive throat clearing and even shouted words which may have a sexual connotation (coprolalia), may occur in people with autism.

It has even been suggested that there may be a common genetic basis involving particular neurotransmitters such as serotonin, dopamine and neuropeptides (endogenous opiates). There may also be a link with obsessive compulsive disorders in which there are complex rituals or checking behaviours.

Self-injurious behaviour occurs in a proportion of people with autism and is seen in a third of people with Tourette syndrome. Recent advances in treatment, using neurotransmitter antagonists hold out hope for more focused treatment.

Schizophrenia

In the past, chronic schizophrenia was often mistaken for autism, particularly in adults living in institutions. There are many similarities between the two conditions and there are also similarities between Asperger syndrome and schizoid personality disorder – the latter is thought to be a precursor to some forms of functional psychosis.

Because of the communication difficulties suffered by the autistic person, it is often difficult to say whether there is lack of insight, which is the cardinal requisite for the diagnosis of severe functional psychosis such as schizophrenia, manic depressive psychosis or organic confusional states.

A very careful developmental history and assessment, together with an account of an abrupt change in behaviour and emotional status is essential in diagnosis. Such is the difficulty in distinguishing these conditions on occasions, that it has been said that schizophrenia never occurs in people with autism and it may be that the underlying cognitive deficits which characterise autism preclude the forms of thought disorder which are diagnostic of schizophrenia. In spite of this, occasional cases are seen where a person with autism develops clear-cut hallucinations or delusions symptomatic of schizophrenia, toxic confusional states and other organic psychoses.

Sometimes, a trial of antipsychotic medication is indicated and a rapid response to such treatment may be diagnostic.

CHAPTER SUMMARY

Autism is a developmental disorder and not an illness, but people with autistic problems are prone to both physical and mental disorders and these will often be more difficult to diagnose and treat than is the case for people who do not suffer from pervasive developmental disorders of the autistic type.

Adults with autism require access to developmental psychiatric services and this can only be achieved if more people are empowered with more knowledge about the health problems of autistic people.

BIBLIOGRAPHY

Corbett, J. (1982). Epilepsy and the encephalogram in early childhood psychoses. In J.K. Wing and L. Wing (eds.) *Handbook of Psychiatry*, volume 3. Cambridge, Cambridge University Press, pp. 198-202.

Corbett, J. (1983). An epidemiological approach to the evaluation of services for children with mental retardation. In M.H. Remschimdt (ed.) *Epidemiological Approaches in Child Psychiatry*. Stuttgart, Theime.

Dalldorf, J. (1983). Medical needs of the autistic adolescent. In E. Schopler and G.B. Mesibov (eds.) *Autism in Adolescents and Adults*. New York, Plenum Press, pp. 149-168.

Gillberg, C. (1984). Infantile autism and other childhood psychoses in a Swedish urban region. Epidemiological aspects. *Journal of Child Psychology and Psychiatry*, **25**, 35-43.

Gillberg, C. (1991). The treatment of epilepsy in autism. *Journal of Autism and Developmental Disorders*, **21**, 61-77.

Gillberg, C. (1992). The Emmanuel Miller Lecture 1991: autism and autistic-like conditions-subgroups of disorders of empathy. *Journal of Child Psychology and Psychiatry*, **31**, 99-119.

Gillberg, C. and Coleman, M. (1995). *Biological Aspects of Autism*. Mac Keith Press, London, distributed by Cambridge University Press, Cambridge.

Gillberg, C. and Schaumann, H. (1983). Epilepsy presenting as infantile autism? Two case studies. *Neuropaediatrics*, **14**, 206-222.

Gillberg, C., Steffenburg, S. and Jakobsson, G. (1987). Neurobiologic findings in 20 relatively gifted children with Kanner-type autism or Asperger syndrome. *Developmental Medicine and Child Neurology*, **29**, 641-649.

Kopel, H.M. (1997). The autistic child in dental practice. *Journal of Current Adolescent Medicine*, **2**, 38-42.

Olsson, I., Steffenburg, S. and Gillberg, C. (1988). Epilepsy in autism and autistic-like conditions: a popular based study. *Archives of Neurology*, **45**, 666-668.

Riikonen, R. and Amnell, G. (1981). Psychiatric disorders in children with earlier infantile spasms. *Developmental Medicine and Child Neurology*, **23**, 747-760.

Rutter, M. (1970). Autistic children. Infancy to adulthood. *Seminars in Psychiatry*, **2**, 435-450.

Steffenburg S. (1991). Neuropsychiatric assessment of children with autism: a population based study. *Developmental Medicine and Child Neurology*, **33**, 495-511.

Steffenburg, S. and Gillberg, C. (1986). Autism and autistic-like conditions in Swedish rural and urban areas: a population-based study. *British Journal of Psychiatry*, **149**, 81-87.

Stiver, and Dobbins, (1980)

Taft, L.T. and Cohen, H.J. (1971). Hypsarrhythmia and childhood autism: a clinical report. *Journal of Autism and Childhood Schizophrenia*, **1**, 327-336.

Volkmar, F.R. and Nelson, D.S. (1990). Seizure disorders in autism. *Journal of the American Academy of Child and Adolescent Psychiatry*, **29**, 127-129.

10

Psychiatric and behavioural problems and pharmacological treatments

David J. Clarke

PSYCHIATRIC AND behavioural disorders are not uncommon among adults with autism and related disorders (Clarke *et al.* 1989). *Learning disability* also increases vulnerability to psychiatric disorder (Corbett 1979), and may be associated with autism. A substantial minority of adults with autism have epilepsy, and this may also increase vulnerability or cause diagnostic confusion.

Carers and professionals can do much to improve the quality of life of people with autistic disorders by recognising the clinical features of such additional disorders, and taking appropriate action to have them assessed and treated. It is important to distinguish between an additional psychiatric disorder and behavioural abnormalities which result directly from the autistic Triad of Impairments. Eccentric behaviour resulting from unusual preoccupations, or associated with social and language impairments, may easily be mistaken for psychotic illness. Maladaptive behaviours may result from emotional reactions to environmental changes (such as severe anxiety following a change in routine or staffing) and may be perplexing unless a knowledge of autism is combined with an acquaintance with psychiatric disorders and their presentation.

Behavioural disorders (such as inappropriate sexual behaviour, aggressive behaviour and self-injury) may limit opportunities and create challenges for services. Non-specific behavioural disorders such as abnormal aggression or loss of temper usually reflect the outcome of an interaction between an adult with autism and their environment. Such interactions may be complex (humans have the capacity to change their environment), and factors which initiate a behaviour may differ from those which predispose to it or maintain it. This is illustrated in Figure 10.1, using severe self-injurious behaviour by a man with fragile-X syndrome as an example. Fragile-X syndrome is a genetic disorder due to abnormal expansion of parts of the DNA 'genetic code' that has been found to be associated with social anxiety, autistic-like features (and sometimes autism) and a characteristic pattern of behaviour that often includes hand-biting in response to anxiety (Turk

1992). An episode of self-injury (such as abnormally severe wrist-biting) may start as a response to an anxiety-provoking environmental change (such as a change in key worker at a day centre). Men with fragile-X syndrome have a vulnerability to self-injury, and this *predisposition* may be increased when sensory impairments are also present (self-stimulation may increase among people with sensory impairments when there is a low level of external stimulation). Fragile-X syndrome causes soft-tissue laxity, which may lead to ear infections and hearing impairments, and the soft, velvety skin characteristic of fragile-X syndrome may be more vulnerable to injury. Self-injury through hand-biting may be *maintained* by its association with a reduction in anxiety and 'escape' from contact with an unfamiliar worker. Further factors (such as enjoying the attention of a familiar staff member attempting to provide comfort or terminate the self-injury) may then come into play. Secondary changes may eventually occur, one mechanism that is thought to play a part in maintaining some severe self-injury being a change in the opiate-like neuropeptide systems that are involved in the regulation of pain sensation. It has been suggested that some severe self-injury results in the release of such natural opiate-like substances, resulting in a reduction in pain sensation and a pleasant change in emotional state, reinforcing the behaviour and effectively creating a state of 'addiction' to self-injury. This hypothesis has led to the use of opiate-blocking substances in the treatment of self-injury, with benefits in some cases. Local irritation due to infection may cause itching and further injury through biting or scratching if not recognised and treated. The factors predisposing to, precipitating, and maintaining such behaviours must therefore be identified for each individual, so that management can be based on factors that remain operative and that are amenable to manipulation.

This chapter deals with the *pharmacological* (drug- or medication-based) treatment of psychiatric and behavioural disorders. In the case of severe (psychotic) psychiatric disorders, drug treatments are of proven value, and a major component in management. The evidence for the efficacy of pharmacological treatments in the management of non-specific behavioural problems is less well established. Some relevant studies are reviewed below. The emphasis in this chapter on psychopharmacology should not be taken as implying that such treatments are always appropriate, or should be used in isolation. In view of the complexities of many behavioural disorders, a pharmacological approach is often best combined with other interventions such as psychologically based strategies and environmental manipulations.

Special attention should be given to the balance between risk and benefit when using medications for unlicensed indications or in situations where efficacy has not been firmly established, and it is always necessary to tailor the treatment to the individual, and to take account of additional disabilities or

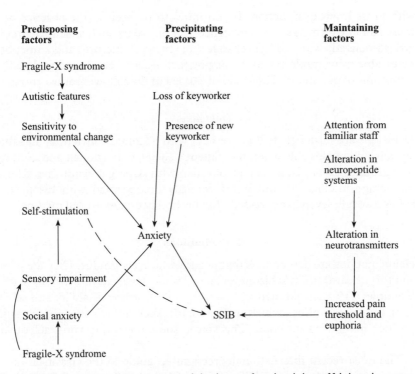

Figure 10.1 *Factors predisposing to, precipitating, and maintaining self-injury in a man with autism and the fragile-X syndrome. SSIB Seriously self-injurious behaviour*

disorders that are relevant to the selection of a particular drug. It is, for example, necessary to be aware of the relative effects of compounds on the seizure threshold when prescribing for someone with epilepsy, and similar considerations apply to other conditions such as constipation and cerebral palsy.

THE CLASSIFICATION OF PSYCHIATRIC DISORDERS AND THEIR CLINICAL FEATURES

Psychiatric disorders have been classified in many ways, most authors making a distinction between severe disorders (including 'psychotic' disorders in which reality-testing is impaired) and less severe disorders (such as 'neuroses'). Psychoses may be symptomatic (such as the dementias accompanying diseases such as Alzheimer's disease or Huntington's disease, or the delirious states secondary to infections or to drug use) or 'functional' (such as severe depression, schizophrenia or paranoid psychoses). The term 'functional' was used to describe psychotic disorders that were not associated with gross brain dysfunction. It continues to be used in the absence of a more suitable term in spite of evidence that disorders such as schizophrenia are associated with subtle changes in brain structure and function, detectable using modern neuro-imaging techniques. Terms used to describe symptoms of psychiatric illness are discussed in the following subsections.

Delusions

Delusions are false beliefs that are held with absolute conviction, and that are not understandable given the patient's social, educational, and cultural background. Example: a 36-year-old man with Asperger syndrome, who is of average intelligence and not previously preoccupied with his health, believes, while severely depressed, that his bodily organs are 'all missing'.

Hallucinations

Hallucinations are perceptions that occur without a stimulus. They are often auditory (heard), as in schizophrenia, or visual (seen), as in delirious states. Example: a 19-year-old man with autism, mild learning disability and schizophrenia hears 'voices', which make remarks such as 'he's washing his stuff up' 'he's never been any good'. The 'voices' sometimes argue with each other.

The most recent internationally recognised guide to the classification of psychiatric disorders is the *ICD-10 Classification of Mental and Behavioural Disorders*, published by the World Health Organisation (1992). 'ICD-10' stands for the Tenth Revision of the International Classification of Diseases. The following disorders are included within the classification, and readers are advised to consult the Clinical Guidelines if a detailed description of a disorder is required.

Dementias

Dementias are characterised by progressive impairments in memory and other cognitive abilities, leading to impaired judgment and thinking. There is (at least initially), no reduction in the level of consciousness as seen in delirium, and other symptoms (such as emotional lability, irritability, apathy or coarsening of social behaviour) may be present. For a confident diagnosis, symptoms should have been present for at least six months.

Delirium

Delirium is characterised by a reduction in awareness of the environment ('clouded consciousness'), memory impairments, disorientation, changes in the pattern of activity (such as increased reaction time) and disturbance of the sleep-wake cycle.

Schizophrenia

Schizophrenia is characterised by fragmentation of thought (often manifest as disordered speech, sometimes by the experiences of having thoughts inserted into or withdrawn from the mind), delusions of control or influence, or other bizarre delusions, specific types of auditory hallucinations, movement abnormalities, emotional abnormalities and disorders of the perception of free will, so that acts or emotions may be perceived as made or imposed by some external agency ('passivity experiences'). Different types of schizophrenia are recognised, each with a characteristic pattern of symptoms and course.

Schizophrenia is *not* 'a split personality' and it is very rarely associated with dangerously aggressive behaviour to other people (when this does occur in association with schizophrenia, the person concerned usually has other problems such as alcohol abuse or a personality disorder).

Delusional disorders

Delusional disorders are characterised by the presence of circumscribed delusions, without other symptoms characteristic of schizophrenia.

Acute and transient psychotic disorders

These are characterised by a sudden onset of psychotic symptoms (delusions, hallucinations, etc.), without an organic cause. Symptoms otherwise suggestive of schizophrenia may appear (usually fleetingly) but the disorder resolves within a month. In some people the disorder may apparently occur as a response to severely stressful events.

Mood disorders

Mood disorders include *manic* and *hypomanic* states, characterised by elated mood (sustained for several days) accompanied by features such as overactivity, talkativeness, disinhibition, decreased need for sleep and distractibility. Mania is the more severe form of the disorder, and may be accompanied by delusions or hallucinations.

Depressive disorders

Depressive disorders are characterised by low mood, loss of interest or pleasure in activities which are normally pleasurable, early waking, worsening of low mood in the morning, reduction in activity and appetite, weight loss and reduction in libido. Depressive disorders (or 'clinical depression') differ from everyday unhappiness or understandable low mood through the presence of these additional features, although a depressive syndrome may be *precipitated* by an event (such as bereavement) that would be expected to cause unhappiness. Severe depressive episodes may be accompanied by psychotic features such as delusions or hallucinations. Depressive disorders are associated with a much increased risk of self-harm. This may take the form of suicide or, more commonly among people with learning disabilities, severely self-injurious behaviour such as head-banging.

Bipolar disorders

Bipolar disorders are characterised by recurrent episodes of mania and/or depression.

Neurotic, stress-related and somatoform disorders

These include *phobias* (fears of objects or situations), *panic* disorder (characterised by unpredictable, intense episodes of fear with an abrupt onset, lasting minutes, and with features such as palpitations, sweating, or a feeling of 'going mad'), *generalised anxiety*, *conversion* ('hysterical') disorders, and *obsessive-compulsive disorder* which is characterised by obsessions (recurrent, unpleasant, intrusive, thoughts which are resisted and which cause distress) or compulsions (actions which the person carries out repetitively while acknowledging that there is no reason to do so). Example: a 33-year-old man has, for many years, switched the lights in each room in his house on and off five times before going to bed. He realises this serves no purpose, but feels so anxious that he cannot sleep if he has not performed the *compulsive ritual*. Rituals may be difficult to distinguish from stereotyped activities, which are usual among people with autism. The history of a *change* in behaviour, and the presence of *resistance* to the activity, may help diagnosis. Some pharmacological research (e.g. Gordon *et al.* 1993) suggests that rituals and stereotyped, repetitive behaviours occurring in autistic disorders may share underlying biological mechanisms.

Behavioural syndromes associated with physiological disturbances and physical factors

These include the eating disorders *anorexia nervosa* and *bulimia nervosa*. These are more common in women and are characterised by altered attitudes to eating and body image.

Personality disorder

Many types of personality disorder are listed in the classification. Three are of relevance when considering the differential diagnosis of autism (i.e. conditions which share some features, and should be distinguished because they do not include the Triad of Impairments seen in autism). Paranoid personality disorder is characterised by excessive sensitivity to setbacks or criticism, suspiciousness, ideas of self-reference and a tendency to misconstrue neutral or friendly actions as hostile or contemptuous. Schizoid personality disorder is characterised by emotional coldness, flattened affectivity, a limited capacity to express tender feelings, a consistent choice of solitary activities and an insensitivity to prevailing social norms and conventions. Dissocial personality disorder is characterised by unconcern for the feelings of others, persistent irresponsibility and disregard for social norms or rules, very low tolerance of frustration, incapacity to experience guilt or to profit from adverse experience and a proneness to blame others for behaviours causing conflict. In practice, features of several types of personality disorder often cause problems for any one individual.

Mental retardation/learning disability

Mental retardation (learning disability in the UK) is subdivided according to severity. Mild mental retardation usually results in delay in the understanding and use of language and difficulties with academic school work, but with well-preserved self-care skills and the ability to carry out practical and domestic tasks. Mild learning disability is associated with an IQ between 50 and 69 if formal testing is performed with a standardised test. Moderate, severe and profound retardation are also defined, although in practice they are often grouped together, the term 'severe learning disability' being used to describe people with IQs below 50. Many adults with autism also have a learning disability, both disorders being markers of underlying brain dysfunction which may result from a structural or functional abnormality. Some adults with autism have a specific genetic disorder (such as tuberous sclerosis). Such disorders may predispose to patterns of behaviour or emotional reaction, including behaviours which may be severely challenging.

Autistic disorders

The autistic disorders, termed *pervasive developmental disorders* in the ICD-10 classification, include childhood autism, atypical autism, Rett syndrome, Asperger syndrome, and some other categories.

Disorders with onset in childhood or adolesence

The behavioural and psychiatric disorders with onset usually occurring in childhood and adolescence include *hyperkinetic* disorders, characterised by overactivity and deficits in attention; *conduct* and *emotional* disorders, and other disorders with an onset that is usually in childhood such as enuresis (bedwetting), *tics* (sudden, involuntary, rapid, non-rhythmic, stereotyped movements or vocalisations) and *Tourette syndrome* (combined vocal and multiple motor tics). Some of these disorders (such as hyperkinetic syndromes and tics) are not uncommon among adults with autism, especially if the autistic disorder results from a genetic or metabolic abnormality. Hyperkinesis and autistic disorders are documented among children with tuberous sclerosis (Hunt and Dennis 1987), and may persist into adult life. Tourette syndrome has been described in association with autism in several reports (e.g. Kerbeshian and Burd 1986; Littlejohns *et al.* 1990), and the presence of tics may indicate a favourable response to dopamine-blocking medications (Fisher *et al.* 1986).

PHARMACOLOGICAL TREATMENTS

The efficacy of pharmacological treatments in the treatment of severe psychiatric disorders has been clearly established. The trials demonstrating efficacy have usually involved people with schizophrenia or other psychoses who did not also have autism or a learning disability, although there is no reason to assume that efficacy would differ markedly for a population of adults with autism and psychotic disorders. The evidence for the efficacy of drugs in treating behavioural disorders (such as abnormally aggressive or severely self-injurious behaviour) is less well established, although drug treatments can undoubtedly help *some* people with such problems.

The efficacy of antipsychotics and antidepressants

Davis and Garver (1978) summarised the results of over 200 double-blind studies comparing the antipsychotic drugs with placebo; antipsychotic medication was more effective in 85% of the trials. Cole *et al.* (1964), in a large trial of antipsychotic medication in acute schizophrenia, found that

75% of people receiving antipsychotics improved considerably, compared to 25% of people receiving placebo. A substantial proportion of those receiving placebo experienced a worsening of their mental state during the trial. The efficacy of antidepressant medication in the treatment of affective disorders has also been established beyond doubt. However, all effective medications have the potential to cause adverse effects ('side effects'), and so a choice of medication must take into account individual patient characteristics as well as the psychiatric diagnosis. In some cases (e.g. where a schizophrenic disorder is suspected, but the patient's limited use of language means that it is not possible to be certain of the clinical features), a trial of medication may be justified. Where there is uncertainty, the risk of treating a disorder without being sure of the diagnosis must be balanced against the risk of not treating a condition which may be associated with severe emotional distress and markedly abnormal behaviour (such as self-harm or aggressive behaviour) and which may result in injury, or markedly curtail opportunities.

Information about individual drugs that are used to treat psychiatric and behavioural problems is given below. Information about novel or controversial treatments is given in the section relating to the disorder in which they have been used. Full prescribing information for all drugs is available in the manufacturers' data sheets (Walker 1994).

Antipsychotics

Antipsychotic drugs abolish, or reduce the impact of, symptoms of psychosis such as delusions and hallucinations. Their efficacy in this respect is well established. They are also referred to as 'neuroleptics' or 'major tranquillisers', but they do not usually impair consciousness or cause paradoxical effects (such as impulsive behaviour which may follow disinhibition when alcohol or benzodiazepines are used). Their effects on depressive disorders are less clearly established: some may benefit depression in the absence of psychotic features (e.g. low dose flupenthixol), and depression which is accompanied by delusions and hallucinations is often treated with a combination of an antidepressant and an antipsychotic.

The conventional antipsychotic drugs, such as chlorpromazine, thioridazine, haloperidol and trifluoperazine, are useful treatments for positive symptoms of schizophrenic and other psychoses (delusions, auditory hallucinations, thought disorder, passivity experiences, etc.), but have relatively little effect on *negative* features such as social withdrawal and lack of motivation. Long-term ('maintenance') treatment may be necessary to prevent relapse in some forms of schizophrenia.

Antipsychotics vary in their *potency*, which reflects their ability to block the activity of a neurotransmitter (dopamine) in specific sites within the brain. Highly potent antipsychotics require a smaller dose for a given effect, and usually have a more specific dopamine-blocking action than less potent compounds. Specificity of dopamine blockade results in some advantages (e.g. fewer adverse effects such as sedation and constipation which result from the blockade of other receptors) but also some disadvantages (movement disorders such as muscular spasms, and a 'Parkinsonian' syndrome). The tendency to produce clinical features which resemble those of Parkinson's disease (muscular tremor and rigidity) is one of the most common adverse effects of antipsychotic medication, and results from an imbalance between brain dopaminergic and cholinergic systems. Acetylcholine is also a neurotransmitter, and selective blockade of cholinergic receptors can cause a Parkinsonian syndrome. This may, if necessary, be overcome by prescribing *anticholinergic* drugs, which correct the imbalance and prevent Parkinsonian side effects. However, blockade of cholinergic receptors may in turn cause additional adverse effects (such as dry mouth, blurred vision and constipation), and may reduce the effectiveness of antipsychotics (Johnstone et al. 1983). Antipsychotics with a less specific dopamine-blocking action are less likely to produce Parkinsonism, but may be associated with other adverse effects. Thioridazine, for example, has both dopamine-blocking and anticholinergic effects, so it rarely produces movement disorders, but commonly causes constipation. It is important to prescribe an antipsychotic that is likely to be tolerated well by the individual patient, by doing so, adverse effects are minimised and compliance is improved. A drug that the patient does not take, because of an adverse effect, stands no chance of doing good.

Other potential adverse effects of antipsychotics include sedation, a lowering of blood pressure when rising from a lying or sitting position, photosensitivity (skin protection is often advisable if exposure to bright sunlight is likely) and (rarely) interference with the production of some blood cells. The *neuroleptic malignant syndrome* (NMS) is a rare but potentially fatal complication of treatment with antipsychotics, and consists of fever, muscular rigidity, an alteration in consciousness, and features indicating dysfunction of the autonomic nervous system (sweating, rapid heart rate, changes in blood pressure, etc.) (Rosebush and Stewart 1989). NMS usually occurs immediately after antipsychotic treatment is started, or the dose increased. Early recognition and treatment is important. Other adverse effects of antipsychotics are listed in the relevant data sheets (Walker 1994).

Antipsychotics that differ from those used for the past 40 years are now becoming available, with claims of fewer adverse effects, or a broader spectrum of activity (e.g. against negative as well as positive symptoms). One of these compounds, clozapine, is licensed specifically for the treatment of schizophrenia resistant to other drugs. It has a beneficial effect on both positive and negative symptoms, and is as effective as other antipsychotics. However, it is associated with neutropenia and agranulocytosis (failure to produce white blood cells) in a small minority of those treated, and so stringent monitoring to allow early detection of this problem is necessary. Clozapine may be effective in up to 60% of people with schizophrenia unresponsive to other medications (Ereshefsky *et al.* 1989). Another consideration when prescribing for adults with autism is that clozapine lowers the convulsive threshold. About 30% of people with autism have seizures during adolescence or early adult life, and about 4% of patients receiving between 300 mg and 600 mg of clozapine per day develop seizures, so it seems likely that the drug may adversely affect seizure control in some people with autism who have epilepsy.

Antipsychotics are also used 'to quieten disturbed patients' (British Medical Association and the Royal Pharmaceutical Society 1995), and they are widely used as adjuncts to the management of non-specific 'challenging' behaviours. The evidence for efficacy when used in this way is reviewed below.

Tricyclic antidepressants (TCAs)

These compounds, which include amitriptyline, imipramine, clomipramine and dothiepin, are very effective treatments for the syndrome of 'clinical' depression described above. They have no impact on unhappiness or misery, but reverse the syndrome of low mood associated with loss of appetite and weight, distorted thinking (often with unjustified pessimism, guilt, and suicidal ideation), poor sleep, etc., after a time lag of about two weeks. This delay in therapeutic effect is poorly understood, but may arise because the antidepressant effect of the compounds depends on an alteration in the number or sensitivity of receptors for particular neurotransmitters (serotonin and noradrenaline) within the brain, which takes time to occur. The practical importance is that patients receiving antidepressants, and their carers, should be told that the beneficial effects will not occur immediately, and that it is important to continue with the treatment. Unfortunately, the *adverse* effects of these compounds usually occur immediately, and patients may abandon treatment as a result. The commonest adverse effects are sedation or a feeling of dizziness, or effects related to anticholinergic activity (dry mouth, blurred vision, constipation and problems with urination). The TCAs are very dangerous if taken in overdose, many have very marked cardio-toxic effects. Psychiatrists have long been aware of the paradox of treating a condition (severe depression) which is strongly associated with suicidal ideas and attempt with drugs which cause death very readily if taken in excessive amounts. TCAs are not effective treatments for manic illnesses, which may be made worse if they are prescribed.

Specific serotonin re-uptake inhibitors (SSRIs)

These compounds are as effective as the TCAs in the treatment of depression, but differ in their chemical composition and adverse effect profile, which is more favourable. They have far fewer anticholinergic or cardiotoxic effects, are usually better tolerated as a result, and are much safer if taken in overdose. They include fluoxetine and paroxetine, and some are licensed for the treatment of eating disorders and obsessive-compulsive disorder, as well as depression. They share with clomipramine (a TCA) a relative specificity for serotonin receptors (hence their name), and there is some preliminary evidence that they may have a beneficial effect on some features of autism, although there is debate about the extent to which positive effects reflect the relief of underlying depression (Ghaziuddin *et al.* 1991; Mehlinger *et al.* 1990).

Carbamazepine

Carbamazepine is an anticonvulsant drug, structurally related to TCA's that is used in the treatment of focal and generalised seizures and also as a prophylactic treatment to prevent recurrence of bipolar affective disorder. Adverse effects include gastrointestinal disturbances, dizziness, drowsiness, rashes and (rarely) blood abnormalities. The concentration of carbamazepine in blood can be used to assess the correct dose for each person treated. Carbamazepine may be of benefit for some adults with developmental disorders (including autism) who have abnormally aggressive behaviour of some specific types. This use is reviewed below.

Lithium

Lithium is a naturally occurring element, closely related to sodium and potassium. It is used in the form of a salt, usually lithium carbonate or lithium citrate, and is effective in the acute and prophylactic treatment of depressive and bipolar affective disorders. Lithium salts are highly effective treatments for these conditions, and, if the correct dose is given, are relatively free of adverse effects (the most common being a fine tremor, thirst and excessive urination, and gastrointestinal disturbances). However, lithium salts have a very narrow therapeutic/toxic ratio (i.e. the dose causing toxicity is a low multiple of the therapeutic dose). Blood tests are necessary before and during treatment, to check the level of lithium (so that the dose can be adjusted to the individual) and to ensure that kidney function is adequate and thyroid function is not being adversely affected by treatment with lithium. Lithium toxicity causes blurred vision, drowsiness, weakness, slurred speech and loss of co-ordination, which may progress to seizures, circulatory collapse and death if not recognised. For these reasons, patients receiving lithium and/or their carers need information about action to be taken in circumstances where lithium toxicity may develop (e.g. when fluid loss follows diarrhoea and vomiting) and about drug interactions which may cause toxicity. Research has shown that patients and carers value such information, are not deterred from treatment by a knowledge of potential adverse effects, and have a more positive attitude to the use of medication if a full explanation of the risks and benefits of treatment are given (Clarke and Pickles 1994). Written information may be helpful for carers, and lithium information cards are available from pharmacies and psychiatrists. Lithium has been used to treat aggressive and severely self-injurious behaviour among people with learning disability (e.g. Craft *et al.* 1987), and this use is considered below, in the subsection entitled 'Aggressive behaviour'.

Propranolol

Propranolol is a beta-adrenoceptor blocking agent ('beta-blocker') used predominantly as an antihypertensive agent (it reduces abnormally high blood pressure). Its effects include slowing of heart rate, and a blocking of the physical sensations which accompany panic. For this reason it is also used as an anxiety-reducing ('anxiolytic') medication which has an advantage over compounds such as diazepam (Valium) because it does not produce dependence and is not associated with a withdrawal syndrome. It probably acts in ways other than by reducing the physical sensations which accompany panic (thus breaking the 'vicious cycle' of spiralling anxiety), because it is one of the beta- blockers which readily enter the brain, and is a more effective anxiolytic than beta-blockers which do not. This implies a central action, as well as peripheral effects. Because it enters the brain readily, propranolol may cause vivid dreams in addition to the adverse effects common to beta-blockers (such as cold hands and feet). Beta-adrenoceptors are found in lung tissue, and mediate the response to stress which dilates the airways (for example, during an asthmatic attack). Beta-blockers, by preventing this response, may be very dangerous if prescribed to people with respiratory disease. They may also cause heart failure in people who are vulnerable. Their use, therefore, requires close medical supervision, especially when treatment is initiated.

Beta-blockers have been used to treat adults with autism, the rationale being that many people with autism have severe anxiety caused by environmental change, sometimes with accompanying severely challenging behaviour.

Opiate antagonists

Naloxone and naltrexone are compounds that reverse the effect of opiates such as morphine and diamorphine (heroin) that are derived from the opium poppy or synthesised; they also reverse the effect of opiate-like substances such as β-endorphin that are produced by the human nervous system (see Figure 10.2). They are licensed for the adjunctive treatment of people formerly dependent on opiates (naltrexone) or the reversal of opiate-induced nervous system depression (naloxone). Naltrexone is given orally, and naloxone by intravenous, intramuscular or subcutaneous injection. The adverse effects of these compounds closely resemble the features of the opiate withdrawal syndrome (insomnia, dysphoria, nausea, joint pain, sweating, etc.). Other adverse effects are listed in the relevant data sheets. They have been used to treat severely self-injurious behaviour in people with developmental disorders, including autism (e.g. Barrett *et al.* 1989) and this use is reviewed below (in the section titled 'Self-injurious behaviour').

BEHAVIOURAL DISORDERS AND AUTISM

The term 'behavioural disorder' or 'challenging behaviour' is sometimes used to describe any behaviour which is:

of such an intensity, frequency or duration that the physical safety of the person or others is likely to be placed in serious jeopardy, or behaviour that is likely to seriously limit or delay access to or use of ordinary community facilities.

(Emerson *et al.* 1987)

Psychiatrists tend to use the term to describe behaviour that challenges services, but that is not a result of a diagnosable psychiatric disorder. There is obviously some overlap, but the concept of psychiatric 'illnesses' which usually respond well to drug treatments, and non-specific 'challenging' behaviours, in which medication may play some part in the overall management, is useful given the present limited state of knowledge about the causes of both these types of disorder. Some of the more commonly encountered clinical problems will be discussed to illustrate the ways in which medication can contribute to a reduction in some aberrant or socially undesirable behaviours, with a concomitant increase in quality of life, and to show how knowledge of drug effects can contribute to advances in the understanding of the aetiology and pathogenesis of behavioural problems associated with autism. Relatively little research has been conducted into the effects of drugs when used to treat behavioural disorders associated with autism. The conclusions discussed relate primarily to behavioural disorders associated with learning disability. The extrapolation usually appears to be clinically justified, but there may be exceptions.

PHARMACOLOGICAL TREATMENT OF BEHAVIOURAL DISORDERS

Aggressive behaviour

Aggressive behaviours are some of the most difficult for relatives and carers to cope with. They often seriously limit opportunities, and may lead to sanctions ranging from social disapproval to the involvement of the police or admission to hospital. Strategies based on psychological principles such as relaxation, anger management or the adoption of low-arousal approaches may be effective, especially where aggressive behaviour results from anxiety provoked by environmental change, unwanted social interaction or an emotionally charged atmosphere.

Evidence is accumulating that some compounds may help some people with autism and/or learning disability who have aggressive behaviour, especially where the aggression follows escalating anxiety or seems to be associated with such extreme arousal that the usual constraints on behaviour are overridden. The evidence for efficacy is usually derived from case studies or series, or small controlled studies, and attention must be given to the risk/benefit ratio when considering prescribing.

Zuclopenthixol, an antipsychotic, has been found to reduce the frequency and severity of aggressive behaviours among people with learning disability in a number of studies (Izmeth *et al.* 1988; Malt *et al.* 1995; Mlele and Wiley 1986; Singh and Owino 1992) but data concerning efficacy in treating such behavioural disorders among adults with autism have not been reviewed. Following reports that aggressive behaviour among people with schizophrenia improved when they were treated with zuclopenthixol, Yar-Khan (1981) reported a beneficial effect on the aggressive behaviour of 15 people with learning disability. A further study (Mlele and Wiley 1986) found marked reductions in aggressive behaviour among ten in-patients with learning disability, but the authors pointed out that other variables may also have influenced the subjects' behaviour (at the time of the study the wards in the unit were being refurbished). Malt *et al.* (1995) reported a comparison of the effects of zuclopenthixol or haloperidol (versus placebo) in a double-blind crossover trial involving 34 people with learning disability. The authors reported reductions in scores of an instrument derived from the Schedule of Handicaps, Behaviours and Skills (HBS) but no change in scores obtained using the Clinical Global Improvement Scales. The choice of a modification of the HBS to assess changes in maladaptive behaviour related to drug treatment seems unusual; instruments such as the Aberrant Behaviour Checklist (Aman *et al.* 1985) have been designed and evaluated specifically for this purpose. Malt *et al.* (1995) reported beneficial effects from relatively low doses of zuclopenthixol (the mean daily doses after eight weeks of treatment were 5.5mg and 5.13mg for the two phases of the trial). Aggressive behaviour was a problem for 11 of the 34 subjects, other maladaptive behaviours included anxiety, psychomotor agitation, self-injury, and 'psychotic symptoms, hallucinations or both'. In view of the established efficacy of antipsychotics in reducing psychotic phenomena, the results of this study pertaining to the treatment of non-psychotic behaviour disorders such as aggression must be treated with caution. Further controlled studies with more tightly defined inclusion criteria are necessary before firm conclusions can be drawn about the benefits of zuclopenthixol in the treatment of aggressive behaviours. However, as antipsychotics are widely used to attempt to treat such disorders when other measures have proven ineffective or impractical, zuclopenthixol would appear to be one of the antipsychotics for which there is most evidence for efficacy.

Some reports have suggested that some people with aggressive behaviour with a sudden onset and apparent loss of control ('episodic dyscontrol') have a relatively high prevalence of electroencephalogram (EEG) abnormalities, and that aggressive behaviour with these characteristics may be reduced following treatment with anticonvulsants, especially carbamazepine (e.g. Stone *et al.* 1986). The successful use of carbamazepine to treat aggressive behaviour with a sudden onset has been reported among people with EEG abnormalities (Tunks and Dermer 1977) and those with rage reactions but normal EEGs (Mattes *et al.* 1984). Mattes (1986) reviewed the psychopharmacological management of temper outbursts, and concluded that there was some evidence from case reports and controlled studies that carbamazepine reduced aggressive behaviours in some people irrespective of EEG changes or diagnosis. Reports also suggest benefit from carbamazepine treatment for some people with learning disabilities and aggressive behaviour which is 'explosive' in nature. Langee (1989) reported a retrospective study of 76 learning disabled people with behavioural problems including aggression, of whom 30 had a complete or nearly complete loss of the abnormal behaviour during treatment. Laminack (1990) re-examined Langee's data, suggested that carbamazepine appeared to be without benefit for subjects without epilepsy and with a normal EEG, and concluded that an EEG may be a useful screen when considering the use of carbamazepine in the treatment of severe behavioural disorders. Other reports have described the successful treatment of rages associated with learning disability with carbamazepine (e.g. Gupta *et al.* 1987) or carbamazepine combined with other agents (e.g. Buck and Havey 1986). Adequate research into the effects of carbamazepine on aggressive behaviour associated with autism, however, has not been reported, and conclusions must therefore necessarily be limited. The evidence suggests that carbamazepine may benefit aggressive behaviour of sudden onset, with a 'rage' quality to it, especially if EEG abnormalities are found.

Propranolol is an antihypertensive (blood pressure lowering) agent that has an anxiety-reducing effect, but must not be used to treat people with chest disease or certain heart problems. One study describes the effects of adding propranolol to the existing medication received by eight adults with autism.

The immediate result across all patients was a rapid diminution in aggressivity … as the individual becomes less anxious, defensive and dearousing behaviors are relinquished and more social and adaptive behaviors appear. There is a concomitant improvement in language, although it is unclear whether lost skills are recouped or new ones developed. Further research is indicated.

(Ratey *et al.* 1987)

The hypothesis underlying this study, which was not controlled, was that beta-blockers reduce 'a painful state of hyperarousal'. Although propranolol has a useful anxiolytic effect for some adults with autism, its potential adverse effects limit its use. Clinical experience suggests that it is of considerable benefit for a minority of adults with autism who have severe anxiety, and sometimes reduces anxiety-related behaviours such as stereotypies or aggression, stereotypies being repetitive movements with no apparent purpose, such as hand-flapping. In many cases, however, it does not alter apparently anxiety-related behaviours, and it occasionally produces undesirable behavioural changes.

Mehlinger *et al.* (1990) described a 26-year-old white female with autism with temper outbursts and aggressive behaviour at a sheltered workshop. Her placement was in jeopardy because of a two-month escalation in aggression. She had previously received treatment with imipramine, with an initial improvement (for two weeks) followed by a reversion to her previous behaviour. The imipramine had therefore been stopped. She was treated with fluoxetine 20 mg every other day. She became more interactive, socially appropriate and tolerant of human contact. Behaviours such as the ordering of objects and other repetitive, stereotyped behaviours declined in frequency and severity and her temper outbursts became less frequent. She was happier and no longer enuretic. When the dose was increased, her anxiety and stereotypies increased. The dose was subsequently reduced to 20 mg per day and improvement was maintained. The authors noted the use of fluoxetine to treat obsessive symptomatology, and speculated about 'similar pathophysiology' in the two disorders (see discussion of the use of clomipramine below). Friedman (1991) suggested that the worsening of stereotypies noted by Mehlinger *et al.* may have been due to 'serotonergic-mediated inhibition of dopamine lateralized to the right hemisphere of the brain' and that it could be avoided by gradual dose titration. Ghaziuddin *et al.* (1991) reported four cases in which a person with autism had been treated with fluoxetine, and concluded:

fluoxetine seems to be most useful when a clear-cut superimposed depressive illness is present. This appears to be all the more true when there is a family history of the disorder. Second, compulsive rituals and other non-specific behaviours, such as stereotypies do not seem to respond well, although irritability might decrease (clomipramine might be a more suitable drug to use in such circumstances). Third, in some cases, as in Cases 1 and 4 above, there is a danger that side effects of the medication, such as agitation and nervousness, might be confused with symptoms...in view of the limited experience of this drug in people with developmental disorders, a cautious approach is recommended.

Lithium has also been used to treat aggressive behaviour in people with learning disabilities. Spreat *et al.* (1989) reviewed the records of 38 people with learning disability and aggressive behaviour treated with lithium. A reduction in the frequency of aggressive outbursts of 30% or more was observed among 24 of the people treated. A more favourable response was found among people with more severe aggression and hyperactivity before treatment, and those who had higher serum lithium concentrations during treatment. Other studies of the use of lithium to reduce abnormally aggressive behaviour were reviewed by Craft *et al.* (1987), who conducted a double-blind trial of lithium in 42 people with learning disability. Nearly three-quarters of the patients in the lithium-treated group showed a reduction in aggressive behaviour, with few adverse effects. Patients had to have had at least, 'two episodes of overt aggression in two separate weeks of the run-in period' to be included in the trial, and the severity of aggression during the trial was rated on a five-point scale ranging from 'well behaved' to 'seclusion required'. Patients with a cyclical pattern of behavioural disturbance (indicating a possible underlying affective disorder) were excluded from the trial. The authors note that, 'these were difficult patients, many of whom had not responded to other therapies' and concluded that lithium was a potentially useful agent in the treatment of adults with learning disability and 'uncontrollable aggressiveness'.

Inappropriate sexual behaviour

Inappropriate sexual behaviour (i.e. behaviour that has the potential to bring the individual into conflict with the law, or that is socially unacceptable) causes problems for a small proportion of men with autism. Such behaviour may arise from ignorance of social norms or a lack of education or understanding (especially where the person concerned also has a learning disability). It may be associated with the social impairments characteristic of the autistic Triad of Impairments, and reflect a failure to comprehend the conventions governing social interaction and interpersonal relationships. Education and counselling are important, and are often all that is required. Other psychologically based interventions may also be required. For a small number of men with inappropriate sexual behaviour that has proved unresponsive to such measures in isolation, or where they cannot be used, the prescription of libido-reducing medication (LRM) may be appropriate as the least restrictive alternative. The issue of consent to the use of LRM is important, but essentially no different to consideration of consent to the use of other medication given to favourably influence behaviour or emotional state. Further details can be found in Clarke (1989).

It is often assumed that male sexual responsiveness and, among offenders, 'sexual aggression' are related to plasma testosterone concentrations. Research suggests that this is not so and that, although plasma testosterone concentration does influence such measures as recidivism among sex offenders (Bremer 1959), it is only one factor influencing sexual behaviour. It has been shown, for example, that castration does not invariably eliminate sexual drive (Heim and Hursch 1979) and that serious sexually motivated offences may be carried out by men with demonstrably low plasma testosterone concentrations (Raboch *et al.* 1987). However, even a small reduction in libido may enable men to control impulses that would otherwise lead to unacceptable sexual behaviour (Freund 1980) and LRM may be helpful to some men with autism and unacceptable sexual behaviour for this reason.

Many compounds have been used to reduce male libido, including non-specific sedatives and antipsychotic drugs (Bartholomew 1968; Kamm 1965), oestrogens and progestogens (female sex hormones) (Cooper 1986; Field and Williams 1970) and compounds marketed as having a more specific antilibidinal effect such as benperidol and cyproterone acetate (CPA). Of the LRMs available, the evidence for efficacy is greatest for medroxyprogesterone acetate (MPA) and CPA (Clarke 1989). CPA has a more specific libido-reducing action, and fewer adverse effects than MPA. Benperidol is an antipsychotic agent related to haloperidol, and appears to have weaker libido-reducing effects than CPA. One double-blind placebo-controlled trial of its effect on penile responsiveness and other measures in 12 paedophilic sexual offenders found no significant difference between benperidol, chlorpromazine and placebo, except for a reduction in self-reporting of sexual thoughts when receiving benperidol. The authors concluded that the libido-reducing effects of benperidol were weak and unlikely to be sufficient to control serious antisocial sexual behaviour (Tennent *et al.* 1974).

CPA is a steroid analogue, with two actions that contribute to its libido-reducing properties: competitive antagonism of testosterone (at receptors in cell nuclei) and progestogenic activity leading to a reduction in the release of gonadotrophins from the hypothalamus, and thus to a reduction in the production of testosterone in the testes. There are numerous reports suggesting the CPA has significant libido-reducing effects, including controlled studies (e.g. Bancroft *et al.* 1974; Cooper 1981) but there have been no methodologically sound studies of its use among adult men with autism. There is no reason to assume its efficacy would be reduced among men with autism, but caution or dose adjustment may be necessary where the person concerned receives other medication. CPA may cause transient fatigue when treatment is initiated, and may cause gynaecomastia (breast enlargement). The manufacturers recommend that a sperm count is carried out before treatment (CPA causes a reversible inhibition of sperm formation), but this rarely seems to be carried out in practice. Electrolytes, liver function and blood count should be monitored during treatment.

Treatment with an LRM may reduce the intensity of sexual drive, but will have no effect on its direction. Men with autism and inappropriate or potentially offending sexual behaviour may be helped by the prescription of LRM, but will usually require education, supervision and other strategies as well.

Self-injurious behaviour

The complexity of the aetiology and pathogenesis of severely self-injurious behaviour (SSIB) has been discussed in the Introduction (see Figure 10.1), and pharmacological strategies are often usefully combined with other management components devised to address issues such as the reinforcing value of SSIB in avoiding unwanted social interaction for someone with autism. SSIB of a specific nature (such as hand-head contact) may have many different functions at different times for one individual, and an understanding of operant and biological theories and their probable interaction is necessary to maximise therapeutic effect (Oliver and Head 1990).

SSIB may result from physical illness (such as tooth- and ear-ache) or psychiatric illness (especially depression) and careful assessment of these and other possible underlying factors is necessary (Bridgen and Todd 1990). Sovner *et al.* (1993) described the successful use of fluoxetine to treat self-injury associated with depression in two adults with learning disability.

Pharmacological strategies to reduce SSIB such as head-banging were once limited to the use of sedatives such as opium (in the nineteenth and early twentieth centuries) and later barbiturates and other compounds to reduce motor activity generally and hence limit tissue damage. When antipsychotic agents became available in the 1950s, they were used in a similar way, although some evidence now suggests that the effect of such compounds on transmitters within the nervous system may confer more specific beneficial effects. Some reports have suggested a role for antipsychotic medication in the treatment of SSIB, an area reviewed by Aman (1987) who felt that evidence for efficacy was probably greatest for thioridazine. In some animal studies, self-injury has been induced by destroying dopaminergic neurons and then challenging with L-dopa (e.g. Breese *et al.* 1989). However, as King (1993) noted, the evidence for the efficacy of antipsychotics in the treatment of SSIB is not strong (other than via a non-specific sedative effect) and no syndrome of SSIB has ever been described as part of an 'antipsychotic withdrawal syndrome'. Singh and Millichamp (1985) concluded that, 'there was some indication that antipsychotics and antimanics may prove to be useful in the treatment of self-injury...', but emphasised the need for methodologically rigorous studies with random assignment of subjects to treatment conditions, control groups, placebo comparisons, double-blind procedures, standardised doses prescribed on the basis of dose per unit body weight, as well as appropriate experimental design, assessment measures and statistical analyses. These criticisms still apply, with the possible exception that trials against other treatments thought to be effective may be considered more ethically appropriate than the use of placebo.

There is some evidence that SSIB may, in some instances, be a form of compulsive behaviour (King 1993) and, like compulsive behaviour, respond to treatment with serotonin re-uptake blocking agents such as fluoxetine. Ricketts *et al.* (1993) reported four adults with learning disability whose SSIB responded to treatment with fluoxetine, and noted that of 44 cases of SSIB treated with fluoxetine previously reported in the literature, 42 had a beneficial response.

Sovner and Hurley (1981) described the beneficial response of two subjects with severe learning disability to lithium treatment, which was associated with a reduction in self-injury. Other reports of a positive response of SSIB to lithium treatment have been reported (e.g. Cooper and Fowlie 1973). Winchel and Stanley (1991) concluded that, 'despite the tentative nature of the data, considerable support is emerging for the use of lithium and carbamazepine with mentally retarded patients who injure themselves.'

In some people with autism and learning disabilities, SSIB may be maintained in part by changes in endogenous opiate-like neuroregulatory systems. In 1978 Kalat described similarities between behaviours seen in autism and those observed among people taking opiates on a long-term basis. Other authors have also explored these similarities, including Deutsch (1986) who described reduced pain sensitivity, diminished crying, a reduction in social behaviour, instability of mood, and abnormal motor activity including repetitive stereotyped behaviours, concluding:

> In view of the beneficial effects of haloperidol in autism and its synergism with naloxone, the ability of neuroleptics to increase levels of β-endorphin in plasma, the presence of 'autistic' features in opiate addicts and opiate-treated animals, and the dysregulation of opioid activity in autism, a rationale exists for a clinical trial of opiate antagonist administration to autistic patients ... in addition to their possible role in enhancing attention in autistic patients, opiate antagonists may also have a specific indication for autistic patients exhibiting self-injurious behaviour.
>
> (Deutsch 1986)

There is also evidence from treatment trials that the self-injury that is so problematic for some people with autism may be related to opioid neuroregulatory abnormalities, and may be successfully treated with opioid blocking drugs such as naltrexone. Abnormalities in opioid neuroregulatory systems have also been hypothesised to contribute to other features of autism, and the evidence for this is reviewed in the section entitled, 'Treatment of features of autism', in which the role of fragments derived from pro-opiomelanocortin (POMC) in learning and social behaviour is considered (see Figure 10.2).

Gillberg *et al.* (1985) found that children with autism who injured themselves severely had higher concentrations of β-endorphin in cerebrospinal fluid (CSF; the fluid surrounding the brain and spinal cord) than children with autism who did not have SSIB, and Sandman *et al.* (1990) found that people with learning disability who had stereotyped behaviour and SSIB had higher CSF β-endorphin concentrations than matched control subjects. Three studies published in 1983 describe reductions in SSIB among people with learning disability who were treated with the opiate antagonist naloxone (Davidson *et al.* 1983; Richardson and Zaleski 1983; Sandman *et al.* 1983). Further reports followed (Bernstein *et al.* 1987; e.g. Sandyk 1985). More recent reports have described the use of naltrexone, an opiate antagonist which is relatively long-acting and has the advantage over naloxone of being active when taken by mouth. Campbell *et al.* (1988) treated seven children with autism using naltrexone, and concluded that five had benefitted, with reductions in SSIB and aggressive behaviours. Walters *et al.* (1990) described a 14-year-old male with autism, learning disability and SSIB, and reported a marked decrease in SSIB during two phases of treatment with naltrexone. Interestingly, the SSIB did not revert to baseline levels during a second placebo phase. An increase in social relatedness was also observed during the phases of active drug treatment. Herman *et al.* (1987) noted a dose-dependent reduction in SSIB in three children after treatment with naltrexone. Some of the studies reporting reductions in SSIB used double-blind controlled methodology (e.g. Sandman *et al.* 1990). However, some studies have failed to find reductions in SSIB after treatment with naloxone or naltrexone (e.g. Beckwith *et al.* 1986; Szymanski *et al.* 1987). There therefore seems to be evidence in favour of the efficacy of opiate antagonists in the treatment of SSIB in some people with learning disability, including people with autism. However, such treatment is not universally successful and, in view of the relatively small number of people reported and the complexities of the aetiology of SSIB, little can be deduced about the characteristics that imply a positive response.

Similar reservations apply to the use of other medications in the management of SSIB among adults with autism. It is often the case that SSIB is associated with tissue damage which limits function and may be irreversible or even life-threatening, and, in such circumstances, clinicians will be justified in using almost any management strategy which is ethically appropriate, for which there is some evidence of efficacy, and which seems likely to be associated with an acceptable risk of adverse effects. Where the need for treatment is less pressing, however, it can be difficult to evaluate the potential effectiveness of treatments given the small number of studies of individual drugs reported in the literature, and the almost complete lack of information about treatments used for adults with autism. As Ruedrich *et al.* (1990), considering the use of beta-blockers to treat SSIB and aggressive behaviour associated with learning disability, concluded:

The psychopharmacologic treatment of persons with mental retardation who exhibit aggressive or self-injurious syndromes is varied and controversial. Many psychotropic agents have been used ... none of these have been studied sufficiently to recommend them unequivocally ... blockers of beta-adrenergic function of the sympathetic nervous system have been postulated to have efficacy in some aggressive or self-injurious persons. This literature was reviewed, a relevant case report presented, and concerns raised concerning the premature endorsement of beta-blocking medications before they have been adequately studied.

Pica

Research has shown that abnormal eating behaviour is not uncommon among people with learning disability and autism, although much of the literature consists of case reports or studies specifically of pica (the consumption of abnormal food items such as frozen food, 'food pica' or non-food items, 'non-food pica'. The term pica is derived from a latin word meaning a magpie. Pica has been found to lead to disorders such as gastrointestinal obstruction and parasite infestation. O'Brien and Whitehouse (1990) found only two subjects with pica (both of whom had autism) in a survey of 48 adults with learning disability in three community settings. Other eating abnormalities were found among the adults with autism, notably a tendency to search incessantly for food. Lofts *et al.* (1990) found that 15.5% of 806 adults with learning disability in a residential facility in the USA had pica, and 54% of those with pica had serum zinc levels below the normal range (compared to 7% of controls). After two weeks of baseline data collection, the authors treated subjects in the pica group with 100mg of chelated zinc. The average number of incidents of pica per person fell from 23 in the two-week baseline period to 4.3 during treatment with zinc. Lofts *et al.* (1990) concluded that serum copper and zinc concentrations should be measured and deficiencies corrected before behavioural techniques are used to treat pica. Laboratory monitoring is necessary because high doses of zinc have been found to produce copper deficiency and a macrocytic anaemia.

These data suggest that biological factors need to be taken into account in the assessment of pica, and that zinc treatment may be beneficial for adults with autism and pica who are found to have low serum zinc concentrations. Further research is needed before firm recommendations can be made concerning treatment.

TREATMENT OF FEATURES OF AUTISM

The core triad of autistic impairments has traditionally been felt to be relatively resistant to medication-based interventions. Some treatments for behavioural abnormalities associated with autism have sometimes been found to have a beneficial effect on other areas of functioning, others have been developed in response to research findings concerning neurotransmitter abnormalities.

Haloperidol, a dopamine antagonist, has been found to significantly reduce hyperactivity, stereotyped behaviours and withdrawal, and to facilitate learning in some subjects with autism (Anderson *et al.* 1984; Campbell 1987). Anderson *et al.* (1989) found that haloperidol significantly reduced hyperactivity, temper tantrums, social withdrawal and stereotypies among 45 children with a DSM-III (American Psychiatric Association 1980) diagnosis of infantile autism in a double-blind, placebo-controlled crossover trial. The children, aged 2.02 to 7.58 years, were randomly assigned to haloperidol or placebo, in a double-blind crossover design. The authors concluded:

Haloperidol was shown to be a powerful therapeutic agent when administered for four weeks and free of side effects: at doses ranging from 0.25 to 4.0 mg/day, there was a clinically and statistically significant reduction of a variety of symptoms. The children were calmer without being sedated, showed decreases in hyperactivity, temper tantrums, withdrawal, and stereotypies, and showed an increase in relatedness. These findings are in agreement with our previous findings.

(Anderson *et al.* 1989)

Haloperidol was not found to facilitate (discriminatory) learning in this trial. The utility of haloperidol is limited by potential adverse effects, notably tardive dyskinesia.

Fenfluramine is an anorexigenic amine and a serotonin antagonist. It was proposed as a treatment for autism after abnormally high concentrations of serotonin were found in the blood of some subjects with autism. This finding was associated with some evidence that autistic children with hyperserotoninaemia had more severe cognitive impairments and more severe behavioural abnormalities than those with normal blood serotonin levels (Campbell *et al.* 1975). DuVerglas *et al.* (1988) noted that:

an observation that it increased IQ scores and reduced maladaptive behaviours among three patients with autism (Geller *et al.* 1982) led to a multicentre double-blind controlled study against placebo in crossover or comparison designs coordinated by investigators at the UCLA Neuropsychiatric Institute. These and other data were reviewed by the authors, who concluded that fenfluramine had positive effects (notably the reduction of hyperactivity and stereotypic behaviours) in 33% of subjects, and that those with the best response had higher baseline IQs and hyperactivity with motor stereotypies.

These conclusions have been challenged by others. Stern *et al.* (1990) carried out a 12-month double-blind randomised crossover trial of fenfluramine in 20 children with autism. Some children showed improvements in cognitive and language functioning, but the improvements were not statistically significant. They concluded that, 'fenfluramine may have a limited place in the management of some patients with autistic disorder.'

In an extensive review of the literature on the use of fenfluramine in autism, Campbell (1988) concluded that,

only carefully designed and controlled studies, with adequate and homogeneous patient samples employing measures sensitive to change due to drug, and careful clinical monitoring, will determine the role of fenfluramine in the treatment of infantile autism.

Ekman *et al.* (1989) compared the effects of fenfluramine on 20 children with autism over 48 weeks, analysed using a double-blind placebo-controlled crossover design, with ratings using the Griffiths Developmental Scales and Real Life Rating Scale. The authors concluded that,

the only significant improvement was a decrease in abnormal motor behaviour. We did not find any significant improvement in intellectual functioning or any correlation between good clinical response and low baseline serotonin levels or high baseline IQ.

Gillberg (1990) concluded that,

at the present stage it does not appear that fenfluramine has a clear place in the treatment of autism.

Clomipramine is a tricyclic antidepressant (TCA) with a potent serotonin re-uptake blocking action. It has been used to treat obsessive-compulsive disorder and other maladaptive repetitive behaviours such as hair-pulling (Swedo *et al.* 1989) and nail-biting (Leonard *et al.* 1991). It is a much more effective anti-obsessional agent than desipramine (a TCA with an effect predominantly on the re-uptake of noradrenaline) or placebo. This led Gordon *et al.* (1993) to perform a double-blind comparison of clomipramine, desipramine and placebo in the treatment of 24 autistic subjects (12 treated with clomipramine versus desipramine; 12 with clomipramine versus placebo). The authors found a reduction in stereotyped behaviour, abnormal reciprocal social interaction, anger and compulsive behaviours when treatment was with clomipramine, but not when desipramine or placebo were used. Both TCA's were superior to placebo in the reduction of hyperactivity. Reductions in self-injury were also noted, but these were not systematically assessed. Gordon *et al.* (1993) concluded that biological links between compulsions and stereotyped repetitive behaviours in autistic disorder should be explored, and added that:

An ongoing clomipramine/desipramine study in non-autistic, mentally retarded children with prominent motor stereotypies will ascertain whether these repetitive behaviours are also differentially responsive to clomipramine therapy in the absence of autism. Controlled trials of other potent serotonin reuptake inhibitors (fluoxetine, sertraline and paroxetine) in the treatment of autistic and mentally retarded subjects will be important because of the potential for relatively fewer side effects, including insomnia, sedation, and cardiac conduction delay.

In addition to the hypotheses linking features of autism to dysfunction in opioid neuroregulatory systems (e.g. Sahley and Panksepp 1987; and the papers referred to in the section entitled, 'Self-injurious behaviour') research has also been conducted into the effects of fragments derived from pro-opiomelanocortin (POMC) on cognition and behaviour in autism. Figure 10.2 shows the relationship between POMC, endogenous morphine-like substances (endorphins and encephalins) and adrenocorticotrophic hormone (ACTH) which regulates the release of steroid hormones. POMC fragments consist of amino-acid sequences, the biological activity of the compound varying according to the exact sequence of amino-acids present. Some fragments derived from ACTH have been shown not to have ACTH-like activity, but to promote learning and to have behavioural

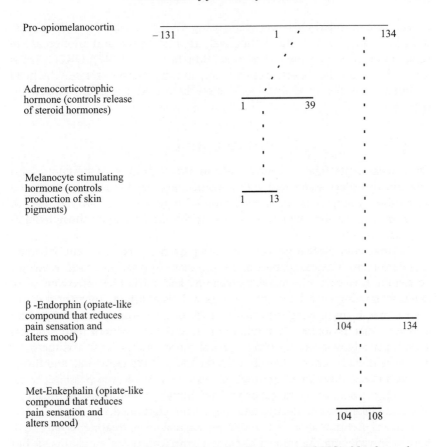

Figure 10.2 *Fragments derived from pro-opiomelanocortin (POMC). Numbers refer to the positions of amino-acids in POMC. Met-enkephalin, for example, consists of the amino-acid sequence: tyrosine-glycine-glycine-phenylalanine-methionine. This sequence is also found in POMC, being the 104th to 108th amino-acids respectively*

effects in non-human mammals. One compound, ORG 2766, is an analogue of ACTH 4–9 (i.e. the fragment of ACTH from the fourth to the ninth amino-acids). It has been found to be effective after administration by mouth (amino-acid sequences form peptides, which are usually digested and lose their activity when taken by mouth), and to improve information processing, adaptation and social behaviour in animal and human studies (De Wied and Jolles 1982; Niesink and Van Ree 1983). In a controlled study of 14 children with autism, Buitelaar *et al.* (1990) found ORG 2766 treatment (20 mg per day) to be associated with increased locomotion, speech and appropriate play activities, and a reduction in stereotyped behaviours.

A second controlled crossover trial (using 40 mg per day for eight weeks) found a reduction in social withdrawal, improved play, and an increase in social interaction and the use of gaze (Buitelaar *et al.* 1992). ORG 2766 is not available for the treatment of autism, and the authors stressed the need for further studies of efficacy and safety before its use could be recommended.

CONCLUSIONS

Drug treatments have a central role in the treatment of psychotic and affective disorders associated with autism. They may be usefully combined with other strategies (such as reduction of expressed emotion, removal of environmental stressors or techniques for the masking of auditory hallucinations).

Pharmacological treatments may play a part in the management of behavioural problems including abnormally aggressive and seriously self- injurious behaviour unacceptable sexual behaviour, and pica. The effectiveness of drugs in treating such behaviours is less well established, but they seem to offer scope for improving the quality of life of *some* adults with autism who also have such problems. Careful attention to the risk/benefit ratio is necessary, especially when using drugs for unlicensed indications, and the drug and dose must be chosen carefully on the basis of the individual and his or her additional disabilities or medical disorders. Wherever possible, some objective measure of the target behaviour should be used to assess the effect of treatment, so that ineffective treatment is not continued.

There is preliminary evidence that pharmacological treatments *may* be of benefit in reducing the impact of some of the features of autism itself, but further research is needed before firm conclusions can be drawn. Such research may help to clarify the biological basis for autistic symptomatology, and the ways in which biological factors interact with environmental and other variables to produce maladaptive behaviours.

BIBLIOGRAPHY

Aman, M.G. (1987). Overview of pharmacotherapy: current status and future directions. *Journal of Mental Deficiency Research*, **31**, 120–130.

Aman, M.G., Singh, N.N., Stewart, A.W. and Field, C.J. (1985). The aberrant behaviour checklist: a BEHAVIOUR rating scale for the assessment of treatment effects. *American Journal of Mental Deficiency*, **89**, 485491.

American Psychiatric Association (APA) (1980). *Diagnostic and Statistical Manual of Mental Disorders* (third edition) (DSM-III). Washington, DC, APA.

Anderson, L.T., Campbell, M., Adams, P., Small, A.M., Perry, R. and Shell, J. (1989). The effects of haloperidol on discrimination learning and behavioral symptoms in autistic children. *Journal of Autism and Developmental Disorders*, **19**, 227–239.

Anderson, L.T., Campbell, M., Grega, D.M., Perry, R., Small, A.M. and Green, W.H. (1984). Haloperidol in infantile autism: effects on learning and behavioral symptoms. *American Journal of Psychiatry*, **141**, 1195–1202.

Bancroft, J., Tennent, G., Loucas, K. and Cass, J. (1974). The control of deviant sexual behaviour by drugs: 1. Behavioural changes following oestrogens and antiandrogens. *British Journal of Psychiatry*, **125**, 310–315.

Barrett, R.P., Feinstein, C. and Hole, W.T. (1989). Effects of naloxone and naltrexone on self-injury: a double-blind, placebo-controlled analysis. *American Journal on Mental Retardation*, **93**, 644–651.

Bartholomew, A.A. (1968). A long acting phenothiazine as a possible agent to control deviant sexual behavior. *American Journal of Psychiatry*, **124**, 917–923.

Beckwith, B.E., Couk, D.I. and Schumacher, K. (1986). Failure of naloxone to reduce self-injurious behaviour in two developmentally disabled females. *Applied Research in Mental Retardation*, **7**, 183–188.

Bernstein, G.A., Hughes, J.R., Mitchell, J.E. and Thompson, T. (1987). Effects of narcotic antagonists on self-injurious behavior: a single case study. *Journal of the American Academy of Child and Adolescent Psychiatry*, **26**, 886–889.

Breese, G.R., Criswell, H.E., Duncan, G.E. and Mueller, R.A. (1989). Dopamine deficiency in self-injurious behaviour. *Psychopharmacology Bulletin*, **25**, 353–357.

Bremer, J. (1959). *Asexualization*. NewYork, Macmillan.

Bridgen, P. and Todd, M. (1990). Challenging behaviour: introducing a preadmission checklist, problem analysis flow chart, and intervention flow chart to guide decision making in a multidisciplinary team. *Mental Handicap*, **18**, 99–104.

British Medical Association and the Royal Pharmaceutical Society (RPS) of Great Britain (1995). *British National Formulary*. London, BMA and RPS.

Buck, O.D. and Havey, P. (1986). Combined carbamazepine and lithium therapy for violent behavior. *American Journal of Psychiatry*, **143**, 1487.

Buitelaar, J.K., Van Engeland, H., Van Ree, J.M. and De Wied, D. (1990). Behavioral effects of ORG 2766, a synthetic analog of the adrenocorticotrophic hormone (4–9), in 14 outpatient autistic children. *Journal of Autism and Developmental Disorders*, **20**, 467–478.

Buitelaar, J.K., Van Engelend, H., De Kogel, K., De Vries, H., Van Hoof, J. and Van Ree, J. (1992). The adrenocorticotrophic hormone (4–9) analog ORG 2766 benefits autistic children: report on a second controlled clinical trial. *Journal of the American Academy of Child and Adolescent Psychiatry*, **31**, 1149–1156.

Campbell, M. (1987). Drug treatment of infantile autism: the past decade. In H.Y. Meltzer (ed.) *Handbook of Autism and Pervasive Developmental Disorders*. New York, Wiley.

Campbell, M. (1988). Fenfluramine treatment of autism. *Journal of Child Psychology and Psychiatry*, **29**, 1–10.

Campbell, M., Adams, P., Small, A.M., Tesch, L.M. and Curren, E.L. (1988). Naltrexone in infantile autism. *Psychopharmacology Bulletin*, **24**, 135–139.

Campbell, M., Friedman, E., Green, W.H., Collins, P.J., Small, A.M. and Breuer, H. (1975). Blood serotonin in schizophrenic children. A preliminary study. *International Pharmacopsychiatry*, **10**, 213–221.

Clarke, D.J. (1989). Antilibidinal drugs and mental retardation: a review. *Medicine, Science and the Law*, **29**, 136–146.

Clarke, D.J., Littlejohns, C.S., Corbett, J.A. and Joseph, S. (1989). Pervasive developmental disorders and psychoses in adult life. *British Journal of Psychiatry*, 155,
692–699.

Clarke, D.J. and Pickles, K.J. (1994). Lithium treatment for people with learning
disability: patients' and carers' knowledge of hazards and attitudes to treatment.
Journal of Intellectual Disability Research, 38, 187–194.

Cole, J., Klerman, C.L. and Goldberg, S.C. (1964). Phenothiazine treatment of
acute schizophrenia. *Archives of General Psychiatry*, 10, 246–261.

Cooper, A.F. and Fowlie, H.C. (1973). Control of gross self-mutilation with lithium
carbonate. *British Journal of Psychiatry*, 122, 370–371.

Cooper, A.J. (1981). A placebo-controlled trial of the antiandrogen cyproterone
acetate in deviant hypersexuality. *Comprehensive Psychiatry*, 22, 458–465.

Cooper, A.J. (1986). Progestogens in the treatment of male sex offenders: a review.
Canadian Journal of Psychiatry, 31, 73–79.

Corbett, J.A. (1979). Psychiatric morbidity and mental retardation. In P. Snaith and
F.E. James (eds.) *Psychiatric Illness and Mental Handicap*. Ashford, Headley
Brothers.

Craft, M., Ismail, I.A., Krishnamurti, D., Mathews, J., Regan, A., Seth, R.V.
and North, P.M. (1987). Lithium in the treatment of aggression in mentally
handicapped patients: a double-blind trial. *British Journal of Psychiatry*, 150,
685–689.

Davidson, P.W., Kleene, B.M., Carroll, M. and Rockowitz, R.J. (1983). Effects of
naloxone on self-injurious behaviour: a case study. *Applied Research in Mental
Retardation*, 4, 1–4.

Davis, J.M. and Garver, D.L. (1978). Neuroleptics: clinical use in psychiatry. In
L.L. Iversen and S.D. Iversen (eds.) *Handbook of Psychopharmacology*, volume 10,
Neuroleptics and Schizophrenia. New York, Plenum Press.

Deutsch, S.I. (1986). Rationale for the administration of opiate antagonists in treating infantile autism. *American Journal of Mental Deficiency*, 90, 631–635.

De Wied, D. and Jolles, J. (1982). Neuropeptides derived from the pro-opiocortin:
behavioral, physiological, and neurochemical effects. *Physiological Reviews*, 62,
976–1059.

Du Verglas, G., Banks, S.R. and Guyer, K.E. (1988). Clinical effects of fenfluramine
on children with autism: a review of the research. *Journal of Autism and
Developmental Disorders*, 18, 297–308.

Ekman, G., Miranda-Linne, F., Gillberg, C., Garle, M. and Wetterberg, L. (1989).
Fenfluramine treatment of twenty children with autism. *Journal of Autism and
Developmental Disorders*, 19, 511–532.

Emerson, E., Barnett, S., Bell, C., Cummings, R., McCool, C., Toogood, A. and
Mansell, J. (1987). *Developing Services for People with Severe Learning Difficulties
and Challenging Behaviours*. Canterbury, University of Kent.

Ereshefsky, L., Watanabe, M.D. and Tran-Johnson, T.K. (1989). Clozapine: an atypical antipsychotic agent. *Clinical Pharmacy*, 8, 691–709.

Field, L.H. and Williams, M. (1970). The hormonal treatment of sexual offenders.
Medicine, Science and the Law, 10, 27–34.

Fisher, W., Kerbeshian, J. and Burd, L. (1986). A treatable language disorder: pharmacological treatment of pervasive developmental disorder. *Journal of
Developmental and Behavioral Paediatrics*, 7, 73–76.

Freund, K. (1980). Therapeutic sex drive reduction. *Acta Psychiatrica Scandinavica*,
Supplement, 287, 5–38.

Friedman, E.H. (1991). Adverse effects of fluoxetine. *Journal of the American Academy of Child and Adolescent Psychiatry*, **30**, 508.

Geller, E., Ritvo, E.R. Freeman, B.J. and Yuwiler, A. (1982). Preliminary observations on the effects of fenfluramine on blood serotonin and symptoms in three autistic boys. *New England Journal of Medicine*, **307**, 165–169.

Ghaziuddin, M., Tsai, L. and Ghaziuddin, N. (1991). Fluoxetine in autism with depression. *Journal of the American Academy of Child and Adolescent Psychiatry*, **30**, 508.

Gillberg, C. (1990). Autism and pervasive developmental disorders. *Journal of Child Psychology and Psychiatry*, **31**, 99–119.

Gillberg, C., Terenius, L. and Lonnerholm, G. (1985). Endorphin activity in childhood psychosis. *Archives of General Psychiatry*, **42**, 780–783.

Gordon, C.T., State, R.C., Nelson, J.E., Hamburger, S.D. and Rapoport, J.L. (1993). A double-blind comparison of climipramine, desipramine, and placebo in the treatment of autistic disorder. *Archives of General Psychiatry*, **50**, 441–447.

Gupta, B.K., Fish, D.N. and Yerevanian, B.I. (1987). Carbamazepine for intermittent explosive disorder in a Prader-Willi syndrome patient. *Journal of Clinical Psychiatry*, **48**, 423.

Heim, N. and Hursch, C.J. (1979). Castration for sex offenders: treatment or punishment? A review and critique of recent European literature. *Archives of Sexual Behaviour*, **8**, 281–304.

Herman, B.J., Hammock, M.K., Arthur-Smith, A., Egan, J., Chatoor, I., Werner, A. and Zelnick, N. (1987). Naltrexone decreases self-injurious behavior. *Annals of Neurology*, **22**, 550–552.

Hunt, A. and Dennis, J. (1987). Psychiatric disorder among children with tuberous sclerosis. *Developmental Medicine and Child Neurology*, **29**, 190–198.

Izmeth, M.G., Khan, S.Y. and Kumarajeewa, D.I. (1988). Neuroleptic treatment of oligophrenic patients. *Pharmatherapeutica*, **5**, 217–227.

Johnstone, E.C., Crow, T.J., Ferrier, I.M., Frith, C.D., Owens, D.G.C., Bourne, R.C. and Gamble, S.J. (1983). Adverse effects of anticholinergic medication on positive schizophrenic symptoms. *Psychological Medicine*, **13**, 513–527.

Kalat, J.W. (1978). Speculations on similarities between autism and opiate addiction. *Journal of Autism and Childhood Schizophrenia*, **8**, 477–479.

Kamm, I. (1965). Control of sexual hyperactivity with thioridazine. *American Journal of Psychiatry*, **121**, 922–923.

Kerbeshian, J. and Burd, L. (1986). Asperger's syndrome and Tourette syndrome: the case of the pinball wizard. *British Journal of Psychiatry*, **148**, 731–736.

King, B.H. (1993). Self-injury by people with mental retardation: a compulsive behavior hypothesis. *American Journal on Mental Retardation*, **98**, 93–112.

Laminack, L. (1990). Carbamazepine for behavioral disorders. *American Journal on Mental Retardation*, **94**, 563–564.

Langee, H.R. (1989). A retrospective study of mentally retarded patients with behavioral disorders who were treated with carbamazepine. *American Journal on Mental Retardation*, **93**, 640–643.

Leonard, H., Lenane, M., Swedo, S., Rettew, D.C. and Rapoport, J.L. (1991). A double-blind comparison of clomipramine and desipramine in the treatment of onychophagia. *Archives of General Psychiatry*, **48**, 821–827.

Littlejohns, C.S., Clarke, D.J. and Corbett, J.A. (1990). Tourette-like disorder in Asperger's syndrome. *British Journal of Psychiatry*, **156**, 430–433.

Lofts, R.H., Schroeder, S.R. and Maier, R.H. (1990). Effects of serum zinc supplementation on pica behavior of persons with mental retardation. *American Journal on Mental Retardation*, **95**, 103–109.

Malt, U.F., Nystad, R., Bache, T., Norsen, O., Sjaastad, M., Solberg, K.O., Tonseth, S., Zachariassen, P. and Maehlum, E. (1995). Effectiveness of zuclopenthixol compared with haloperidol in the treatment of behavioural disturbances in learning disabled patients. *British Journal of Psychiatry*, **166**, 374–377.

Mattes, J.A. (1986). Psychopharmacology of temper outbursts: a review. *Journal of Nervous and Mental Disease*, **174**, 464–470.

Mattes, J.A., Rosenberg, J. and Mayes, D. (1984). Carbamazepine vs propranolol in patients with uncontrolled rage outbursts: a random assignment study. *Psychopharmacology Bulletin*, **20**, 98–100.

Mehlinger, R., Sceftner, W.A. and Poznanski, E. (1990). Fluoxetine and autism. *Journal of the American Academy of Child and Adolescent Psychiatry*, **29**, 985.

Mlele, T.J. and Wiley, Y.V. (1986). Clopenthixol decanoate in the management of aggressive mentally handicapped patients. *British Journal of Psychiatry*, **149**, 373–376.

Niesink, R.J.M. and Van Ree, J.M. (1983). Normalizing effect of an adrenocorticotropic hormone (4–9) analog ORG 2766 on disturbed social behaviour in rats. *Science*, **221**, 960–962.

O'Brien, G. and Whitehouse, A.M. (1990). A psychiatric study of deviant eating behaviour among mentally handicapped adults. *British Journal of Psychiatry*, **157**, 281–284.

Oliver, C. and Head, D. (1990). Self-injurious behaviour in people with learning disabilities: determinants and interventions. *International Review of Psychiatry*, **2**, 99–114.

Raboch, J., Cerna, H. and Zamek, P. (1987). Sexual aggressivity and androgens. *British Journal of Psychiatry*, **151**, 398–400.

Ratey, J.J., Bemporad, J., Sorgi, P., Bick, P., Polakoff, S., O'Driscoll, G. and Mikkelsen, E. (1987). Open trial effects of beta-blockers on speech and social behaviors in 8 autistic adults. *Journal of Autism and Developmental Disorders*, **17**, 439–446.

Richardson, J.F. and Zaleski, W.A. (1983). Naloxone and self-mutilation. *Biological Psychiatry*, **18**, 99–101.

Ricketts, R.W., Goza, A.B., Ellis, C.R., Singh, Y.N., Singh, N.N. and Cooke, J.C. (1993). Fluoxetine treatment of severe self-injury in young adults with mental retardation. *Journal of the American Academy of Child and Adolescent Psychiatry*, **32**, 865–869.

Rosebush, P. and Stewart, T. (1989). A prospective analysis of 24 episodes of neuroleptic malignant syndrome. *American Journal of Psychiatry*, **146**, 717–725.

Ruedrich, S.L., Grush, L. and Wilson, J. (1990). Beta adrenergic blocking medications for aggressive or self-injurious mentally retarded persons. *American Journal on Mental Retardation*, **95**, 110–119.

Sahley, T.L. and Panksepp, J. (1987). Brain opioids and autism: an updated analysis of possible linkages. *Journal of Autism and Developmental Disorders*, **17**, 201–216.

Sandman, C.A., Barron, J.L. and Colman, H. (1990). An orally administered opiate blocker, naltrexone, attenuates self-injurious behavior. *American Journal on Mental Retardation*, **95**, 93–102.

Sandman, C.A., Datta, P., Barron, J.L., Hoehler, F., Williams, C. and Swanson, J. (1983). Naloxone attenuates self-abusive behavior in developmentally disabled clients. *Applied Research in Mental Retardation*, 4, 5–11.

Sandyk, R. (1985). Naloxone abolished self-injuring in a mentally retarded child. *Annals of Neurology*, 17, 520.

Singh, I. and Owino, W.J. (1992). A double-blind comparison of zuclopenthixol tablets with placebo in the treatment of mentally handicapped in-patients with associated behavioural problems. *Journal of Intellectual Disability Research*, 36, 541–549.

Singh, N.N. and Millichamp, D.J. (1985). Pharmacological treatment of self-injurious behavior in mentally retarded persons. *Journal of Autism and Developmental Disorders*, 15, 257–267.

Sovner, R., Fox, C.J., Lowry, M.J. and Lowry, M.A. (1993). Fluoxetine treatment of depression and associated self-injury in two adults with mental retardation. *Journal of Intellectual Disability Research*, 37, 301–311.

Sovner, R. and Hurley, A. (1981). The management of chronic behavior disorders in mentally retarded adults with lithium carbonate. *Journal of Nervous and Mental Disease*, 169, 191–195.

Spreat, S., Behar, D., Reneski, B. and Miazzo, P. (1989). Lithium carbonate for aggression in mentally retarded persons. *Comprehensive Psychiatry*, 30, 505–511.

Stern, L.M., Walker, M.J., Sawyer, M.G., Oades, R.D., Badcock, N.R. and Spence, J.G. (1990). A controlled crossover trial of fenfluramine in autism. *Journal of Child Psychology and Psychiatry*, 31, 569–585.

Stone, J.L., McDaniel, K.D., Hughes, J.R. and Hermann, B.P. (1986). Episodic dyscontrol disorder and paroxysmal EEG abnormalities: successful treatment with carbamazepine. *Biological Psychiatry*, 21, 208–212.

Swedo, S., Leonard, H., Rapoport, J.L., Lenane, M.C., Goldberger, E.L. and Cheslow, D.L. (1989). A double-blind comparison of clomipramine and desipramine in the treatment of trichotillomania (hair pulling). *New England Journal of Medicine*, 321, 497–501.

Szymanski, L., Kedesdy, J., Sulkes, S. and Cutler, A. (1987). Naltrexone in treatment of self injurious behaviour: a clinical study. *Research in Developmental Disabilities*, 8, 179–190.

Tennent, G., Bancroft, J. and Cass, J. (1974). The control of deviant sexual behavior by drugs: a double-blind controlled study of benperidol, chlorpromazine and placebo. *Archives of Sexual Behaviour*, 3, 261–271.

Tunks, E.R. and Dermer, S.W. (1977). Carbamazepine in the dyscontrol syndrome associated with limbic system dysfunction. *Journal of Nervous and Mental Disease*, 164, 56–63.

Turk, J. (1992). The fragile-X syndrome: on the way to a behavioural phenotype. *British Journal of Psychiatry*, 160, 24–35.

Walker, G. (1994). *ABPI Data Sheet Compendium*. London, Datapharm Publications.

Walters, A.S., Barrett, R.P., Feinstein, C., Mercurio, A. and Hole, W.T. (1990). A case report of naltrexone treatment of self-injury and social withdrawal in autism. *Journal of Autism and Developmental Disorders*, 20, 169–176.

Winchel, R.M. and Stanley, M. (1991). Self-injurious behavior: a review of the behavior and biology of self-mutilation. *American Journal of Psychiatry*, 148, 306–317.

World Health Organisation (WHO) (1992). *ICD-10 Classification of Mental and Behavioural Disorders: Clinical Descriptions and Diagnostic Guidelines*. Geneva, WHO.

Yar-Khan, S. (1981). The psychiatrically violent patient. *British Medical Journal*, **282**, 1400–1401.

11

Appreciating the style of perception and learning as a basis for anticipating and responding to the challenging behaviour of adults with autism

Hugh Morgan

IT HAS been seen already that pharmacological interventions can play a significant role in the treatment of the symptomatic behaviour sometimes displayed by people with autism. In Chapter Ten, for example, David Clarke illustrates the predisposing factors leading to, and maintaining, seriously self-injurious behaviour in a man with autism and the fragile-X syndrome. His analysis includes consideration of the inter-relationship between cognitive, environmental and biochemical factors. This chapter extends and develops the psychological side of this theme by considering the style of autistic perception and learning as predisposing factors leading to the symptomatic and sometimes challenging behaviour so characteristic of people with autism. Symptomatic behaviours, including self-injurious, stereotypical and ritualistic behaviours, even repeated and determined questioning of others, may often arise because the person with autism feels under threat, frustrated, unable to communicate with others, and is therefore unable to predict what will happen next. This chapter will argue that behaviour should not be seen in isolation from cognition.

Traditional treatments used in autism have tended to focus on visible behaviour alone, that is the symptoms associated with autism, rather than on the underlying reasons for the anxiety which produces the overt displays of behaviour. It will be argued that the challenge in providing therapeutic services for adults with autism lies *not* in the success or failure with which we, as practitioners, apply intervention strategies in attempts to ameliorate the problematic behaviour of people with autism, but in how we can create the conditions to enable people with autism to predict their world with a degree of confidence, by beginning from the premise that the autistic perception of the world is qualitatively different to our own. It seems ironic that we accuse people with autism of being lacking in the intuitive skill of empathy, yet it is our own lack of empathy - our apparent inability to place our-

231

selves in the shoes of the person with autism – that has hampered our ability, as practitioners, to understand the reasons for displays of behaviours which challenge services.

This chapter therefore identifies and considers underlying reasons which may contribute to behaviours which are seen to challenge services. Any strategy for helping the individual with autism to achieve predictability and control in his or her life will need to be based on an understanding of the style of autistic learning. Enabling strategies then can be developed by providing answers to the questions that the person with autism is likely to have. This method will be referred to as signposting. There is, however, the recognition that practitioners sometimes encounter, and must to respond to, some very difficult situations. Acknowledgement of these pressures is made and general guidelines are detailed for intervening in challenging circumstances. It may be helpful to begin with a brief glance at traditional approaches to the symptomatic behaviour of autism: psychodynamic, educational and behavioural.

PSYCHODYNAMIC APPROACHES TO TREATMENT

It was seen in Chapter One that in the two decades following the end of the Second World War, psychodynamic explanations and responses to autism were dominant in many countries. For example, Bettleheim (1967) proposed that autism was derived from the parents having death wishes towards the child, and, today, in some countries, particularly in Southern Europe, the psychoanalytical model still prevails and proponents of this approach still talk in terms of 'curing' autism (for one example see Athanassios and Panopoulou-Maratou 1995). However, there has been little or no systematic evaluation of this form of treatment and subsequent research has failed to support the value of the psychoanalytical explanation for the origin of autism or its treatment (Howlin *et al.* 1987). Such theories appear to have failed to explain the highly specific nature of cognitive and communicative defects associated with autism.

PHARMACOLOGICAL APPROACHES TO TREATMENT

Howlin *et al.* (1987) appraised the efficacy of medication in the treatment of the symptomatic behaviour of autism and indicated that what limited evidence there is suggests that drug treatments for autism are far from being essential and do very little to affect the basic disorder. Medication has continued to be given to individuals with autism in the management of behavioural problems, particularly those seen to arise from extreme anxiety or disruptive behaviour (Le Couteur 1990). There seems to be a significant use of medication in the current treatment of the symptomology associated with autism. For example, a report on the services provided by GAUTENA to children and adults with autism in the Basque region of Spain illustrates that 40% of children and adults receive some form of medication. This figure includes medication for allergies, tranquillisers and sleeping pills (Scott 1995). Howlin *et al.* (1987) suggested that pharmaceutical intervention may be useful in reducing the non-specific symptoms aligned with autism. Clarke agrees (Chapter Ten), though cautions that further research is required before firm conclusions can be drawn.

What are the general concerns about the applications of taking medication to treat the symptomatic behaviours found in autism ?

Shattock (1995), a senior lecturer in pharmacy and Director of the Autism Research Unit at the University of Sunderland, has raised the following general concerns on the use of medications to treat the symptomatic behaviour of autism:

1 There are biological, and probably biochemical, abnormalities in people with autism when compared to the general population and, therefore, it is difficult to predict what will be the consequence of taking a particular medication.
2 Because of the individual differences between people with autism, their symptoms and underlying problems will differ, and the application of medication which is appropriate for one may not be appropriate for another.
3 The medications used to treat the symptomatic behaviour of autism were not designed specifically for people with autism and the effects of variations in dosage are often profound. It is not necessarily the case that by increasing the dose there will be a parallel increase in effect.
4 The drug without side effects does not exist. Drugs with similar structures and modes of action will, when taken together, have an additive effect and thus an increased potential for side effects. Shattock likened the effects of drugs upon the brain as being more related to the blunderbuss than to the rapier (Shattock and Burrows 1995).

EDUCATIONAL APPROACHES TO TREATMENT

The recognition that autistic children have specific cognitive restrictions had a marked influence on methods of treatment in the 1960s and 1970s and, indeed, ever since. Early educational programmes tended to rely on psychological and regressive techniques, i.e. psychotherapeutic approaches, but these came to be replaced by methods of more direct teaching. It has been demonstrated (Bartak and Rutter 1973; Rutter and Bartak 1973) that children with autism responded well and made most progress in their academic and behavioural development within structured educational settings, rather than in those employing psychodynamic approaches. Take, for example, the teaching of self-recognition: the psychotherapeutic method might be to use play or drama therapy to unmask the 'self', whereas an educational strategy might use photographs and questions at key stages of a task to encourage the individual to recognise their own role in the activity, and, subsequently, their feelings of these experiences. Educational and behavioural methods have been the mainstay of current treatment used in the care of individuals with autism and Andersson *et al.* (1989) have recommended that any treatment plan must include educational and behavioural approaches.

BEHAVIOURAL APPROACHES TO TREATMENT

In order to be objective, the behavioural approach has sought to look at behaviour, i.e. at what is actually done. As soon as one looks at the circumstances in which behaviour occurs and the consequences of its occurrence, the possibility of introducing a technology can immediately be seen (Blackman 1976). Behaviour modification seeks to empirically measure human behaviour and descriptions therefore consist of what actually happens rather than interpreting the behaviour in terms of cognition, physiological factors and so on. Descriptions of behaviour take little account of the underlying desires, deficits, handicaps, damage or illness of an individual. Under this model, challenging behaviour is viewed as learned behaviour which can be explained by examining the associations between the antecedents, the behaviour, and the consequences of this behaviour. In the field of learning disabilities, challenging behaviour is now perceived to be serving four functions - attention, escape, tangible reinforcement,and sensory stimulation (Durand 1990, see McGill 1993).

Whilst behavioural interventions have been used widely in autism, many practitioners still harbour residual doubts about the effectiveness of their applications. The early work of the behaviourists in the field of autism was not evaluated effectively (Howlin *et al.* 1987). In autism especially, there have been on-going concerns that changes in patterns of behaviour learned in one setting are rarely transferred to another. McGill (1993) remarks that whilst there has been considerable evidence of the short-term effectiveness of behavioural methods with a wide range of individuals, such methods have produced disappointing amounts of maintenance and generalisation. Howlin *et al.* (1987) found that there was also no longer-term follow-up, although a recent study by Luce and Niemann (1995) attempts to replicate work on intensive behavioural intervention with young children with autism.

The value of the behavioural approach has been to instil a rigour in the way in which we, practitioners, record our observations, making us aware of the dangers of subjective interpretation. In recent years there has been a 'mellowing' of intensive and strictly behavioural approaches as exemplified by the growth of cognitive behaviourism. Aversions, i.e. the use of electric shocks, smacking, etc., can no longer be used in many countries. A good example of the contemporary behavioural interventions used specifically in preparing adults with autism for community life can be found in Datlow Smith (1990). But whilst behaviour modification has emerged from one attempt to understand behaviour, it is not the only way to do so. Behavioural approaches are certainly useful for teaching new skills, but not for teaching understanding, and this is particularly important when applied to people with autism. It has been suggested that people with autism possess unusual nervous systems and do not learn from the everyday environment as do others (Lovass *et al.* 1989), and they appear to have a different style of thinking and learning (Grandin and Scariano 1986; Sinclair 1992; Jordan and Powell 1994). It is therefore not enough to apply teaching approaches focusing on symptomatic behaviour alone, yet ignoring the cognitive make-up of the person with autism and their unconventional style of learning.

OTHER INTERVENTIONS

There is little empirical evidence that other methods of intervention including facilitated communication, play therapy, music therapy, pet therapy, daily life therapy, or holding therapy, offer any particular advantages (Howlin 1995). Parents' expectations are often raised by the bold statements of proponents of therapies purporting to offer 'cures' (for a recent example, see Sellin 1995). In order to make sense of, and assess, the potential benefits of a particular approach, it is necessary to consider the:

1 extent to which the new intervention strategy addresses the specific impairments found in autism
2 rationale and main principles of practice
3 evidence for its effects
4 ways in which the new approach differs from one's own practice
5 need to make a considered judgment to assess the potential effects of the new approach by collecting information before, during and after, the intervention is employed (Jones 1995).

Furthermore, the value of on-going collaborative work compared with the singular forms of treatment has been emphasised. A multidisciplinary integration of approaches, in which family/carers are actively involved, is recommended by Andersson *et al.* (1989), i.e. all significant persons who interact with the person with autism (Lovass *et al.* 1989). Le Couteur (1990) identified three significant elements which comprise an effective treatment programme for intervening when children with autism exhibit behavioural difficulties. These very general guidelines, which would also seem to be as relevant for many adolescents and young adults are: (1) assess the child's skills and difficulties within the natural environment; (2) utilise parents as co-therapists; (3) introduce change gradually, with the minimum of distress. For adults with autism, we should perhaps include practitioners and befrienders in the second point.

Even so, the application of assessment to adults with autism in naturalistic settings is not as straightforward as it may seem at first. Different types of assessment may be required for different types of treatment. Naturalistic observations may lead to unrealistic conclusions being reached as to the abilities of the adult with autism, because the behaviour may be tied to the situation in which it was learned and may not be representative of a general ability (Edwards *et al.* 1995). Edwards *et al.* also point out that observers should be aware of the potential role played by familiar staff (and this would also apply to parents/carers/befrienders) in structuring and supporting the communication of the adult with autism, and be aware of the implications in situations where there is no such structure. Although in naturalistic settings – at home possibly, in which individuals are able to feel confident, secure and relaxed – then such circumstances provide a better opportunity to observe and assess the strengths and skills of people with autism (Morgan 1994).

ACHIEVING LEVELS OF UNDERSTANDING RATHER THAN RESPONDING TO SYMPTOMS

Generally, it can be summarised so far that, with the exception of educational approaches, the emphasis of attention has been upon changing the behavioural patterns of the individual but not upon seeking ways to improve their levels of understanding, or indeed upon ways of adapting our behaviours to make ourselves more understandable to the individual with autism.

The challenge in working with people with autism should be to find intervention strategies which are based upon an understanding of the nature of autism. Peeters (1995 and unpublished material) talks about autism as being analogous to an iceberg. The visible tip of the iceberg is representative of the symptoms of autism, but the bulk of the iceberg, lying hidden beneath the water, is representative of the reasons for behaviour. By inter-

Illustration 237

vening at the level of symptoms alone, perhaps by pharmaceutical or operant conditioning techniques, the tip of the iceberg may dissipate, but, even so, support for the individual may not necessarily be helpful, because the levels of understanding of autism have been ignored. Peeters' iceberg analogy is orientated towards children – what might it look like if it is applied to adults with autism?

ILLUSTRATION

Visible tip of the iceberg

Symptoms

Obsessive interests
Repetitive actions
Aggression to others and self
Does not interact with peers
Becomes anxious when previously held meanings are disrupted and challenged
Inappropriate sexual behaviour in public
Appears unfeeling to the needs of others
Laughs at, but not with, others
Repeatedly questions others

Invisible part of the iceberg

Causes

Does not understand the rules of the game
Cannot make sense of much of the social behaviour used by others
Understands little of the verbal and non-verbal language used by others
Has psychosexual drives but does not understand the social taboos and meanings
Has difficulty in 'experiencing self' and as a consequence has difficulty in self-control
Lacks social empathy, of intuitive and shared understanding
Restricted imagination fails to add meaning to perception
Unable to control environment, is unable to predict events, events seem to happen by chance
Learning is specific and does not generalise to other settings
Attachments to objects, routine, space and people provide predictability and security

Intervention strategies should therefore take into account the perceptual disabilities of autism and the consequential impact upon learning.

SIGNPOSTING

It is the task of practitioners to answer the questions that the person with autism has but is unlikely to have the means by which to communicate them, or the intuitive understanding of the context in which questions are relevant. Signposts encourage individuals with autism to predict, with confidence, their daily activities. We need to find methods of signposting which reflect a cognition requiring regularity. We also need to be conscious that the development of communication, including receptive language, and social awareness is inseparable (Claiborne Park 1986). Practitioners should become aware of their own behaviour in this process, of the verbal and non-verbal language that is used, the tone of voice and the clarity of the message.

The person with autism is likely to need answers to several distinct questions including 'Where should I be?', 'What do I have to do?', 'When do I do it?', 'How long will it last?', 'Who do I do it with?'. The answers to these questions will have implications for the organisation of the environments in which they live, work, study and spend their leisure time.

A key task for practitioners will be to help people with autism learn to manage time. Duration is an abstract concept, 'wait until next week' for many people with autism is likely to be unimaginable. Often the management of time can be achieved by scheduling, by task organisation and daily timetables, which are simply alternative forms of communication. But, for many people with autism, reading timetables, whether written or pictorial, will be difficult. In these situations it may be helpful to begin with sequencing two activities using pictures. There must be an end in sight, for, without the certainty of a finishing point, then anxiety-induced behaviour may occur.

There are, of course, alternative or augmentative methods of communication including the use of rote learning, bliss symbols, or sign language (Wilbur 1985). But the key to effective use will be the concrete relationship between, say, the sign used and the meaning *behind* the gesture used. Makaton, which is often used in services for adults with autism, and which is a derivative of the British Sign Language for the Deaf, rarely makes use of signs which truly look like the meanings they represent.

The transition from child to adulthood is likely to raise all sorts of other questions for the person with autism. 'Will I be able to have a four-bedroomed house?', 'Will I have a partner?', 'Will I be able to drive my own car?'. Haracopos (1989) remarks that, in Denmark, it is not unusual for adults with autism to undergo a serious crisis in their early- to mid-twenties.

Haracopos says that a well-functioning person with autism, can, concurrently with positive development, reach a painful recognition of their own limitations, and begin to experience problems in coping with the norms and expectations of society.

There is therefore a need for predictability. Life, for the person with autism, appears to be dictated by chance, and they must learn to see that, normally, events do not occur randomly. Too often, insecurity, lack of confidence, and nervous energy are expended in the search for predictability and stability. Therefore purpose in life for people with autism is essential, for, without the organisation and support necessary, withdrawal into stereotypical and obsessive patterns of behaviour can occur. It is often seen that people with autism react to the smallest change in their environment, but this adds weight to the suggestion that attachments for people with autism are based upon the need for predictability and security. When one brick in the wall is missing, the whole wall, for the person with autism, can come tumbling down.

In the following scenario, the perspective of the person with autism living in a residential and Day Centre community is used as an example to highlight the need for clarity and predictability.

VIGNETTE 11.1

Imagine you are in the art room. It is relatively quiet and you are drawing a favourite picture. The picture is of a house, which you are drawing from the roof downwards – this is because you like to look upwards at things, as you like to know that you are safely on the ground. You have already drawn the roof and the top storey, and are just finishing the windows when someone asks you to do something, the words are indistinct but you manage to catch the words 'milk' and 'kitchen'.

Your immediate reaction is to go to the kitchen (which is next door in the house in which you live) to get some milk, but on the way a variety of thoughts suddenly fill your mind, 'which kitchen did they mean?', 'how much milk do they want?', 'where do they want it?'. Worse still, you didn't finish the house, 'how will the roof stay up with no ground floor?', 'what if it hasn't got a door', 'how will you get in?', or 'what if it has got a door and it's open not shut?', 'what's behind it?', or, 'who's behind it?', 'is anything behind it?', 'how much milk?', 'where?', which kitchen?

On reaching the kitchen, the member of staff who is tidying up, says something to you. You catch the words 'Day Centre'. (What they have actually said is, 'Shouldn't you be in the Day Centre?'.) So you obediently turn round and go back towards the Day Centre; this time you are not only worried about your picture and whether it will still be there, but also if you have done something wrong. 'What will happen if your cup of tea has no milk?', 'maybe it has all gone for ever and that's why the person in the kitchen didn't give you any, so what will you do about breakfast, what will you put on your two Weetabix with two spoonfuls of sugar?'.

When you get back in the Day Centre your first concern is your picture, upon which, you are horrified to find, someone has scribbled; 'How can you finish it now so that it looks like it did when you drew it yesterday?'. Then a voice, a trifle impatiently, asks you why you haven't brought back any milk. You try to explain, but can't find the words to express yourself and begin to get frightened. Your mind locks into previous experiences from your life, some unsettling, others giving you a degree of security. Somebody is asking you again to fetch more milk, but they didn't say where from or how much. How will the roof stay on and where did the scribble come from, maybe the house is cracked and is going to fall down in which case how can you draw an identical house tomorrow because it won't be the same as yesterday and how much milk and ..... wouldn't life be so much easier if you could just go and sit somewhere quiet and familiar and safe (the toilet), until everything is alright again?

This situation could have been made so much more comfortable for the person with autism had practitioners signposted the way forward to him: i.e. the practitioner calls the individual by name, who is then asked to go to the kitchen to fetch two pints of milk and then to come back to the art room. The practitioner lays particular emphasis upon 'kitchen', 'house', 'two', 'milk' and 'art room' and says they will look after the picture. The person with autism understands 'where', and 'how much', and also has the security of knowing that his/her picture is safe. The member of staff should speak clearly and unambiguously, and could use sign language or gestures to emphasise what is wanted.

RELATING DIFFICULT BEHAVIOUR TO THE TRIAD OF IMPAIRMENTS

Moving on from demonstrating the need to try to understand the world through the eyes of people with autism, we must accept that sometimes situations do break down and anxiety-induced behaviour is displayed by the person with autism. Those who support and work with people with autism have a responsibility to ensure that both they and the person with autism are as physically and emotionally safe as possible under such circumstances. Adults are physically bigger and stronger than children and the chances are high of injury occurring to both the practitioner and the person with autism.

There is, as yet, no definition of 'challenging behaviour' applied specifically in the field of autism. Those who work closely with people with autism will, through the processes of observation and record keeping, have identified the behaviours in the individuals they work with which are seen to challenge services. Such behaviours will include those not so prevalent within the broader field of learning disabilities including repeated questioning, obsessional and ritualistic behaviour and self-injurious behaviour.

Each of the three essential features of autism, i.e. restricted socialisation, imagination and communication, can lead to behavioural difficulties, but, additionally, often as a consequence of these impairments, there are secondary behavioural problems. Gould (1988) says that when problem behaviours occur in adults these are not so easily dealt with as in children. She identified that the problem of social interaction – illustrated by Wing and Gould's (1979) categories of the aloof person, the passive person and the active but odd person – can lead to differences in the type of problem behaviours displayed. Their clarification represented a broadening of the concept of autism, as identified by Kanner (1943). Gould (1988) acknowledged that these three descriptions were not fixed and static, as individuals with autism may change as they grow older. Wing (1988) identified that the largest group within the triad were those who tended to continue to remain severely impaired in skills and behaviour from child to adulthood. A minority of this group were passive, or active but odd, in their social interaction. Behavioural difficulties associated with this group of people with severe impairments include pica, self-injury, destructiveness and random aggression. It was suggested that behavioural problems became less marked from around 30 years of age (Wing 1989). Wing (1989) also describes a severely aggressive subgroup, as:

a tiny minority who are extremely, even dangerously, aggressive, sometimes self-injuring as well as attacking others

(Wing 1989, p.423)

PRACTITIONER STRESS

Cornish (1986) undertook a qualitative survey of stress encountered by practitioners working with adults with autism. Cornish points out that when working with difficult people in difficult situations, practitioners may experience frustration, helplessness, fatigue, despair and surrender. Although these are all indicators of stress, they are hardly ever measured in physiological terms, except, perhaps, as when a member of staff goes on sick leave. They identified that communication was a key problem, and the inability of practitioners to communicate effectively with the person with autism was described as restricting and disabling. The implication is, presumably, that they receive little positive feedback resulting from their attempts to communicate with their clients. Cornish reported that practitioners experience stress in a variety of forms including: (1) guessing what the person with autism wants; (2) managing obsessional behaviour; (3) searching for appropriate levels of communication; (4) working with people who have an erratic learning pattern, i.e. what is established one day may not transfer to the next (and, one might add, to other settings); (5) lack of feedback (it is often difficult to tell how much the client absorbs or enjoys); (6) echolalia (repetition of what has been said); (7) size and strength of adults with autism can be fear-provoking; (8) noise levels with group settings have knock-on effects to trigger behaviour in others.

These examples seem to illustrate a *range of overt and passive behaviours* which trouble practitioners. To be added to this list should be: (1) seriously self-injurious behaviour (which in itself produces several stressful situations for practitioners, including supporting the self-injuring individual, coming to terms with one's own distress, and explaining and reassuring parents/carers and other practitioners); (2) repeated questioning; (3) intense curiosity; and (4) behaviour arising from the inability of the person with autism to communicate effectively. It would be helpful to look at how a team of practitioners rationalised and approached the latter three behaviours. These illustrations are examples of how these behaviours can be tackled, but, by no means are they intended to be prescriptive.

VIGNETTE 11.2

REPETITIVE QUESTIONING

Tim has lived in a residential unit with 19 other adults with autism for the past six years. He has always been repetitive in his questions to others and occasionally becomes obsessive and persistent to the point where he will display self-injurious behaviour if he is not answered to his satisfaction.

Practitioners felt his questions fell into two categories. Firstly, there is direct repetition:

Q. 'What do you call a long nose?'
A. 'A trunk'
Q. 'Is that what you call it yes?'
A. 'Yes'
Q. 'Yes?'
And so on......
Secondly, there are questions when he is anxious:
Q. 'Why do people talk?'
A. 'People like to talk.'
Q. 'Why do people have to keep talking?'
And so on.......

The increase in intensity of Tim's questioning was observed to be directly correlated to recent events in his life. For example, Tim enjoyed close contact with a relatively small family group, one of whom had died two years previously after a protracted illness, and also, within the residential unit, four long-term residents had moved on to a new home nearby. These examples were felt to be significant life events. One of his questions/phrases is 'like living in houses, best not staying in them,' while a second is:

Q. 'Why do people go to sleep ?'
A. 'Because they are tired.'
Q. 'Nothing wrong with them is there, no?'
And so on....

Through the process of observation and recording it was felt that Tim's questioning served several functions: for reassurance by generating a familiar response, to initiate conversation/interaction and to express his anxieties. The approach adopted was to allot Tim specific times of the day based within his daily routine, when, for a period of five minutes he would have all his questions answered on a one-to-one level in his own room. At other times he would be answered only once, and not at all in certain environments in relation to his direct repetition, for example, when he was out for a drink in the pub. This imposed environmental constraint has been found to have a beneficial effect in that he will increase the range of questions to ask when he knows his usual ones will not be answered.

VIGNETTE 11.3

CURIOSITY

Dave has lived in residential units for the past ten years and his most problematic behaviour results from his intense curiosity. On occasions Dave has entered his peers' rooms to look, touch, but not take, their possessions. He has been observed frequently approaching people not only in the home, but also outside in the community, to look at the labels on their clothes or the contents of their pockets. Dave's curiosity has been especially disconcerting because when the inappropriateness of his actions is pointed out he displays negative behaviour, becoming self-injurious and damaging to property and the personal possessions of others.

The approach adopted by practitioners was twofold, both structured and informal. The structured approach was to teach augmented methods of communication to encourage more appropriate social behaviours, through slides, photographs and role-play. These guidelines were reinforced by, for example, the use of signs on doors saying 'please knock and wait', through practitioners consciously acting as role models, and through verbal praise. Whilst reinforcing such concepts, practitioners also adopted more informal approaches:

It was agreed that, at times, Dave needed to be given an appropriate phrase to use. To elaborate, if Dave went to look at the labels on clothes he would receive the prompt, 'what do you say Dave?You say, can I have a look please?'. A further approach was to 'signpost', to leave written messages, as it was agreed that Dave was more likely to understand or follow written messages than those given verbally. For example, one of Dave's interests was to tune every radio he could find in the home to Radio One, so the message left on a radio would be, 'Have you remembered to ask? Can I change the channel please?'.

VIGNETTE 11.4

FAILURE TO COMMUNICATE

His previous home having been closed at short notice, Patrick was moved into a new residential home. Within a short period of time Patrick began to exhibit adverse behaviours, flapping his hands and arms vigorously; if approached while doing this he became aggressive to others but, worryingly, if left alone he sometimes became seriously self-injurious.

After a period of observation, record keeping and discussion, it was decided that there was a build-up and function to this behaviour. Patrick would begin by pacing ritualistically, he would then begin to stare at his hands, and this would progress to flapping, before explosive self-injurious behaviour, including propelling himself through closed windows.

In the build-up to such behaviour, Patrick's limited speech would become clearer and he would usually ask for coffee. The short-term approach used was to advise him that he could make himself a coffee only after he had sat down and stopped flapping. Given Patrick's perceived level of cognitive ability this would be phrased clearly and unambiguously, he would be asked to 'sit down – stop flapping'. Once sitting down he would be asked to, 'stop flapping, breathe deeply', with practitioners demonstrating this to him. When he was sufficiently relaxed he was given a cup of coffee.

It was felt that the function of the behaviour was to attract attention to a 'want', the behaviour becoming more extreme as he failed to gain a response. With this in mind when practitioners saw Patrick begin to pace, they would ask him what he wanted; Patrick is verbal to a limited degree and it was felt he needed prompting to state what he wanted. Simultaneously, teaching approaches were employed to teach him more appropriate ways of attracting attention to obtain a need. These approaches encouraged the development of a routine with which Patrick felt comfortable, and, together with a steadily increased knowledge of Patrick as an individual by practitioners, the behaviour ceased.

RESPONDING TO DIFFICULT SITUATIONS – GENERAL GUIDELINES FOR PRACTITIONERS

It has been acknowledged that sometimes difficult situations can develop, despite the best efforts to anticipate and create the conditions in which the person with autism can feel secure and confident. Working with people with autism is not an exact science. Any organisation providing services for people with autism should have clear and unambiguous guidelines for the management of behaviours which are seen to challenge services. It is only through clear and consistently applied practices that both practitioners and individuals with autism can gain confidence in their living and working environments. The following guidelines represent some general principles and ways of behaving towards people with autism in residential and Day Centre settings. Again, this information is not meant to be prescriptive, but represents one organisation's approach to managing difficult behaviours by taking account of the style of autistic learning and the need to protect both the individual with autism and the practitioner:

Be extremely aware of your verbal and non-verbal communication. Remember that a person with autism may misunderstand or misinterpret any signals that you may unintentionally give. This is especially important as they are likely to be in an extremely high state of arousal.

1. Decrease the vulnerability of the practitioner and the person with autism: never leave a practitioner alone in a room with an individual with autism who has developed, for whatever reason, an anxiety about the practitioner. An insecurity is easily transferred to the person with autism, who will quickly notice those who feel anxious with him/her (Rusten 1989). In such situations it is better to have another person manage the situation.

2. Encourage other people to move to another area. There are two reasons for doing this: firstly to reduce the number of 'eyes' which the aroused individual feels are upon them, i.e. lessening the intimidation they may feel, secondly to prevent this particular difficulty becoming a trigger for adverse behaviour in others at the same time.

3. Stay calm: be aware of your own bodily responses to the stressful situation. Avoid tensing groups of muscles, e.g. folding arms, clenching fists, etc.

4. Eye contact: avoid staring at the anxious person, this may be construed as a signal of aggression. Try to maintain intermittent eye contact.

5. Keep a safe distance: try to maintain a safe distance between yourself and the anxious person. It is difficult to be specific about this distance. A person with autism may well find distances of three or four feet too intimidating.

6. Speech: tone of voice is extremely important. Use a soft, calming tone (a raised voice serves only to increase the threat that the individual feels, by conveying the practitioner's heightened arousal level, and therefore increases the upward spiral of aggression). Use only short, clear and unambiguous messages. Ensure that the instruction or other message you are giving cannot be misunderstood.

7. Touch: people with autism often dislike being touched by others. Generally, touch is perceived by others as being a signal of warmth, but can also be a sign of dominance. Avoid touching when the individual with autism in a high state of arousal, as this may well give the opposite message to the intended one of reassurance.

8. Listen to the person with autism: they may be trying to tell you something. Alternatively, a person with autism in a high state of arousal will often recount bad experiences which happened a long time ago, and which will have little or no relevance to the current situation.

9. Distraction: try to deflect the attention of the person with autism onto something which they find more pleasurable. Distraction should focus on something which enables the individual to regain some control and predictability over their environment. For example, 'Try to relax and then we will ...'.

10. Instruction: 'Relax, breathe slowly.' Demonstrate these bodily movements to the person with autism. Again this helps to distract attention away from the initial problem.

11. Record the problem: this is the record of the event. Record observations

and actions objectively. In the UK such records are considered legal documents.

12. Debrief: convey to other practitioners how the problem was diffused – good points, negative points. The aim should be to develop a consistency in the approach that all staff use. The individual with autism will gain security from the knowledge that he/she will be responded to and helped in a calm, reassuring and predictable manner by all practitioners.

CHAPTER SUMMARY

This chapter has considered the impact of cognition as a predisposing factor leading to challenging behaviour by adults with autism. It has been recognised that, for those with autism, symptomatic behaviour may be derived from a mismatch between the expectations arising from individual perception and the organisation of the environment around them. This is a helpful way of understanding the reasons for some of the difficult behaviours found when working with adults with autism and for constructing consistent intervention strategies. It has been argued that we should help to enable people with autism to make sense of their world, by beginning from the basis that they have great restrictions in their capacity to understand the social and communication rules defined by our society. By 'signposting' – providing answers to the questions that individuals will have, i.e. 'where should I be?', 'when will it start and finish?', 'what do I have to do', etc., – in concrete situations and locations, and by adopting alternative forms of communication, i.e. visually augmented systems, we may make messages and meanings more understandable. By doing so, we may, of course, anticipate and prevent many of the displays of behaviour which challenge services. However, it was recognised and acknowledged that sometimes difficult situations can develop in working with people with autism and that practitioners are under great pressure to find solutions quickly. Therefore, practical guidelines for responding to the immediate and symptomatic behaviour were presented.

ACKNOWLEDGEMENTS

Theo Peeters, David Tiesdell.

BIBLIOGRAPHY

Andersson, L., Bohman, M., Campbell, M., Coleman, M., Frith, U., Gillberg, C., Hagerman, R., Haracopos, D., Howlin, P., Lansing, M., Lelord, G., Lovass, I., Pelling, H., Plioplys, A., Rusten, B., Schopler, E., Spensley, S., Steffenburg, S.,

Tsai, L., Waterhouse, L. and Wing, L. (1989). The state of the art, May 1989. In C. Gillberg (ed.) *Autism: Diagnosis and Treatment*. New York, Plenum Press.

Athanassios, A. & Panopoulou-Maratou, O. (1995). The operation of the therapeutic community 'Little Garden' for psychotic and autistic children. Paper presented at The First European Conference for Autism, University of Athens, 13–15 January 1995.

Bartak, L. and Rutter, M. (1973). Design of study and characteristics of units, *Journal of Child Psychology and Psychiatry*, **14**, 161–179.

Bettleheim, B. (1967). *The Empty Fortress*. London, Free Press.

Blackman, D. (1976). Introduction and outline of behaviour modification with its basis in the scientific study of behaviour. In *Ethical Implications of Behaviour Modification*. Kidderminster, British Institute of Mental Handicap.

Claiborne Park, C. (1986). Social growth in autism. In E. Schopler and G.B. Mesibov (eds.) *Social Behaviour in Autism*. New York, Plenum Press.

Cornish, V. (1986). *The Autistic Adolescent and Adult*. Collection of papers. London, The Inge Wakehurst Memorial Trust Fund.

Datlow Smith, M. (1990). *Autism and Life in the Community: Successful Interventions for Behavioural Challenges*. Baltimore, Paul H. Brookes Publishing.

Durand, (1990). Cited in McGill, P. (1993). Understanding severe challenging behaviour. In *The Autistic Continuum in Adolescence and Adulthood*. Collection of papers from study weekends. London, The Inge Wakehurst Trust.

Edwards, G., Evans, G., Jordan, R., Knott, F., Lewis, C. and Williams, T. (1995). Observation, Assessment, Recording and Evaluation. Module 3. Unit 1, Distance Education Course in Autism (Adults). Birmingham, University of Birmingham, School of Education.

Gould, J. (1988). *Coping with Behaviour Problems. Adolescents and Adults with Autism*. Collection of Papers from Study Weekends. London, The Inge Wakehurst Trust.

Grandin, T. and Scariano, M.M. (1986). *Emergence Labeled Autistic*. California, Arena Press.

Haracopos, D. (1989). Comprehensive treatment programme for autistic children and Adults in Denmark. In C. Gillberg (ed.) *Autism: Diagnosis and Treatment*. New York, Plenum Press.

Howlin, P. (1996). *Autism in Adulthood: the Way Ahead*. London, Routledge.

Howlin, P., Rutter, M., Bergin, M., Hemsley, K., Hersor, L., and Yule, W. (1987). *Treatment of Autistic Children*. Chichester, John Wiley and Sons.

Jones, G.E. (1995). *Approaches to Autism. Distance Education Course for Professionals Working with Individuals with Autism*. Birmingham, University of Birmingham.

Jordan, R. (1995). Educational programmes with individuals with autism. Paper presented at the Research Day of the Midlands Branch of the Association for Child Psychology and Psychiatry, Birmingham, 1995.

Jordan, R. and Powell, S. (1994). Module 1. Unit 3, Distance Education Course in Autism (Adults). Birmingham, University of Birmingham, School of Education.

Kanner, L. (1943). Autistic disturbances of affective contact. *Nervous Child*, **2**, 217–250.

Le Couteur, A. (1990). Autism: current understanding and management. British Journal of Hospital Medicine, **43**, 448–452.

Lovass, I., Calouri, K. and Jada, J. (1989). In C. Gillberg (ed.) *Autism: Diagnosis and Treatment*. New York, Plenum Press.

Luce, S. and Niemann, G.W. (1995). Intensive behavioural intervention with young children with autism: preliminary data from a replication study. Paper presented at the Research Day of the Midlands Branch of the Association for Child Psychology and Psychiatry, Birmingham, 1995.

McGill, P. (1993). Understanding severe challenging behaviour. In *The Autistic Continuum in Adolescence and Adulthood:* Collection of Papers from Study Weekends. London, The Inge Wakehurst Trust.

Morgan, S.H.(1994). Can adults with autism empathise with others? (Master of Medical Science Degree Thesis. University of Birmingham, 1994).

Peeters, T. (1995). The best treatment of behaviour problems in autism is prevention. Paper presented at The First European Conference for Autism, University of Athens, 13–15 January 1995.

Rusten, B. (1989). Educational issues in adolescence. In C. Gillberg (ed.). *Autism: Diagnosis and Treatment.* New York, Plenum Press.

Rutter, M. and Bartak, L. (1973). Follow-up and findings and implications for services. *Journal of Child Psychology and Psychiatry,* **14,** 241–270.

Scott, L. (1995). GAUTENA: an exemplary system of services. *Link,* **16,** 9–11.

Sellin, B. (1995). *In Dark Hours I Find My Way.* London, Gollancz.

Shattock, P. (1995). In P. Shattock and T. Burrows (eds.) Promoting Physical and Material Well-Being. Module 2. Unit 3, Distance Education Course in Autism (Adults). Birmingham, University of Birmingham, School of Education.

Sinclair, J. (1992). Bridging the gaps: an inside-out view of autism (or do you know what I don't know?) In E. Schopler and G.B. Mesibov (eds.) *High-Functioning Individuals with Autism.* New York, Plenum Press.

Wilbur, R.B.(1985). Sign language and autism. In E. Schopler and G.B. Mesibov (eds.) *Communication Problems in Autism.* New York, Plenum Press.

Wing, L. (1988). The continuum of autistic characteristics. In E. Schopler and G.B. Mesibov (eds.) *Diagnosis and Assessment in Autism.* New York, Plenum Press.

Wing, L. and Gould, J. (1979). Severe impairments of social classification and associated abnormalities in children: epidemiology and classification. *Journal of Autism and Developmental Disorder,* **9,** 11–29.

12

Working with adults with autism in residential settings: a strategy for practitioner training

Hugh Morgan

INTRODUCTION

R ESIDENTIAL PROVISION is a significant means of support for many adults with autism. In 1995, no less than 1200 people with autism were living in services registered under the Autism Quality Audit and Accreditation programme in the UK. It could also be argued that with greater awareness and diagnosis of autism, there will be an increasing requirement for residential services for adults with autism. The success of all residential programmes for people with autism will be determined largely by the quality of practitioners who are recruited, and the capacity of the employing organisation to provide on-going support and training for their staff, so as to maintain a low turnover and stable environment.

This chapter has four main aims. Firstly, to investigate the need for training of practitioners working with adults with autism in residential settings. Secondly, to identify several of the essential training components for inclusion in a programme seeking to develop skills in good care practice for work with adults. Thirdly, to evaluate strategies for training which can be utilised by organisations providing services to adults with autism. The final objective is to identify the development of professional courses in autism-specific training for practitioners and to present a profile of one such course operated by the University of Birmingham.

INFLUENCES ON TRAINING

Internationally, there are very few training opportunities for staff wishing to obtain professional qualifications in autism. In some countries, university or college degree courses are prerequisites for employment in service provision for adults with autism and within other areas of the learning disabilities field. For example, Giddan and Giddan (1993) surveyed European farm communities for people with autism and found that degrees or qualifications obtained from courses in Social or Ortho Pedagogics were basic requirements for employment in communities operating in La Pradelle, France; Dr Leo Kannerhuis Wolfheze, Holland; Ny Allerodgard, Denmark; and La Garriga, Spain. Giddan and Giddan also surveyed the residential communities of Somerset Court, the Dunfirth Community and Hof Mayerweide, in England, Eire and Germany respectively, but discovered that recruitment policies encouraged applications from persons with other types of practice-based skills, not necessarily including academic qualifications. There is therefore a lack of consistency, at least at a superficial level, in the skills required by applicants for work in residential settings with adults with autism, between countries. So, whilst the situation in certain European countries can appear impressive, the completion of a university degree course would not, in its own right, equip an employee for work in the specific field of autism, for unless course curricula included in-depth, theoretical and practical expositions of autism, the value of application to work with people with autism is likely to be limited. Without this, there is a danger of confusing education with specialist training. Alternatively, it could be argued that the benefit of an academic background predisposes a practitioner to think and communicate in an organised manner and will help them to effectively assimilate practical experience.

Once in employment, the opportunities for practitioners to analyse and evaluate their practice and thus to gain insight into the reasons why they perform certain tasks in certain ways, can be comparatively restricted. In the UK an extensive study of services for children and adults with autism, undertaken by Jones and Newson (1992) showed that training for the majority of staff was derived from direct on-the-job experience, i.e. working alongside and observing the work of, experienced colleagues, and by participation in case discussions. What little research there is, has been applied to generic, rather than to autism-specific, residential practice.

'On-the-job' training is the most accessible form of training for residential practitioners who work tremendously unsocial hours. Other forms of training are less adaptable to the hours of work and the tasks of residential workers. Skills acquired from 'on-the-job' experiences should not be underestimated, for many practitioners working in settings with adults with autism have, by sheer dint of their practical experience, developed areas of expertise. Indeed, Henderson and Crowhurst (1991) highlight the importance of 'on-the-job' training and recommend that the role of managers as in-house trainers in residential work should be expanded. They suggest that 'on-the-job' training can be improved through the development of a structured system which increases the opportunities for training and feedback in four areas:

1 Pre-planning of activities of shift work
2 Household and community activities

3 Teaching skills
4 Coping strategies, i.e. of difficult behaviour

Mittler (1984) also values 'on-the-job' training, believing that it must be practical and designed to equip people with learning disabilities with the whole range of skills sufficient for community living. Record keeping should be a key priority for 'on-the-job' training, as a method of demonstrating to practitioners the effectiveness of their actions. It is imperative that practitioners should have the support of their managers so that the training is consistently translated into practice. A particular weakness of 'on-the-job' training arises from a lack of evaluation of the process, for without evaluation, recognition and acknowledgement of practitioners' practice skills can be sadly missing. Jones and Newson (1992) ask the pertinent question

'How can staff evaluate the work that they do? Is it possible to develop an evaluation package which provides staff with a structure and ideas on how they might assess the effect of particular interventions or ways of working within their establishment?'
(Jones and Newson, p. 32)

Due to the lack of any systematic approach to training, there is a need to develop strategic planning at both local and national levels. Cullen (1988) is critical of traditional training techniques, i.e. lectures, and workshops which often focus on one-to-one situations with service-users. The effectiveness of such training needs to be measured against positive changes in the lives of their clients and Cullen believes that there is little evidence to this effect and therefore new methods must be used and evaluated. In the USA, Anderson (1987) has also been critical of traditional training models for residential workers, but found that the inclusion of written or verbal feedback to practitioners was an important component in training schedules.

This chapter is therefore concerned with comparing and contrasting the traditional modes of training for practitioners employed in residential settings with adults with autism and thus enabling practitioners working within residential settings to develop a coherent and resource-effective strategy for training.

THE CLOSE RELATIONSHIP BETWEEN GENERIC CARE PRACTICE AND AUTISM-SPECIFIC PRACTICE

There is a very close relationship between generic residential or day care practice and the capacity of an employee and an agency to provide specific care for adults with autism. Autism-specific practice cannot operate without good residential care practice, which itself becomes the underpinning experience upon which the application of autism-specific practice can be laid.

Practitioners supporting adults with autism in residential and day settings will need to acquire skills and knowledge in both generic care and also autism-specific practice. Take communication for example – the ability of a member of staff to communicate clearly and objectively with other staff, both verbally and in writing, is an essential skill for work both with people with autism and, of course, in any other area of the caring professions. Wall (1990) identifies that, despite many positives in the operation of the TEACCH group homes, a major source of frustration appears to be the lack of effective skills in working with people with autism, including communication problems with co-workers. But one can look beyond provision in North Carolina and see that, traditionally, communication problems between co-workers is a major problem with any type of work in the caring professions, doubtless in every country, and not just something peculiar to autism. It is something that practitioners often get wrong, yet must continually strive to get right. Within the field of autism, however, the need for excellent communication systems between co-workers has added impact, for without consistency from practitioners, the potential for ambiguity being passed on to clients with autism is enormous. People with autism often appear to be inordinately perceptive and alive to inconsistencies within their environment and between staff. Poor communication between practitioners is therefore likely to lead to an inconsistent living environment – one in which adults with autism will become increasingly confused and anxious.

Training for work in the more continuously intense areas of work with adults with autism, i.e. for practitioners in residential homes or day care centres, can be planned strategically and may be approached at two levels. Level-one training should be organised to facilitate the development of underpinning skills in good quality residential/day care practice. Level-two training should equip practitioners with an appropriate knowledge base for working together with adults with autism. With the increasing numbers of adults now receiving a diagnosis of autism, one of the exciting tasks ahead must be to identify the special characteristics which are essential for working with adults with autism.

DEMONSTRATING THE NEED

How well equipped are staff working with adults with autism in the underpinning knowledge of good residential care practice?

A high proportion of people with a diagnosis of autism will also have an associated learning disability. Therefore, as there is a paucity of previous and detailed studies investigating the training of practitioners working with adults with autism, it would seem reasonable to draw upon findings obtained from research which has looked at the training requirements of practitioners working with people with learning disabilities.

Smith *et al.* (1994) reported on the training needs and aspirations of both managerial and front-line practitioners (referred to in the study as, 'care staff') working in community residential care for adults with learning disabilities who were resettled from hospitals in the West Midlands region of the UK. The report drew on a larger survey carried out by Wun and Cumella (1993) and included staff employed in four different agencies: The National Health Service (NHS), Social Services, voluntary (i.e. not for profit) and private (i.e. for profit) sectors. A total of 222 support staff and 75 managerial staff responded to the survey.

Care staff

Of the care staff (mean age 36 years and mean length of service 32 months) 94.6% held no relevant professional qualification (i.e. in nursing or social work). Without formal qualifications, the significance of induction programmes assumes great importance. Indeed, induction training has been seen as producing a positive effect for staff involved in resettlement programmes for people with learning disabilities (Allen *et al.* 1990). Yet, in three of the four employing organisations, care staff who received induction training were in the minority – 85.8% failing to receive any at all. Furthermore, in the private sector, none had received any induction training.

Staff were asked to rate their need for training and to identify their training priorities for a list of training topics. Overall, 49.8% of care staff believed that more training was required and top of their list was the need for training in the management of challenging behaviour. Conversely, philosophy and attitudes to learning disability were scored as one of the low priority areas for training.

Managerial staff

In the Smith *et al.* (1994) study, 58% of managerial staff overall held nursing or social work qualifications. As in the case of care staff, only a small proportion of managers working in NHS, Social Services and voluntary establishments received induction training. Not one private sector manager had received induction training. Of the managers, 49% felt that more training was needed, priorities being managerial training (including the area of finance as well as training in therapeutic techniques). Like their care staff, philosophy and attitudes to learning disabilities featured as low priority training needs for managers.

So what conclusions relevant to work with people with autism can be drawn?

If one accepts that the design and delivery of services for people with autism traditionally tends to be very comparable to those for people with learning disabilities, then the following points will be pertinent. The provision of training for staff working in the field of learning disabilities continues to be given a low priority by service-provider organisations and, as a consequence, staff tend to have low expectations for training. Staff priorities are often understandably focused on receiving greater guidance to help them to cope with their most traumatic episodes at work, which are likely to revolve around the area of clients' problematic behaviours. There is therefore a need for the development of coherent training strategies for both the induction and on-going needs of practitioners.

LEVEL ONE – TRAINING DESIGNED TO DEVELOP AN UNDERPINNING KNOWLEDGE FOR PRACTITIONERS WORKING WITH ADULTS WITH AUTISM

The training process for practitioners working in the TEACCH Group Homes in North Carolina commences with an involved staff selection process prior to any appointment being made. Thereafter, training is largely governed by the licensing agency for Group Homes in North Carolina – the Division of Facility Services of the State Department of Social Services – the equivalent of the Local Authority Registration Department in the UK. Staff are required to receive training in areas including medication administration, fire prevention, resuscitation techniques and first aid. By contrast, autism-specific training falls outside the jurisdiction of the licensing authority and becomes the responsibility of the organisation managing the Group Homes, i.e. TEACCH (Wall 1990).

A comparable position operates in England and Wales, whereby units providing residential care for adults with autism are instructed to adhere to the standards laid down under *Home Life: a Code of Practice for Residential Care* (DHSS 1984), a document which falls under the terms of reference of the 1984 *Registered Homes Act*. Often erroneously believed to be a charter for older persons' services, it covers several other client groups, including those with learning disabilities. This document states that the general safety of the residents is the responsibility of the home owner, who must ensure that staff receive training in appropriate areas. As in the USA, there is no legal requirement for practitioners to undertake autism-specific training. The initial emphasis is placed on training, including fire prevention, first aid, health and safety, etc. So what basic skills in good care practice should be expected of staff working with adults with autism ?

Training should go well beyond areas of basic skills laid down by State or National legislative authorities. Although fire prevention and first aid are clearly important skills, it would be reasonable to expect that all practitioners could have the opportunity to explore the areas identified below.

Level-one training topics

- Historical aspects of the project - what circumstances led to the development of the project in which they find themselves employed
- Philosophy of an establishment, i.e. objectives and methods of achievement
- Rights of their client group
- Learning disabilities and the law
- Observation and record keeping. Formal and informal systems of communication
- An appreciation of the value of multidisciplinary work by looking at the role of the clinical psychologist, field work social worker, community nurse
- Parents' perspective
- Team building
- Role evaluation
- Role of the key worker
- Equal opportunities
- Fire prevention
- Health and safety
- First aid
- Supervision skills
- Epilepsy
- Food hygiene
- Knowledge of normal child development and ageing processes.

The astute manager or training officer can often arrange for these topics to be provided on an in-house basis by professionals from other agencies at minimal or no cost. Practitioner rotas can be organised effectively to ensure that once per week staff have the opportunity to meet together. Most, if not all subjects, should be repeated on an annual basis to ensure that practitioners are being up-dated with new regulations and to ensure that good practices are being maintained. Of course, this much of this information can be reinforced in a manual, given to each practitioner when they commence employment and undertake their induction programme. It is possible that, in the UK, the recent and evolving introduction of National Vocational

Qualifications (NVQs), by the National Council for Vocational Qualifications (1988), will encourage the development of general competencies in some, if not all, of the above-mentioned subjects. However, as yet, NVQs do not address autism-specific practice, because they focus on the development of generic work-based competencies.

Strategies for training

The work of practitioners with adults with autism can be multifaceted. Elements of social work can be required, including a knowledge of welfare rights and of working in partnership with families. Likewise nursing skills are useful, for practitioners need to know the uses and side effects of the medicines they administer and to be able to recognise and appropriately support individuals suffering epileptic seizures. Practitioners also require teaching skills based upon the unconventional style of autistic learning to enable individuals with autism to acquire new skills, and for appropriate recording and observation to take place. Management skills for those practitioners leading teams may also be useful and can help practitioners to retain structure and objectivity in staff management situations. We ask a lot of practitioners working with adults with autism!

So, it is important that any organisation providing support services for adults with autism should have a coherent strategy for training. This plan must be understood and agreed by all practitioners and also by the employing organisation, so ensuring that expectations for training are realistic and are tailored to reflect the needs of the client group and their staff. We can learn much from innovative practitioner training operated in developing countries by following easily understood principles for training. These were summarised by Cullen (1995) as:

> Compatible
> Decentralised
> Effective and observable
> Inexpensive
> Flexible
> Simple
> Sustainable.

The message implied is to keep practitioner training focused on the skills, knowledge and needs required by the specific client group, i.e. in this case, adults with autism. Focus is lost as soon as there is movement into training which does not reflect the needs of the people being supported. In residential settings there are four key avenues that will be available, not all of these meeting the principles outlined by Cullen (1995):

1 In-house training
2 Training which takes place outside the establishment consisting of one-day or short courses
3 External training courses which offer the opportunity for staff to undertake a relevant professional qualification
4 Distance learning approach.

By exploring these strategies in greater depth it is possbile to outline some of the advantages or disadvantages inherent in each method.

In-house training

The in-house training method has several appealing advantages for practitioners employed in residential settings for adults with autism. Logistically, it is possible to maximise the number of staff taking part in the training session and to minimise the disruption caused to the autistic client group. Furthermore, the impact on an organisation's training budget, caused by bringing in outside speakers, can be fairly low when tutors' fees are divided between the maximum number of places on the course. Travel costs and time away from the client are kept to a minimum by this method.

The in-house method can also have advantages in terms of the content of teaching, whereby invited speakers have an opportunity to see an establishment in concrete terms rather than as an abstract concept, thereby enabling them to have a clearer grasp of the environment in which staff are employed, and any discussion can then be centred on the needs of the establishment. It is important also for practitioners to know that they have all been taught the same subject, in the same way, thus adding to the consistency of approach that is essential to enable support to be given to adults with autism.

The in-house approach does have drawbacks, however, which tend to centre on the quality of the teaching environment, for there is a lack of opportunity for staff to receive tuition in an environment free from the immediate pressure of work. Practitioners also lack the opportunity to mix and compare experiences with colleagues from other care settings.

External short course (day and short courses)

Unlike the in-house method, practitioners have the opportunity to move away from their usual work environment and into a different environment, the sole purpose of which is to encourage learning.

This approach to training offers the opportunity for staff to 'compare notes' with staff from other establishments, and it is so often the informal agenda of the external training courses which can be of particular value to staff.

But, the logistical disadvantages of the external short course method of training are significant. In recent years within the UK, a persuasive and apparently highly profitable industry has developed in the provision of external and short training courses for practitioners working with people with learning disabilities. Some courses can look attractive, particularly those purporting to offer 'magic' answers to long-standing problems. Caution should be exercised, as sending staff on these courses can be very expensive in terms of both human and financial resources for the following reasons:

1 Because only small numbers of employees can be released (unless the establishment closes for the duration of the course), it fails to be cost efficient.

2 It can deplete a residential or day service of their staff, thus detrimentally impacting upon the direct care given to people with autism. Jones and Newson (1992) quoted one Principal of a small service for adults with autism,

With such a small staff team, you can't afford for more than one person to attend external courses.

(Jones and Newson 1992, p. 205)

3 The question which employers should seek to address: is, 'is the message of training being passed to all staff in a consistent manner?'. This will be doubtful if only a few members of staff have the opportunity to take these courses.

Secondment for attendance on generic, external courses leading to a professional qualification

Secondment to external courses on a part-time or full-time basis requires considerable commitment from an employer. Often financially expensive, there can also be a requirement that employers replace the seconded student for a temporary period lasting throughout the duration of the course, thus potentially doubling the costs incurred, but, also importantly, introducing a change of personnel into the lives of the client group with autism. In England and Wales this is true of the current regulations set by the Central Council for Education and Training in Social Work (CCETSW) for students seeking secondment onto the two year full-time (or four-year part-time), Diploma in Social Work course.

For employers thinking of seconding individual staff members onto long courses such as these, the 'litmus test' will be the level of significance attached to autism within each of these professional courses. What opportunities on the course will there be for the seconded member of staff to work with children or adults with autism and to complete assignments which closely identify the needs and the quality of service provision required by people with autism? It is therefore important that professional courses recognise autism as a distinct subject compared to learning disabilities, acknowledging, for example, that discourse with people with autism is significantly different. Furthermore, the rhetorical impact of normalisation, taught as the basis of any teaching of learning disability in social work and nursing, can become a practical minefield for staff seeking to apply these principles to people with autism. The goals may be similar, but the methods of achievement may be quite different. There is therefore a need for such topics to be taught in an insightful way as far as autism is concerned.

Distance learning

The clear advantage of the distance learning approach is that practitioners can undertake the course without requiring temporary or long stretches away from their employment. The quality of the distance learning course will be determined largely by the substance of the course materials, i.e. the relevance of the content and the quality of writing, together with the student's motivation and capacity for working alone, and the support networks and opportunities for meeting other students and with tutors on a regular basis. Also important will be the employer's ability to empathise with the pressures that the student will face and thus provide moral support.

For practitioners employed in intensive areas of support for adults with autism, where release from duties may, for their employers and themselves, be difficult, the distance learning approach may increasingly offer an attractive and cost-efficient way of gaining recognised knowledge and skills. A practical example of the distance learning approach applied to the training of practitioners working with adults with autism is discussed later on in this chapter, in the section entitled, 'Advanced Certificate of Education Autism (Adults)'.

LEVEL TWO – AUTISM-SPECIFIC TRAINING

It has been recognised for many years by those working in the field of autism that practitioners require training, over and above basic care practice, which reflects the individual needs of children and adults with autism. The relevant literature contains many short suggestions as to the type of training that practitioners should receive to support people with autism. Staff training should include training in behavioural and instructional techniques (Schopler 1976) and 'care-givers' should also be given the opportunity to participate in the design of treatment plans (Datlow Smith 1990). Induction programmes should include the assimilation of the organisation's philosophy and treatment approach (Simonson and Simonson 1987). Training ought to contain the aetiology of autism, emphasising social and communication deficits (Wall 1990). The latter also stresses the role that management and administrative personnel have to play in determining and communicating a consistent philosophy and providing clear feedback to staff who must be made to feel valued and involved in decision-making processes. There should be a recognition and remediation of staff burnout (Foster 1980; Meldrum 1990). Essentially, the skill of staff will lie in their ability to plan and maintain an environment and programmes that provide appropriate stimulation, minimise behavioural problems and, above all, make life as enjoyable as possible for adults with autism (Wing 1989). In England and Wales, the National Autistic Society, and some local autistic societies, try to meet the training needs of practitioners by organising short courses; Jones and Newson (1992) conveyed that practitioners reported their appreciation of these courses, which stimulated awareness in participants that further, in-depth training was required. Relying on outside organisations to take the initiative in training can often deflect attention away from the responsibilities of employers and their senior managers, who can themselves play a leading role in the development of an autism-specific training programme. One example of the creative way in which a small organisation can implement a training programme in autism, is obtained from Iceland and illustrated in Vignette 12.1.

VIGNETTE 12.1

LEVEL TWO: AUTISM-SPECIFIC TRAINING

One example of training for work in community-based residential settings with adults with autism is provided by the Group Homes and Workshop for people with autism, in Reykjavik, Iceland. The training provided for practitioners has tended to be mainly autism-specific, drawing upon the input of trainers from outside Iceland. Over the past two years, new staff have undertaken an introductory course in autism for three to five hours which runs on a termly basis. The TEACCH philosophy is a major influence and, in addition to teaching programmes given by visiting lecturers, several practitioners from Iceland have been trained in the TEACCH programme in North Carolina, returning to give workshops and lectures themselves on this topic. It is of note that the TEACCH programme is probably the most widely 'copied' model in the world for dealing with diagnostic, treament and follow-up issues in connection with autism spectrum disorders (Gillberg 1989). In the past three years the 'Heimili og vinnustofa einhverfra' (i.e. Group Homes and Workshop for People with Autism) homes have held several training sessions relating to autism, with topics including:

Communication and social handicap among persons with autism and ways and means to improve these skills

Asperger syndrome

Alternative communication systems

Parent and professional collaboration

Theory of mind

Epilepsy/seizures among adolescents and adults with autism

Adolescence and adulthood (based on outcome of long-term follow-up studies)

Puberty and sexual maturation

Autism and Adolescent Psychoeducational Profile (AA-PEP)

Recreation, leisure and educational needs of autistic adolescents

Treatment and management of behavioural problems among children and adults with autism

University of California Los Angeles (UCLA) Young Autism Project

Behaviour modification

Facilitated communication

Living with autism – a personal experience

Service development for adults in North Carolina's TEACCH programme (four of our staff members visited North Carolina and shared their experiences with the others).

As far as residential work with adults with autism is specifically concerned, the aim of an on-going, autism-specific training programme should be to reflect the needs of the client group living within an establishment and also to take account of the strengths and weaknesses of the practitioner group. The quality of the training programme will determine the knowledge base and confidence of the staffing group, who should themselves be encouraged to pass on their skills to other practitioners. It would be appropriate for practitioners to engage in training which enables them to understand what is so special about autism and how people with autism differ fundamentally from other people with learning disabilities, targeting the deficits in socialisation, communication and imagination.

The practical implications of these deficits for behaviour and for appropriate management strategies to be employed should be a high priority in training sessions. Induction programmes for practitioners new to a service can be a useful opportunity to orientate them to good care practices, and also to what is so special about working with people with autism. In the UK, COSPA, the Confederation of Service Providers to People with Autism, have produced an induction training package seeking to enable practitioners to identify the key characteristics of autism and the implications for practice (COSPA 1993), as have the Sussex Autistic Community Trust Ltd (McKernan and Mortlock 1995).

Vignettes can play an important, although not prescriptive, part of staff training. Discussion will help practitioners to conceptualise the link between theory and practice. Practitioners should be made aware that there are no 'magic' answers to the behaviours manifest in the life-long handicap of autism. Rather, they should be encouraged to co-operatively develop consistent strategies based upon their underlying knowledge of autism and good care practice and their knowledge of the individual clients. Some key areas in an autism-specific training programme may include the following.

Philosophy and history of a service

The development of an individual service usually reflects a highly relevant and tailored response to the needs of adults with autism. In the UK, as in other countries, these services have often been established by parents and interested practitioners. It is important that practitioners are motivated to understand the reasons why their service was planned in a particular way, the philosophy upon which it was based, and, of course, to be aware of the inevitable struggles which took place before the unit was established. Practitioners should have some awareness of the range of services required by and delivered to people with autism at international, national and local levels, and be able to see where they 'fit' into the scheme of things. By understanding the underlying philosophies of service design practitioners can be helped to contribute to the on-going debate.

Targeting the range of disabilities to be found within autism

Training which targets the aetiology of autism spectrum disorders should take into account the wide differences in the intellectual and skill levels of individuals with autism. Many establishments will provide services for a range of people with autism and it may be wise to have separate in-house training sessions reflecting the profiles of, say, those with a diagnosis of Asperger syndrome compared to those with autism and an associated severe learning disability. Practitioners should be able to identify the key characteristics of autism arising from the Triad of Impairments and to empathise with the autistic perception of the world. There should be opportunities for the acquisition of skills in observing and managing behaviour, developing and implementing effective teaching and care programmes, establishing collaborative practices with other professionals and parents, as well as establishing and monitoring effective policies for the provision of a service that enhances the quality of life of individuals with autism.

Understanding the unconventional nature of learning by people with autism and the responses that are required

Practitioners should be encouraged to understand that perception and learning appear to be unconventional for people with autism, as compared to other people, and that this has consequences for the way in which programmes are designed and the method by which everyday experiences are approached. The use of augmented forms of communication, as well as teaching in context, will be helpful in these respects, and practitioners should become aware and knowledgeable of the range of strategies and specific techniques that can be employed.

Autism-specific assessments

The assessment process for people with autism should take into account their restrictions in the areas of communication, socialisation and imagination. The process also needs to be pertinent to the specific environments in which the individual lives, works and spends his or her leisure time. Traditional forms of assessment, e.g. the Progress Assessment Chart, or PAC (Gunzberg 1977), the Social Training Achievement Record (STAR) profile (Williams 1985), and the scale for assessing coping skills (Whelan and Speake 1979), are geared towards people with learning disabilities and fail to focus sufficiently on the prime impairments found in autism. Progress has been made on autism-specific assessments for work with children, for example, *An Assessment and Intervention Schedule* (Aarons and Gittens 1992); and, for older people with autism, *The Adolescent and Adult Psychoeducational Profile* (*AAPEP*), reported by Schopler and Mesibov (1988), which was demonstrated to be significantly more helpful compared to individual programme plans (IPPs) in identifying areas of need and recommendations for further development of skills. Recently, in the UK, the National Autistic Society has undertaken development work with the objective of producing an autism-specific assessment and individual local societies, including the West Midlands Autistic Society, have produced their own assessment formats. Practitioners should be able to describe objectively the symptomatic behaviour of autism and understand the underlying reasons for these patterns of behaviour, and also the unusual balance of skill levels often found in many people with autism.

Uses and abuses of medication

Medication has continued to be prescribed for adults with autism in the management of behavioural problems, particularly those seen to arise from extreme anxiety or disruptive behaviour. Very few practitioners have medical or nursing qualifications, yet may administer many different types of medications to many people. Practitioners should be encouraged to understand the medical aspects of autism, particularly focusing on the uses and side effects of medication, and be aware of the effect that medication may have on the individuals with whom they work.

Attachment and loss: transition and bereavement

Practitioners should be enabled to understand why people with autism often seem to become so attached to routine, space, objects, as well as people. The loss of these attachments have clear implications for the support that practitioners are able to provide for the person with autism on a daily basis. Particular emphasis should also be given to the development of supporting mechanisms in transition and when a bereavement is about to, or has, occurred.

Creating a stable anxiety-free environment, but also teaching more flexible behaviours

There is a need to take account of the lack of flexibility that the person with autism has when planning suitable environments and appropriate daily programmes. Practitioners working with individuals with autism have a role in encouraging and developing more creative and flexibile strategies within the adults with autism with whom they work, and, by so doing, may have a major impact on their quality of life and prospects for independence.

Traditionally, practitioners have not been very proficient at teaching people with learning disabilities to interact with others. In the field of autism, there are particular difficulties arising from the specific restrictive ability of social interaction, but, even so, practitioners should begin by teaching the ground rules of social interaction in the settings in which adults with autism live, for these skills will become critical in determining their ability to interact subsequently with others in the wider community. It is recognised that practitioners will need to understand, and build in to such teaching programmes, strategies for skill generalisation.

Self-determination

By developing an understanding of the unconventional style of learning of adults with autism, and by teaching strategies based on this knowledge, practitioners should seek to enable adults with autism to experience everyday life events, to learn how to make *informed* choices, and to demonstrate their own wishes.

Non-aversive approaches to managing difficult behaviour

Displays of behaviours including self-injurious, stereotypical and ritualistic behaviours, even repeated and determined questioning of others, are likely to arise because the person with autism feels under threat, frustrated, unable to communicate with others and is therefore unable to predict what will happen next. Practitioners can play an important role in creating the conditions in which people with autism can predict their world with a degree of confidence. A focus for practitioner training should not only be the problematic behaviour of the individual with autism, but, most importantly, the perceptions and behaviours of the practitioners themselves. Practitioners should understand that they are part of the system which will influence change.

SPECIALIST PROFESSIONAL QUALIFICATIONS FOR WORK WITH ADULTS WITH AUTISM

Progress is being maintained towards the development of an autism-specific distance learning course operated by the European Educautisme Group, funded in part by the EU. Contributors to this iniative have included representatives from France, Spain, Belgium, Portugal and the UK. In at least two academic institutions in the UK, modules on autism are included in special education and social work courses. However, in the UK, at the University of Birmingham, a professional course devoted to autism has been running since 1992 and, during 1994, a one-year course for practitioners providing support services for adults with autism commenced. A closer look at the Birmingham course will follow, to be preceded by a brief decription of the Educautisme programme

European Educautisme training programme

Funded by the EU Horizon programme, the Educautisme group operated for several years until December 1994. The goal of the team was to devise training modules for professionals working in the field of autism. The group, based at the University of Mons, have written four units, which were at the pilot study stage by early 1995. The units were called 'residential autonomy', 'leisure activities', 'behaviour problems' and 'co-ordination' of the natural and professional environment.

Advanced Certificate of Education Autism (Adults)

The University of Birmingham course for practitioners working with adults with autism was a logical progression from the one-year distance/part-time learning course for teachers working with children with autism, operated within the School of Education. These courses represent a co-operative venture, their development being supported by the National, the West Midlands and Leicestershire Autistic Societies, as well as by the university.

The first course for teachers commenced in September 1992 and demand for places quickly led to the development of a part-time course and also to the appointment of a full-time lecturer in the field of autism. During the first three years of operation, students completed the course from as far away from the UK as Luxembourg, Hong Kong and Greece. Those successfully completing the course were awarded the Advanced Certificate Education (ACE) (Autism) qualification and were then eligible to undertake further work subsequently leading to diplomas, undergraduate or master's level degrees in the field of autism. The course thus provided not only a professional training in the field of autism, but also helped to stimulate ongoing practitioner development and formed the basis for research into autism by practitioners in the field.

Identifying the need for a course for practitioners working with adults with autism

In 1993, a survey was undertaken by the steering group within the School of Education in the University of Birmingham, which targeted a small number of adult communities operated by, or affiliated to, the National Autistic Society. It was found that of 274 practitioners working in these units, 238 had no recognised or relevant qualification. These findings are consistent with the findings of the Smith *et al.* (1994) study, reported in the section entitled, 'Demonstrating the need', in units for people with learning disabilities. It could be determined from this that a course specifically designed for practitioners working with adults with autism should enable the staff to access the course at a variety of levels. The starting point for professional courses for those working with adults with autism was the ACE, which commenced in September 1994 and attracted applicants holding a professional qualification. It was planned that, by 1997, candidates without formal academic or professional qualifications would be able to access the course and pursue a certificate, rather than an advanced certificate, qualification. Like the course for teachers, those who successfully complete the course for adults will be eligible to undertake further undergraduate or postgraduate work in the field of autism.

Course content

Course content was determined by a National Steering Committee of practitioners and set out to achieve four main objectives:

1 to present an overview of autism with special reference to adults
2 to enable students to acquire relevant teaching skills and care management skills
3 to present current research findings
4 to encourage practitioners to carry out research in their own workplace.

The curriculum takes the form of study packs designed for home study, which has encouraged students to undertake practical activities in their place of work. There is also an Introductory Handbook, providing an invaluable guide to the contemporary views of theory and practice in the field of autism, emphasising why the specific communication, socialisation and imaginative difficulties inherent in autism sets it apart from other learning disabilities.

Currently, the course consists of three modules, each requiring 100 hours of study time. Module 1 is entitled *The Implications of Autism* and consists of four units looking closely at the autistic spectrum, communication, social skills and interaction and finally flexibility in thinking and behaviour. Module 2 is known as *Autism: Foundations for Practice*, and is concerned with the curriculum of adult service provision, demonstrating how quality of life for the adult with autism can be developed and enhanced. Module 3 addresses the means for monitoring the development of adults with autism and identifying qualitative issues in service provision. Particular emphasis has been placed on the management of 'challenging behaviour' and the module stresses the importance in multidisciplinary and community-based links. This module is called *Autism: Intervention Strategies and Service Development.*

Teaching methods

Several teaching methods have been used to enable the students to acquire new skills and to reinforce their practice with underpinning theoretical knowledge. The main teaching approach employed is distance learning, which has enabled practitioners to undertake the course without the need for secondment from their work or having to leave home. There is however a danger in this approach, for the student can find him or herself isolated. The Birmingham-based course has sought to guard against the potential isolation of distance learning by organising two residential weekends and also by providing a regional tutor to whom each student is ascribed. The residential weekends are designed to enable the student to (1) meet with other students and to compare experiences, (2) facilitate opportunities to seek advice from specialist tutors, and (3) gain an introduction to the course material at the beginning and half-way through the course.

As with all the distance-taught courses, the support of an understanding, reliable and informed regional tutor is of prime importance in helping to ward off the feeling of isolation that many students taking distance-learning courses can encounter. Meeting around six times during the duration of the course, the tutorials are held in reasonable geographical proximity to the homes of the students and at mutually agreed times. Between tutorials, the tutor is available for additional support through telephone and fax communication. The main objectives for the tutorial groups are to enable the students to engage in co-operative activities, to discuss and analyse course material, and to provide an opportunity for questions and support as necessary.

Future developments

Evaluation of the course will be by student, tutor and steering committee. It is likely the assessment process will need to become based more around project and research work, rather than purely by academic submissions in essay form. Residential workshops should ideally be structured around 'live' issues: employment and further education, sexuality, self-determination, bereavement and transition, understanding behaviour and intervention techniques, action research and so on. It is planned to start a certificate level course, the Certificate in Higher Education (Autism) for all professionals working with children and adults with autism who do not have the necessary entrance qualifications for application to the existing ACE course.

CHAPTER SUMMARY

Too often, practitioners working with adults with autism are poorly supported, largely because the employers do not understand the mechanisms of training for work in this field. As a result, a poorly trained staff can lead to a particularly vulnerable client group. Training for practitioners working in residential and day centre settings with adults with autism can be planned strategically and focus on the two levels of good care practice and autism-specific practice.

There are four main strategies that can be employed to facilitate training: in-house, external short courses, external long-term courses which lead to professional qualifications, and distance-learning courses which may also lead to professional qualifications. A fifth strategy, the development of work-based competencies with 'on-the-job' training from practitioner mentors may also be a possibility. Many organisations will have limited financial and personnel resources and it is likely to be the in-house and distance-learning methods which will be the most attractive means of achieving a *relevant* training for all their practitioners, whilst simultaneously causing the minimum amount of disruption to the client group with autism. The impetus obtained from the recent development of autism-specific courses must be maintained. The need for practitioners who are skilled in their understanding and practice of what makes autism so different from other types of learning disabilities assumes increased significance, as an increasing number of countries begin to recognise the condition. It is clear that the routes to training should be both flexible and incremental, reflecting the needs of both the organisation and the individual practitioner.

ACKNOWLEDGEMENTS

Dr Beryl Smith, Department of Psychiatry of Birmingham, UK. Sigriour Lao Jonsdottir, Group Homes and Workshop for People with Autism, Iceland. Rita Jordan, School of Education, University of Birmingham, UK. Professor Ghislaine Magerotte, University of Mons, Belgium.

BIBLIOGRAPHY

Aarons, M. and Gittens, T. (1992). *The Autistic Continuum: an Assessment and Intervention Schedule for Investigation of the Behaviours, Skills and Needs of Children with Autism or Autistic Spectrum Difficulties* (revised edition). Windsor, NFER–NELSON.

Allen, P., Pahl, J. and Quine, L. (1990). *Care Staff in Transition: the Impact on Staff of Changing Services for People with Mental Handicaps*. London, HMSO.

Anderson, S.R. (1987). The management of staff behaviour in residential treatment facilities; a review of staff training techniques. In J. Hogg and P. Mittler (eds.) *Staff Training in Mental Handicap*. Beckenham, Croom Helm.

COSPA (1993). *An Introduction To Working with People with Autism*. Nottingham, The Confederation of Service Providers for People with Autism.

Cullen, C. (1987). Nurse training and institutional constraints. In J. Hogg, and P. Mittler (eds.) *Staff Training in Mental Handicap*. Beckenham, Croom Helm.

Cullen, C. (1988). A review of staff training: the emperor's old clothes. *Irish Journal of Psychology*, **9**, 309–323.

Cullen, C. (1995). Paper presented at the Workshop on Training for Staff working with People with Learning Disability, 29 June 1995. Keele, University of Keele.

DHSS (1984). *Home Life: a Code of Practice for Residential Care*. London, Centre for Policy for Aging.

Datlow Smith, M. (1990). *Autism and Life in the Community: Successful Interventions for Behavioural Challenges*. Baltimore, Paul H. Brookes Publishing.

Foster, A. (1980). In A.J. Wall (1990). Group Homes in North Carolina for children and adults with autism. *Journal of Autism and Developmental Disorders*, **20** (3), 353–367.

Gillberg, C.(ed.) (1989). *Diagnosis and Treatment of Autism*. NewYork, Plenum Press.

Giddan, J.J. and Giddan, N.N. (1993). *European Farm Communities for Autism*. Toledo, Ohio, Medical College of Ohio Press.

Gunzberg, H.C. (1977). *Progress Assessment Chart of Social and Personal Development*. London, Mencap.

Henderson, R. and Crowhurst, G. (1991). On-the-job training for residential staff. *Mental Handicap*, **19** (4), 155–157.

Jones, G.E. and Newson, E. (1992). *Report 3: Provision for Adults with Autism in England and Wales*. Nottingham, Child Development Research Unit.

McKernan, T. and Mortlock, J. (1995). *Autism Focus: the Training Workbook for Carers*. St Leonards-on-Sea, Sussex Autistic Community Trust Ltd/Outset Publishing.

Meldrum, W. (1990). Autism in adulthood. In K. Ellis (ed.) *Autism: Professional Perspectives and Practice*. London, Chapman and Hall (in association with the National Autistic Society).

Mittler, P. (1984). Evaluation of services and staff training. In J. Dobbing (ed.) *Scientific Studies in Mental Retardation*. London, Macmillan.

National Council for Vocational Qualifications (1988). *Introducing National Vocational Qualifications; Implications for Education and Training*. London, NCVQ.

Simonson, L.R. and Simonson, S.M. (1987). Residential programming at Benhaven. In D. Cohen and A. Donnellan (eds.) *Handbook of Autism and Pervasive Developmental Disorders*. New York, John Wiley and Sons.

Schopler, E. (1976). Towards reducing behaviour problems in autistic children. In L. Wing (ed.) *Early Childhood Autism*. Oxford, Pergamon Press.

Schopler, E. and Mesibov, G.B. (1988). *Diagnosis and Assessment in Autism*. New York, Plenum Press.

Smith, B., Wun, W.-L. and Cumella, S. (1994). *Training Strategies for Learning Disability*. Birmingham. Centre for Research and Information into Mental Disability.

Wall, A.J. (1990). Group Homes in North Carolina for children and adults with autism. *Journal of Autism and Developmental Disorders*, **20** (3), 353–367.

Whelan, E. and Speake, B. (1979). *The Scale for Assessing Coping Skills*. Manchester, Copewell Publications.

Williams, C. (1985). *The STAR Profile: Social Training Achievement Record and Manual*. Kidderminster. BIMH publication.

Wing, L. (1989). Autistic adults. In C. Gillberg (ed.) *Diagnosis and Treatment of Autism*. New York, Plenum Press.

Wun, W.-L. and Cumella, S. (1993). *Resettlement from Mental Handicap Hospitals*. Birmingham, Centre for Research and Information into Mental Disability.

Epilogue

Future trends in services for adults with autism within the United Kingdom

Hugh Morgan

W ORK IN the field of autism is still in its infancy, both in terms of our knowledge of the condition and of the practices that are used. In the past 50 years or so, great strides forward have been made, both in the development of services for adults with autism and the practices that are employed. In the UK, as in many other countries, it is the parents of those with autism who have led the way forward. Castellani (1986) identified the dynamic relationship between political ideology, government policy and funding for people with developmental disabilities which underpinned historical change, and Mills (1995) employed a similar analysis with specific reference to autism. By taking a similar historical perspective, it is likely that the development of services for adults with autism in the future will be inextricably linked to government policy, attitudes and ideologies current at the time, but also, it is suggested, to an increasing paucity of resources within a highly competitive economic climate. Against this tense background, need and demand for services will continue to grow as recognition and diagnosis of autism spectrum disorders become further widespread. The implication is that instigators of services, be they parents or practitioners, will need to design increasingly innovative models of practice in order to obtain a meaningful service for adults with autism. Even so, the public sector must not be absolved from the responsibility of providing services for people with autism by the endeavours of the voluntary and private sectors. Indeed, the independent sector can and should seek to enable and educate the public sector of the needs of people with autism.

INFLUENCING THE PUBLIC SECTOR

By harnessing the influence and energies of all those who work with and/or support those with autism in the UK, development of practice can be shaped within both the public sector in, for example, long-stay hospitals, and in social services departments. An illustration of this is the work currently being undertaken by the West Midlands Autistic Society (WMAS), who have proposed to the Association of Directors of Social Services (West Midlands region) that a specialist practitioner in the field of autism should be nominated who will 'act' as a resource person for the relevant public sector department (Morgan *et al.* 1995). Also offered by the WMAS is a package of training for public sector employees, consisting of an introductory day and two follow-up sessions, to enable an in-depth consideration of specific issues in practice, obtained from the course participants' own experiences. The initial uptake for both suggestions has indicated that the proposals are being taking seriously, and it is anticipated that several local authorities will nominate practitioners for the resource role in the near future. So it is clear that original forms of shaping and delivering practice will need to found. One example of innovative practice in direct provision is likely to be found in respite services.

RESPITE CARE

Although residential provision is usually an extremely expensive (and often last!) option, a significant range of services are currently available for adults with autism in the UK, which have been described by Mills (1995), elsewhere. However, the increase in residential accommodation for adults with autism over the past ten years in the UK has not been matched by a similar increase in respite services. Traditionally, some establishments have offered respite beds within long-stay accommodation. This approach can be problematic in terms of the constantly changing 'rhythm' of the routine of an establishment arising both because of the large number of short-stay visits, and also because local authority registration and inspection officers appear increasingly hesitant about mixing long-term with respite accommodation. Many organisations have also been inhibited from developing respite care services due to the need to justify the high cost of bed places without the certainty of having these beds filled. Families, however, continue to require respite care for their sons or daughters with autism – and, in some cases, the son or daughter with autism would wish for respite care from their families! One example of a short-term respite service can be viewed in Sheffield, which is derived from a befriender scheme established by the National Autistic Society (NAS) in the city during 1993/4. Sheffield Hallam University and the NAS have piloted a respite service for families within the family home, which is to be staffed by volunteers and managed by a volunteer co-ordinator based in the university. The pilot programme started in October 1995 and is to be evaluated after one year. The role of the volunteer worker is, after a period of training, to befriend the family and not just the person with autism. This may mean taking the individual with autism out of the house for a few hours, or treating the siblings to some valuable one-to-one time away from the family. It could also mean time spent with the parent(s). The advantage of this scheme appears to be that it is low-cost and, as a model of practice, could be replicated elsewhere.

This respite service touches upon the issue of providing support to family members in addition to the person with autism. Powell *et al.* (1992) consider the types of support that families with a child with autism may need, emphasising that family support needs to be delivered in a sensitive manner, with regard to the family's system of beliefs, needs, values, development, membership and major functions. Their analysis would seem to be just as applicable to families with adults with autism in the UK, as to those with children. They see that the challenge for practitioners will be to support families in flexible ways, including:

1 ensuring support for extended family members
2 ensuring support for single parents
3 harnessing natural sources of support, i.e. from friends and relatives
4 accurately assessing of the needs of families
5 ensuring support for families in rural locations
6 ensuring support for families who have children living in residential care
7 developing methods of measuring and evaluating the quality and effectiveness of the support given to families.

PRACTICE WITH HIGH-FUNCTIONING ADULTS WITH AUTISM/ASPERGER SYNDROME

Recognition of the needs of high-functioning adults with autism who may, or may not, have a diagnosis of Asperger syndrome, is likely to lead to the development of supportive schemes enabling access to education, vocational and leisure activities, as well as to their empowerment to make decisions about their lives. Howlin (1996) looks at the potential outcome for adolescents and adults with Asperger syndrome, which she views as being extremely variable. She stresses that development of informed, supportive networks, and continuing help will be needed throughout life to minimise the impact of social and communication deficits, to reduce the negative impact of ritualistic behaviours and to maximise the value of obsessional interests or special skills. In the process of fostering independence, Howlin writes that it is important to avoid making excessive or unrealistic demands, but, equally, to avoid undervaluing potential ability. Lowndes (1994) makes the point that many people with Asperger syndrome would wish to lead an independent life, but themselves recognise the need for background support in order to do so. One innovative attempt to provide community support for high-functioning adults with autism commenced in January 1996 in Birmingham (Morgan and Jordan 1995). Funded jointly, for three years initially, by the Health and Social Services, this project aims to enable adults with Asperger syndrome/autism to maintain a good quality of life in their own homes or in semi-independent accommodation. A Community Support Practitioner was appointed to provide 'hands-on' support. The prime beneficiaries, therefore, were people with autism themselves and the parents of children and adults with autism/Asperger syndrome who would attend associated workshops. Appendix 1 describes these initiatives in a little more detail.

EDUCATION FOR LIFE

The language that is used in work with people with autism has traditionally reflected public perception of the tasks of services. Education is a term which has been associated with children and school, whereas care has been primarily the domain and function of adult provision. It is unfair to people with autism to divide services on such simplistic terms. Education implies learning and has a positive connotation, whereas care depicts more a 'doing unto others' feel, and is often associated with health care practices. This only serves to devalue the status of the actual work – the educational work that takes place in the adult sector.

Many non-autistic adults take part in continuing education and it is likely that, in future years, educational environments will offer the best chance for adults with autism to develop skills and understanding which they had been unable to acquire in childhood and throughout their school years. Therefore education can continue throughout life. There is, of course, a dynamic relationship between education and care; education cannot function effectively without supportive environments – to ensure that the adult son or daughter is physically and emotionally safe in the educational setting will be the first task of the practitioner. It is upon this foundation that education can flourish and this is as applicable to adults' as well as children's services.

IMPACT OF LITERATURE UPON PRACTICE

In the UK especially, much of the literature published in relation to autism has become the bedrock of theoretical understanding, but not necessarily of practice. The trend for the future is likely to be that, increasingly, publications will be written about practice and the relationship between theory and practice, as, hopefully, practitioners' thirst for improved skills and knowledge will lead to those with hands-on experience contributing to these publications. It is understood that a proposed International Journal of Autism (published by Sage and NAS) will have a practional and research focus. Pat Howlin's book also presents the findings of research and offers numerous practical hints to practitioners and parents of high-functioning adolescents and adults with autism (Howlin 1996). Additionally, the NAS is planning to develop a series of working guides with the objective of informing and influencing practice across the autistic spectrum (G. Peacock 1995, in communication with the author). As more and more people undertake professionally qualifying courses in the field of autism (such as the Birmingham University course), then knowledge and self-confidence will increase the contributions made by practitioners to the literature. Autobiographical writings have become, and will continue to be, a rich source of material for others to learn about the perceptions and outlook of individuals with autism. Happe (1991) suggests that these accounts can sometimes challenge accepted views about people with autism, although she suggests that we need to be cautious in our interpretation, due to the subjective nature of the writings and the difficulty in generalisation.

TRAINING OF PRACTITIONERS

In common with one of the themes of this book, there is increasing recognition that practitioners working in the field of autism require specific training for the work that they do. This was explored in relation to autism in Chapter Twelve, but a wider perspective of training in a political context may also prove to be helpful in the future. Government departments will need to be persuaded that capital resources need not be allocated solely to bricks and mortar, but also to the training and development of the skills of hands-on practitioners. What is becoming certain is that practitioners, whatever the setting in which they work, need to become more knowledgeable about autism. Currently, local authorities inherit from central government more than £30 million per year in the Training Support Programme for training in the field of social provision. The independent sector gets nothing directly from this source. With an ever-increasing proportion of social care being provided by the independent sector, including those services for adults with autism, it has been argued by Churchill (1995) that the resources for training should not be held by central government, but should be devolved to an independent training body. Churchill argues cogently that a proposed training body which he refers to as, 'the Independent Sector Funding Agency for Training' (ISFAT), should receive a grant budget from the statutory sector. Currently in work with adults with autism, the Registered Care Manager (i.e. the person responsible for the home), or Manager of Day Services, would seek to incorporate a budget for training into the overall fees negotiated with local authorities for the placements of people with autism. The danger here is that, in times of economic stringency, it is the training budget which is most vulnerable to cuts. If Churchill's vision were to reach fruition, such a shift of resources would have considerable impact upon the development of specialist courses, certainly offering greater opportunities for more needs-led training and access for organisations to a training budget. However, it would also impact significantly upon the existing professional training of social workers and associated professionals, who would themselves need to focus training more upon specific and practical situations rather than upon theory and ideology, in order to maintain the status of their qualifications.

'MIRACLE CURES'

Over many years autism has been particularly vulnerable to those who seek to explain the condition in simplistic terms and devise miraculous cures based upon very uncertain and sometimes judgmental interpretations of the condition. If anything, these often well-meaning, but highly suspect, panaceas will engage the emotional attention and energies of parents and practitioners, but distract attention away from the concrete practice of day-to-day support for people with autism. In the future, increasing stringency will be applied to the 'quack' panaceas for autism. For example, Howlin (1994), has collated data from many empirical evaluations of Facilitated Communication, for which extraordinary success has been claimed previously. Howlin shows that the body of scientific evidence overwhelmingly fails to support the efficacy of Facilitated Communication for people with autism. Hastings (1996) also appraises the empirical evaluation of Facilitated Communication, concluding that there is insufficient evidence for the validity of 'facilitated' communications. Such analyses give practitioners and parents an objective basis upon which they can make a decision whether to engage in such a therapy. Neither Facilited Communication, nor any other of the unconventional therapies, i.e. Holding therapy, Pet therapy and so on, have gained a stronghold in the UK, and they have certainly never been adopted as a mainstream practice. Based upon the experience of past years, it would not be unreasonable to suggest that further 'innovations' will receive widespread coverage in the media, but will disappear following critical evaluation and increasing disillusionment amongst parents and practitioners, once it has been seen that a particular method does not appear to work.

MAKING THE WORLD MORE UNDERSTANDABLE: NEW TECHNOLOGIES

It will be of most benefit in the future to consider and evaluate current practice, taking the best of what we have – the tried and tested elements of consistency, predictability, calmness and empathy – to improve *our* methods of effective communication with people with autism. It is possible that the use of computor technology may help to enable some practitioners to gain some insight into how messages, full of intuitive human understanding, can be misinterpreted by programmes which are not 'user-friendly' (Jordan 1995). The implication appears to be that practitioners can learn to alter their style of communication to reflect the unconventional understanding of people with autism. Equally, computor technology may have significant applications for teaching communication, socialisation and increased flexibility of thinking and behaviour to adults with autism. Palazzi and Smirne (1995) conveyed that the Electronic Mail systems (E-Mail) can become a communication tool that many people with autism can access from their home, with a consequential positive effect on their quality of life. They explain that because the complex and intuitive use of everyday language, which is shaded by tone, accents and pauses, is not apparent in the E-Mail system, the main message received by the person with autism is most likely to be that intended by the sender. There is therefore a reduced risk of ambiguity and inconsistency. It seems as if the E-Mail system may also have a potential use in improving the social interaction of the individual with autism in an asocial way (Jordan and Powell 1995). In Switzerland, Knabe (cited in Jordan and Powell 1995) has worked with adults with autism who have associated learning disabilities, and has used a multi-media approach to encourage learning and reduction in behavioural problems, founded on individualised programmes and based around daily living activities. Virtual Reality is in the very early stages of application for use with people with autism and may have some potential use as a safe and controllable environment to investigate and surmount fears and anxieties (Jordan 1995). Jordan also introduces a note of caution into its utilisation over the long-term. In North Carolina, Virtual Reality is being used as a learning aid for children with autism, and is seen as an opportunity to permit individuals to explore new methods of responding and learning themselves (Strickland *et al.* 1995).

These are but a few suggestions which may indicate some directions for the future for adults with autism, and the practitioners who work with them. Consolidation of tried and trusted practice needs to be combined with innovative development in an unsympathetic economic climate. There is a need to be aware of the potential impact that new technologies can make, whilst being very mindful of the the need for scrutiny and evaluation of the services that are delivered, in order to measure their effectiveness and thus justify their application.

APPENDIX 1

The need for a Community Support Practitioner (Asperger syndrome) was identified following a survey undertaken by the West Midlands Autistic Society (WMAS) in 1992 and also from feedback from parents with younger autistic/Asperger syndrome children via the parents' support workshop operated by the WMAS.

The WMAS undertook a survey during the latter part of 1992 in order to identify the support services required by those adults with Asperger syndrome living either at home with parents, or in semi-independent or independent accommodation. The geographical spread of the survey was to families living within a radius of ten miles of Birmingham. The response from the survey was as follows:

33 questionnaires were sent out to families known to the WMAS who lived either in, or within close proximity to, south Birmingham
24 replies were received (73% response rate) – consisting of 21 responses from males and three from females
18 of those identified lived at home with their parents and a further three were in independent/semi-independent living situations
16 received no support service at all other than from family.

Summary of parents' additional comments

Parents completing the questionnaire were keen that their sons/daughters should receive the following support:

1. Supervision should be provided on a regular basis by a support person with knowledge of the autistic syndrome and, if possible, experience of autism.

2. An advocate is required who could facilitate contact outside the home situation for the person with Asperger syndrome and who would also visit regularly to monitor domestic and employment progress.

3. A monitoring type of supervision by a person with a knowledge of autism to see that bills are paid, cleanliness maintained, health problems are kept in check, and that contact with the outside world is maintained. An ideal frequency would be to visit once a week and to make an occasional phone call.

4. The person with Asperger syndrome is not able to easily identify his/her own needs and express those needs to others. Therefore, the role of the Community Support Practitioner as a 'facilitator', to encourage and enable the person with Asperger syndrome to make decisions about his/her own life, becomes an important one.

Function of the initiatives

The implementation of parent workshops

1. To develop the understanding of autism in parents and thus increase their understanding of their own child.
2. To help parents develop enabling strategies so that they may aid their child's progress towards a more independent adult life.
3. To help parents deal with problems that arise in managing behaviour and creating a healthy family environment.

The appointment of community Support Practitioner

1. To befriend adults diagnosed as having Asperger syndrome who are living independently or semi-independently at home or in the community.
2. To pay regular visits to ensure that these adults:

 i are managing their financial resources appropriately, e.g. that they are making payments on time, and are able to budget for clothes and other bills
 ii are being supported and encouraged to maintain appropriate levels of hygiene in the home
 iii are living in a safe environment.

Based upon the individual skills of the client, the Community Support Practitioner should ensure that:

 i appropriate support in areas such as shopping, food preparation, etc., is being provided
 ii plans are made for the leisure and social aspects of the client's needs.

3. To provide up-to-date information on matters of welfare rights, such as Housing Benefit, Income Support and Community Care Grants.
4. To form links and liaise on behalf of the person with Asperger syndrome with any statutory bodies and voluntary organisations who are able to offer opportunities in the areas of leisure, further and adult education and employment.
5. To form and initially lead a forum whereby all adults in the scheme can meet on a regular basis to discuss issues relating to their homes.
6. To act as a facilitator to encourage the person with Asperger syndrome to make choices and decisions about the direction of his/her own life.

Evaluation

Parent workshops

The first stage of evaluation of the project will be incorporated into the first workshop, followed by evaluation at the end of the workshop period with a further evaluation some time after that to see if the benefits have been maintained.

Community Support Practitioner

1. Throughout the three years of the programme, specific monitoring will identify the numbers, gender, ages and geographical spread of the client group.

2. Information obtained for Individual Programme Plans will enable an analysis to be undertaken of the success in gaining access to activities which are of most benefit to individuals with Asperger syndrome.

3. The qualitative outcome of the agreed Individual Programme Plans (i.e. whether the action taken in specific activities has led to an improved quality of life and greater self-confidence) may be assessed by involving the service-user and/or his/her parents/advocate in an appraisal of the increased opportunities facilitated by the Community Support Practitioner.

BIBLIOGRAPHY

Castellani, P.T. (1986). *The Political Economy of Developmental Disabilities*. Baltimore, Paul H Brookes.

Churchill, J. (1995). 'A case of who cares loses', *The Guardian*, Wednesday 6 September 1995.

Happe, F.G.E. (1991). The autobiographical writings of three Asperger syndrome adults: problems of interpretation and implications for theory. In U. Frith (ed.) *Autism and Asperger Syndrome*. Cambridge, Cambridge University Press.

Hastings, R. (1996). Does Facilitated Communication free imprisoned minds? *The Psychologist*, **9**, 19–24.

Howlin, P. (1994). Facilitated Communication and autism: are the claims for success justified? *Communication*, **28** (2), 10–12.

Howlin, P. (1996). *Autism Adulthood: the Way Ahead*. London, Routledge.

Jordan, R. (1995). *New Directions in Autism*. Birmingham, University of Birmingham.

Jordan, R. (1995). Communicating with a computer: the use and abuse of computers in developing communication skills in individuals with autism. In Proceedings of Autisme-France Third International Conference. Nice, January 1995. Paris, Autisme-France.

Jordan, R. and Powell, S. (1995). Autism and computer applications. Report on Autisme-France, Third International Conference. Birmingham, University of Birmingham.

Lowndes, R. (1994). Supported living for people with Asperger syndrome. *Communication*, **28**(3), 13.

Mills, R. (1995). Section 2: services to adults with autism in the UK. In L. Wing, R. Jordan, R. Mills, H. Morgan, C. Atkins and R. Reynolds, Module 1. Unit 1, Distance Education Course in Autism (Adults). *The Autistic Spectrum and Range of Provision to Adults with Autism.* Birmingham, University of Birmingham, School of Education.

Morgan, H. and Jordan, R. (1995). *A Community Support Service to People with Autism/Asperger Syndrome and their Families/Carers.* Birmingham, West Midlands Autistic Society.

Morgan, H., Williamson, J. and Price, G. (1995). Submission to the Branch Meeting of the Association of Directors of Social Services for the West Midlands. Dudley, West Midlands Autistic Society.

Palazzi, S. and Smirne, S. (1995). Project of Minitel/Videotel Communication in families and persons with autism. In *Autism and Computer Applications.* Proceedings of Autisme-France Third International Conference. Nice, January 1995. Paris, Autisme-France.

Powell, T.H., Hecimovic, A. and Christensen, L. (1992). Meeting the unique needs of families. In D. Berkell (ed.) *Autism: Identification, Education and Treatment.* New Jersey, Lawrence Erlbaum Associates.

Strickland, D., Marcus, L., Hogan, K., Mesibov, G. and McAllister, D. (1995). Using virtual reality as a learning aid for autistic children. In *Autism and Computer Applications.* Proceedings of Autisme-France Third International Conference. Nice, January 1995. Paris, Autisme-France.

Index